New Historicism and Cultural Materialism

Transitions

General Editor: Julian Wolfreys

Published Titles

Forthcoming Titles

Transitions

New Historicism and Cultural Materialism

John Brannigan

St. Martin's Press
New York

St. Martin's Press, Scholarly and Reference Division, 175 Fifth Avenue, New York, N.Y. 10010

First published in the United States of America in 1998

This book is printed on paper suitable for recycling and made from fully managed and sustained forest sources.

Printed in Hong Kong

ISBN 0–312–21388–3 clothbound
ISBN 0–312–21389–1 paperback

Library of Congress Cataloging-in-Publication Data
Brannigan, John.
New historicism and cultural materialism / John Brannigan.
p. cm. — (Transitions)
Includes bibliographical references and index.
ISBN 0–312–21388–3 (cloth). — ISBN 0–312–21389–1 (paper)
1. Criticism. 2. Historicism. 3. Materialism in literature.
I. Title. II. Series: Transitions (St. Martin's Press)
PN81.B663 1998
801'.95—dc21   97–52610
                                                                     CIP

Contents

General Editor's Preface

Transitions: *transition–em*, n. of action. 1. A passing or passage from one condition, action or (rarely) place, to another. 2. Passage in thought, speech, or writing, from one subject to another. 3. **a.** The passing from one note to another **b.** The passing from one key to another, modulation. 4. The passage from an earlier to a later stage of development or formation ... change from an earlier style to a later; a style of intermediate or mixed character ... the historical passage of language from one well-defined stage to another.

The aim of *Transitions* is to explore passages and movements in critical thought, and in the development of literary and cultural interpretation. This series also seeks to examine the possibilities for reading, analysis and other critical engagements which the very idea of transition makes possible. The writers in this series unfold the movements and modulations of critical thinking over the last generation, from the first emergences of what is now recognised as literary theory. They examine as well how the transitional nature of theoretical and critical thinking is still very much in operation, guaranteed by the hybridity and heterogeneity of the field of literary studies. The authors in the series share the common understanding that, now more than ever, critical thought is both in a state of transition and can best be defined by developing for the student reader an understanding of this protean quality.

This series desires, then, to enable the reader to transform her/his own reading and writing transactions by comprehending past developments. Each book in the series offers a guide to the poetics and politics of interpretative paradigms, schools and bodies of thought, while transforming these, if not into tools or methodologies, then into conduits for directing and channelling thought. As well as transforming the critical past by interpreting it from the perspective of the present day, each study enacts transitional readings of a number of well-known literary texts, all of which are themselves conceivable as having been transitional texts at the moments of their first appearance. The readings offered in these books seek, through close critical reading and theoretical engagement, to demonstrate certain possibilities in critical thinking to the student reader.

It is hoped that the student will find this series liberating because rigid methodologies are not being put into place. As all the dictionary definitions of the idea of transition above suggest, what is important is the action, the passage: of thought, of analysis, of critical response. Rather than seeking to help you locate yourself in relation to any particular school or discipline, this series aims to put you into action, as readers and writers, travellers between positions, where the movement between poles comes to be seen as of more importance than the locations themselves.

Julian Wolfreys

Acknowledgements

Many people have contributed to the formation of this book. My thanks go to the librarians of the University of Luton Learning Resources Centre, the Senate House Library of the University of London, and the British Library. I would also like to thank the students of literary studies at the University of Luton for many fruitful discussions of literature and history, which ventured occasionally into explorations of new historicism and cultural materialism. Some of this material has been presented in papers at seminars and conferences at the University of Luton and University of Kent at Canterbury, and I am grateful for the comments and questions which I received at those sessions. Chapter 8 previously appeared in *Imprimatur*; I am grateful to the editors for permission to reprint that essay in a revised form here. My thanks go also to my colleagues in the department of literary studies at the University of Luton for their helpful suggestions and comments.

I am fortunate to have had the advice, encouragement and the critical mind of the series editor, Julian Wolfreys, throughout the writing of this book, and without whom this volume (and series) would not have been possible. I would like to thank Margaret Bartley, the commissioning editor at Macmillan, and the readers and editors at Macmillan, for their kindness, attention to detail, and for their enthusiasm. Lastly, and most importantly, I have had the invaluable support, encouragement and love of my partner, Moyra Haslett, throughout, and her generous attention and keen intelligence has shaped the thinking and writing of this book at every stage.

JB

Introduction: Literature in History

> we cannot separate literature and art from other kinds of social prac-
> tice, in such a way as to make them subject to quite special and
> distinct laws.
>
> Raymond Williams, *Marxism and Literature*

The chief aim of this volume is to introduce students and the general reader to two theoretical 'movements' which have become prominent and influential practices in all aspects of the discipline of literary studies. Because both theories are very much active, and still contested, even controversial, it is important that this book does not present them as a body of knowledge to be applied to a text, any text, as a formal exercise. It is an important realisation of both new historicism and cultural materialism that its practitioners and its writings are subject to specific historical conditions, and became prominent in specific circumstances at specific times. We might ask, for example, why both emerged in the early 1980s, why both seemed to have come to prominence in Renaissance studies, why both have had large areas and genres of literature to which they have never been 'applied' in critical readings. There are particular types of literary texts in which reading these theories encounters great difficulties. There have also been significant changes in the types of readings produced and the directions in which these theories have been pushed by recent writings that might lead us to question whether or not they are coherent theories any more, if indeed they ever were. It is always worth examining, when one learns of a 'movement' or genre, if the body of texts and practitioners included in the category really have enough in common to warrant such a grouping; given the differences of approach and style of many new historicist and cultural materialist critics, the status of both theories as coherent groupings will be questioned in this volume.

While this volume is primarily engaged, then, in introducing new historicism and cultural materialism, it will do so in a critical and interrogative fashion so that we may discover the blind spots as well as the potential uses, the contradictions as well as the underlying logic, the hidden agendas as well as the explicit assumptions, what they evade as well as what they value. It is important also to realise that the author of even a critical work like this one is far from immune from subjective approaches and selective appropriations. My own position towards these theories is never inseparable from my explanations of them, and for this reason it is best to make this position explicit from the outset. As an academic in a literature department, who teaches and researches in and across the disciplines of literature and history, the work of new historicist and cultural materialist critics has been tremendously influential on my own thinking and critical practice. Moreover, they have become central to my teaching practice in approaching literary texts in relationship to historical context. Although these theories have become unavoidable in academic interest in the relationship between literature and history, and have gained prominence not only to the extent that they are widely taught on literary theory courses but also form substantial methodological bases for a wide variety of other literary, historical and cultural studies courses, I also believe that there are problems with the methodologies and theoretical bases of both new historicism and cultural materialism which we need to bear in mind. It will become clear in the course of this volume that I believe that new historicist and cultural materialist methods and thinking can equip us with very useful ways of looking at literature in history, but that they are not free of troubling and unsatisfactory implications. What I will argue in this volume, then, is that we ought to treat new historicism and cultural materialism with the same degree of suspicion as they afforded previous versions of the past.

Literature *and* history

In their introduction to *New Historicism and Renaissance Drama*, Richard Wilson and Richard Dutton note that new historicist and cultural materialist theories mark the 'return to history' in literary criticism (Wilson and Dutton 1992, 1), and that the focus on the status of history in literary texts is probably the most important contribution which these theories have made to recent work in literary studies. New historicism and cultural materialism share a common preoccupation with the relationship between literature and history, and share an understanding of texts of all kinds as both products and functional components of social and political formations. Where many previous critical approaches to literary texts assumed that texts had some universal significance and essential ahistorical truth to impart, new historicist and cultural materialist critics tend to read literary texts as material products of specific historical conditions. Both theories approach the relationship between text and context with an urgent attention to the political ramifications of literary interpretation. In the eyes of new historicist and cultural materialist critics, texts of all kinds are the vehicles of politics insofar as texts mediate the fabric of social, political and cultural formations. This view is evident in the work of new historicist and cultural materialist critics who read historical context through legal, medical and penal documents, anecdotes, travel writings, ethnological and anthropological narratives and, of course, literary texts. It is important to bear in mind right from the beginning in approaching these theories that they break down the simplistic distinction between literature and history and open up a complex dialogue between them. They refuse to see literary texts against an overriding background of history or to see history as a set of facts outside the written text. To a new historicist or cultural materialist critic, history is not objective knowledge which can be made to explain a literary text. To see history as a secure knowledge which a literary critic can use to fix a text's meanings is clearly a comforting idea, as Jean Howard argues:

> A common way of speaking about literature and history is just that way: literature *and* history, text *and* context. In these binary oppositions, if one term is stable and transparent and the other in some way mirrors it, then that other term can be stabilized and clarified too. (Howard 1986, 24)

Literature is not, however, simply a medium for the expression of historical knowledge. It is an active part of a particular historical moment, or, as Howard says, 'literature is an agent in constructing a culture's sense of reality' (25). For new historicism and cultural materialism the object of study is not the text and its context, not literature and its history, but rather literature *in* history. This is to see literature as a constitutive and inseparable part of history in the making, and therefore rife with the creative forces, disruptions and contradictions of history.

Debates concerning the effects of literature as a form of social expression are far from recent. Plato argued in *The Republic* that poetry ought to be banished from the ideal state because of its corrupting influence (Plato 1987, 70–117, 359–77), a theme that continues in contemporary concerns over the effect that television and cinema have on increases in drug-taking, crime and violence among young people. All states and governments operate some kind of censorship and licensing laws or codes concerning cultural media; and no period in literary history is free of an exemplary case of censorship or controversy where powerful sections of society voice their concern that literature or film or theatre or dance was exerting a corrupting influence. While formalist[1] critics have sought to maintain the idea that literature is a discrete, apolitical and transcendent form of artistic expression, the societies and cultures within which literary texts operate have been busy constraining and censoring such expression out of anxieties that literature would encourage and promote illegal, immoral or undesirable actions. Clearly, we ought to pay attention to the anxieties that governing powers let slip about the effects of literature on social and political behaviour before rushing to accept the idea that literature transcends and has no effect on history, or that history has no effect on literature. New historicist and cultural materialist critics argue that literature does have powerful effects on history, and vice versa, and have paid considerable attention in their work to the effects of literature in both containing and promoting subversion, and to instances of state and hegemonic control over cultural expression.

Both theories emerged in the late 1970s and early 1980s, new historicism in the USA, cultural materialism in Britain. As we shall see in this volume, the issues with which new historicist and cultural materialist critics are most concerned are the role of historical context in interpreting literary texts and the role of literary rhetoric in interpreting history. The work of these critics follows from, and develops further, the interests and beliefs of previous generations of Marxist and historicist critics[2] who re-evaluated the stories that past societies had told of themselves. Historicist critics introduced a degree of scepticism concerning the construction of historical narratives, and the place of the critic or historian within those narratives. Historicism understands the stories of the past as society's way of constructing a narrative which unconsciously fits its own interests. Marxist critics, borrowing from the lessons of historicism, see history as the procession of stories favourable to the victor, the ruling class, with literary texts as much as historical texts taking part in that procession. Walter Benjamin asserts this view in his 'Theses on the Philosophy of History':

> All the rulers are the heirs of those who conquered before them. Hence, empathy with the victor invariably benefits the rulers. Historical materialists know what that means. Whoever has emerged victorious participates to this day in the triumphal procession in which the present rulers step over those who are lying prostrate. According to traditional practice, the spoils are carried along in the procession. They are called cultural treasures, and a historical materialist views them with cautious detachment. For without exception the cultural treasures he surveys have an origin he cannot contemplate without horror. They owe their existence not only to the efforts of the great minds who created them, but also to the anonymous toil of their contemporaries. There is no document of civilization which is not at the same time a document of barbarism. (Benjamin 1992, 248)

Benjamin follows a number of Marxist and historicist thinkers in defining history as a contest of ideologies,[3] and, as a result, follows a radical revision of the notion of truth. Truth, for many nineteenth- and twentieth-century philosophers, is no longer a stable category which is objectively knowable. Nietzsche, for instance, sees truth as a mobile army of metaphors, an image which sees truth operating not only as a flexible weapon defined by and acting in the interests of a ruling ideology, but also as a rhetorical rather than an empirical phenomenon. Truth is constructed as a seemingly objective category, the contents of which are composed of unconsciously partial and preferential versions of the past. This becomes particularly important when the Marxist thinker Louis Althusser claims that literature is one of the institutions which participate in making state power and ideology familiar and acceptable to the state's subjects (Althusser 1984, 1–61). Literature will reflect the values, customs and norms of the dominant interests in its society, according to Althusser's idea, and so is mobilised, mostly unconsciously, by the state as an ideological weapon, an army of metaphors which seek to persuade and manipulate rather than coerce.

In seeing literature as a constitutive part of the way a society orders and governs itself, new historicism and cultural materialism build on Marxist and historicist approaches to literary texts, and are set against formalist approaches to literature which disregard historical context in interpreting literature. According to Paul Hamilton, new historicist and cultural materialist critics are returning the discipline of literary studies to an historically informed base, and the opposition between historically based and formally based interpretations is one which was already central to the discipline: 'Since its acceptance as a respectable academic subject, English literary criticism has alternated between seeing itself as an historical or a formal discipline of thought' (Hamilton 1996, 151). In part this means that new historicist and cultural materialist critics are engaged in uncovering the historical contexts in which literary texts first emerged and were received, but it also means that they are busy interpreting the significance of the past for the present, paying particular attention to the forms of power which operated in the past and how they are replicated in the present. For critics such as Stephen Greenblatt or Alan Sinfield, literary texts are vehicles of power which act as useful objects of study in that they contain the same potential for power and subversion as exist in society generally. In this way literary texts become an important focus for contemporary attempts to resist power, and such critics (particularly cultural materialist critics in Britain) are more often explicit about their own political interests in subverting and resisting power, and employ literature to those ends. New historicism and cultural materialism can be seen therefore using the past as an impetus for political struggle in the present, and making it clear that the discipline of literary studies is not removed from the sphere of politics.

What is new historicism?

New historicism is a mode of critical interpretation which privileges power relations as the most important context for texts of all kinds. As a critical practice it treats literary texts as a space where power relations[4] are made visible. The visibility of power is an important concept when considering Elizabethan theatre and its relationship to the state. Jonathan Dollimore cites for an example Queen Elizabeth's anxiety that a play that implied a criticism of her, *Richard II*, 'was played 40 times in open streets and houses' (Dollimore and Sinfield

1985, 8). As Dollimore points out, Elizabeth's anxiety is that the play was performed in the *open*, in a public place outside the contained and demarcated space of the theatre, breaking down the distinction between art and reality, aesthetics and politics. The play becomes more visible and threatens to reveal through allegory the injustice of the monarch to a wide audience. The theatre itself, although advertising itself as the space of fiction and illusion, also allows certain relations, actions and motives to become visible. In many of Shakespeare's works in particular the theatre visibly presents the power plays and political corruption within a monarchic system, and spectacularly represents the poisoning of a king, the madness of a king, the murder of monarchs in their beds. By making such power plays visible, acted out on stage, theatre presents past political events in the spectrum of the contemporary, alongside, and often geographically close to, the seat of royal power in Elizabethan England. The Globe theatre was only a long stone's-throw away.from the Tower of London, and this might lead us to suspect that the representation of regicide in such proximity to the centre of regal power indicates either that it had been so safely contained as to render it powerless, or that it was tantalisingly close to the point of subversion and dissidence right at the heart of power.

The fact that a queen worried about the public performance of a play, possibly Shakespeare's, reveals that there are powerful political stakes in the effects which literary texts and performances can have. For the most part, new historicist critics are not as interested in power plays between contending monarchs or between monarchs and usurpers as they are interested in the operations of power within self-regulating ideologies. A formative study for new historicism was Claude Lévi-Strauss's recognition that culture is a self-regulating system, just like language, and that a culture polices its own customs and practices in subtle and ideological ways. For new historicists this recognition has been extended to the 'self', particularly in Stephen Greenblatt's early and seminal study, *Renaissance Self-Fashioning*. What makes the operations of power particularly complex is the fact that the self polices and regulates its own desires and repressions. This removes the need for power to be repressive. No physical or military force need be deployed or exercised for power to have operated effectively in the interests of dominant ideological systems when the self, ideologically and linguistically constructed, will reproduce hegemonic[5] operations.

New historicism often makes for grim reading with its insistence that there is no effective space of resistance. Because no self, group or culture exists outside language or society, and because every language and society are self-policing, hegemonic systems, there is no possibility of resistance emerging unchecked. This is not to say that there is no resistance, or, as it is more usually termed in new historicist writing, subversion. But subversion is always produced in the interests of power, according to new historicists. The 'production of subversion' is, writes Stephen Greenblatt in his famous essay 'Invisible Bullets', 'the very condition of power' (Greenblatt 1981, 57). Power needs to have subversion, otherwise it would be without the opportunity to justify itself, and to make itself visible as power. Precisely what 'power', and the force behind it, are we will save for the next part of this volume, but power's pervasiveness is certainly a shared assumption among new historicist critics, and this they borrow from Foucault, when he claimed in 1981 that 'Power is everywhere; not because it embraces everything, but because it comes from everywhere' (Foucault 1981, 93). We might pessimistically ask at this point what use is a critical practice that consistently registers the ineluctable and exhaustive nature of power, the futility of resistance, and the inescapable fact of our containment within linguistic and ideological constraints. New historicists usually see their practice as one of exposition, of revealing the systems and operations of power so that we are more readily equipped to recognise the interests and stakes of power when reading culture. Moreover, it is important to recognise that for new historicists the nature of power may remain the same but the form that it takes does not. Again borrowing from Foucault, new historicists often seek to identify what forms power takes as it changes from one period to another, or as Paul Hamilton refers to it, 'the repetition of power through different epistemés' (Hamilton 1996, 162). Much of the early new historicist work on the English Renaissance period, then, focuses on identifying the transition from a pre-modern to a modern epistemé,[6] in which, for example, the modern bourgeois idea of the individual began to emerge.

Since new historicism expends most of its energies on identifying and exposing these different historical epistemés, and the historical evolution of conceptions of the state, the individual, culture, family, etc., it is easy to see how it has represented for many commentators a turn to history. What is most striking about its methods of analysing history, however, is its widespread privileging of textuality, language and representation as the basis for historical analysis. It is in effect literary criticism turned on history, reading history as a text. One of the most problematic aspects of new historicism for historians, however, is its insistence on the pervasiveness and ineluctability of an overarching power, which pays scant attention as a result to the specificities and complexities of history. Indeed, later in this volume I will look more closely at this criticism and examine the contesting notions of history that prevail between literary critics practising new historicism and various different historians.

What is cultural materialism?

Like new historicism, cultural materialism privileges power relations as the most important context for interpreting texts, but where new historicists deal with the power relations of past societies, cultural materialists explore literary texts within the context of contemporary power relations. For cultural materialists the right-wing politics of Thatcherism in 1980s Britain was the context in which they revisited interpretations of Shakespeare, Webster, Wordsworth, Dickens and post-war British literature. According to cultural materialists, texts always have a material function within contemporary power structures. This is amply demonstrated by Alan Sinfield in *Faultlines* when he examines how a Royal Ordnance advertisement for defence equipment in 1989 utilises Shakespeare in promoting itself as a bastion of security and tradition (Sinfield 1992, 1–7). 'We played the Globe', boasts the advertisement, going on to say that at the same time that Shakespeare was putting on his plays in the Globe Theatre, the Royal Ordnance started supplying Britain's military forces with arms. Shakespeare in this advertisement acts as a guarantee of a secure English tradition, promoting an idea of England that supports imperialism ('playing the globe'), that asserts its cultural superiority over others, and represents the same values over 400 years, thereby endorsing a conservative approach to English politics and society.[7] For cultural materialists, literary texts behave in a direct and meaningful way within contemporary social and political formations.

This is not to say that the writings of emerging new historicists bore no relation to the politics of 1980s America. As we shall see later in the volume, much of new historicist thinking regarding the possibility of radical and dissident perspectives, and the hegemonic operation of the most conservative ideologies, can be traced to left-wing (or, more accurately, liberal left-wing) reactions to the effects of the Reagan administration in the White House. But whereas the relevance of contemporary political situations in new historicist writings is implicit, in cultural materialist readings for the most part the conservative politics dominating Britain from 1979 are in the foreground. Alan Sinfield, in the introduction to his book on post-war British literature (1989), cites Margaret Thatcher's nostalgic view of the 1950s as the last great decade of order and restraint as an impetus for reading dissidence and diversity into the literature of that decade. Julian Wolfreys, in his deconstructive form of cultural materialism in *Being English*, begins with the Thatcherite recuperation of the Victorian period as the epitome of a nostalgic vision of England in order to read the material construction of this sense of Englishness into texts of the Victorian period. In the eyes of cultural materialists, canonical texts and authors are used to validate contemporary political and cultural traditions. The appearance of the head of Dickens on the £10 note in English currency, the hologram image of Shakespeare on certain credit cards, and the stalwart insistence by conservative thinkers to maintain writers like Shakespeare and Austen on the national educational curriculum in Britain has prompted cultural materialists to be alert to the political and cultural appropriations of literary texts and authors and to examine the significance of these appropriations.

Alan Sinfield makes it clear that such appropriations by conservative orthodoxies are likely to be successful, as he maintains that 'the main effect of cultural production will generally be the *reproduction* of an existing order' (Dollimore and Sinfield 1994, 155). Like new historicism, cultural materialism studies the means and methods by which the existing order perpetuates or attempts to transform itself, and proffers a dismal view of the possibility of effective resistance against the dominant order. But whereas for new historicism subversion is always contained by state power, cultural materialism is slightly more hopeful, and for a critic like Sinfield there are sufficient cracks and contradictions in the system to allow for some oppositional intervention. It is possible, according to cultural materialist critics, to expose these contradictions to a degree sufficient to facilitate evasions of the 'structures of containment'. The relationship between power and subversion in cultural materialism is not so complete and closed as in new historicism, and at least justifies the means by which cultural materialist critics have been intervening in contemporary power relations. In some ways, then, cultural materialism takes the implications of new historicist work further in historicising its own practices within power relations.

The uses and applications of new historicism and cultural materialism

New historicism and cultural materialism have been most useful to the discipline of literary studies in exploring the relationship between literature and history, and in demonstrating the ideological and political interests operating through literary texts. In the second section of this volume I will be isolating and criticising the 'typical' strategies of reading and talking about literary texts of new historicist and cultural materialist practice, and demonstrating these strategies through reading a number of literary texts. In that part of the book the uses, potential and limits of such strategies will be made clearer, and will form the basis of a commentary on, and critique of, the critical practice of both theories. In some ways the task of isolating and identifying 'typical' strategies of reading is a reductive and misleading one, as no theory or critical practice is ever so formulaic as to lend itself to such simple application. In this sense it is difficult to talk about applying a theory to a text without some degree of falsification taking place. Inevitably such applications of a shorthand methodology of new historicism or cultural materialism misrepresent the complexities, contradictions and plural practices of various critics, subgroups and interdisciplinary scholars who compose these 'schools' of criticism. Nevertheless, it is an important and useful exercise to try to identify the common themes and methods that form the basis for literary academics labelling themselves 'new historicist' or 'cultural materialist', and it is important to see what they have contributed to the discipline of literary studies and how the critical practices which they have pioneered can be used and adopted as a strategy for reading literary texts.

New historicist methods are useful ways of constructing exchanges between diverse texts in a given historical period. Although in early new historicist work this exchange was often between literary texts and secondary historical sources, later it involved the construction of meaningful dialogues between many primary texts within the same period, including conduct books, penal documents, journal entries and travel narratives, as well as canonical literary texts. The significance of this method of combining texts from many different genres and discourses was not to make the meanings and intentions of a literary text clearer. The new historicist critics were, for the most part, intent on using literary texts as equal sources with other texts in the attempt to describe and examine the linguistic, cultural, social and political fabric of the past in greater detail. It is as a mode of reading history, and the political and social forces at work in historical periods, that new historicist methods are most useful, and this is probably where it best serves literary studies as a critical practice in placing literary texts in an unprivileged exchange with the historical forces in the time of their production. The uses to which Stephen Greenblatt and Louis Montrose have put Shakespeare's texts, as will be discussed later in the volume, of reading them as part of the fabric of Elizabethan society, exemplify this approach.

Cultural materialism, on the other hand, is primarily useful as a series of ways of analysing the material existence of ideology, concentrated in the study of literary texts. For cultural materialist critics ideology works in language and our deployment of language, but more than this, ideology exists in a material form through institutions like the church, the school, the theatre, the university and the museum. What cultural materialists are keen to show is that culture is a field of much ideological contest and contradiction, and that no cultural artefact[8] or practice is outside this political sphere. Furthermore, literary texts do not exist in a fixed moment of production for cultural materialists, as Dollimore and Sinfield explain in the influential 'Foreword' to the first edition of *Political Shakespeare*:

> A play by Shakespeare is related to the contexts of its production – to the economic and political system of Elizabethan and Jacobean England and to the particular institutions of cultural production (the court, patronage, theatre, education, the church). Moreover, the relevant history is not just that of four hundred years ago, for culture is made continuously and Shakespeare's text is reconstructed, reappraised, reassigned all the time through diverse institutions in specific contexts. What the plays signify, how they signify, depends on the cultural field in which they are situated. (Dollimore and Sinfield 1985, viii)

Cultural materialist practices enable us to examine literary texts as part of a wider context of cultural and political institutions. Shakespeare is regarded in the context of his prevalence as a cultural icon, manufactured as a genius and a master figure through the media of education, industry, theatre and the heritage business. For this reason, critics like Alan Sinfield, Jonathan Dollimore and Catherine Belsey are alert to the possibilities of making Shakespeare meaningful in the context of contemporary politics and culture. In the collection of essays, *Political Shakespeare*, from which the above quotation was taken, Dollimore looks at figures of sodomy, prostitution and transvestism in Shakespeare's works, Sinfield looks at the relationship between Shakespeare and contemporary educational curricula and ways of reading, and Graham Holderness examines how Shakespeare has been constructed through cinema and television. The methods which cultural materialists employ are never dissimilar to new historicist methods, but they develop specific strategies for reading the way in which contemporary politics and culture preserves, re-presents and remakes the past, and these strategies will be explored and demonstrated in the second section of this volume.

The volume is structured so as to move from a critical account of the history and practice of both theories, through an account of their relative positions in the contemporary academy, and finally to an extensive and careful demonstration of the readings which new historicism and cultural materialism may produce. This second section takes a number of texts, including Joseph Conrad's *Heart of Darkness*, Charlotte Perkins Gilman's 'The Yellow Wallpaper', Yeats's poem 'Easter 1916', and some of Tennyson's poetry, and demonstrates through readings of these texts the uses and the limitations of the critical practices of both theories. All of these readings are informed by reference to standard and lesser known books and essays in new historicism and cultural materialism, and are also then used to signal how new historicist and cultural materialist critics select and interpret literary texts. Throughout the volume, however, the style and method of my approach is not simply to describe and explain the debates and practices of new historicism and cultural materialism, but also to intervene in those debates, and to work out a means of negotiating the problems as well as the applications of both theoretical approaches. For this reason, I hope that this volume contributes to, as much as it elucidates, the transitions taking place in literary theories today.

Notes

1. Formalism, as its name suggests, is a genre of literary criticism which focuses on the form, style and language of a literary text, and argues that there are specific formal characteristics which make literature distinct from other kinds of writing. Formalist critics attempted to define the 'literariness' of literary language, what marked literature out for special attention. Although it emerged in Russia around 1917, it only became influential in Western literary criticism when its affinities with structuralism became apparent in the 1960s and 1970s. Victor Shklovsky, René Wellek and Roman Jakobson are some of the key figures in the Formalist movement.

2. For explanations of the Marxist and historicist influence on new historicism and cultural materialism, see the discussion in the first section of this volume. See also Moyra Haslett, *Marxist Literary and Cultural Theory*, in the same series as this volume, forthcoming, London: Macmillan, 1998.

3. Ideology is a notoriously difficult and confused term in modern critical theory. In Marx's time, ideology had almost wholly negative connotations as the delusions which others suffered about their own beliefs and values. This meaning still persists today in some forms. The Cold War saw both the USA and the USSR accuse the other of subjecting its peoples to ideological domination, by which was meant the imposition of an oppressive system of values and beliefs, while both also maintained that their own countries were free of ideology. In Marxist literary and cultural studies, ideology has acquired new meanings. It can be used in the sense of a system of ideas belonging to a particular section of society – for example, in Marx's use of 'bourgeois ideology' and 'proletarian ideology'. This gives us the impression of a society in which different group interests of value systems clash with and contradict each other. Ideology in this sense clearly doesn't have pejorative connotations – it is not oppressive – since it refers to a condition in which people identify themselves with particular class or sectional interests, and therefore with the values and beliefs of this class or section. New historicists and cultural materialists are working within a tradition of literary and cultural studies which included many Marxist terms and concepts. See the next chapter on key contexts, included in which is an explanation of the influence of Marxism on the new historicism and cultural materialism. See also Raymond Williams, *Keywords*, London: Fontana, 1983, 153–7, and Tom Bottomore *et al.* (eds.), *A Dictionary of Marxist Thought*, Oxford: Blackwell, 1991, 247–52.

4. Power is perhaps the most elusive term in the new historicist and cultural materialist vocabulary. It is more frequently used by new historicists; cultural materialists tend to use more Marxist terms such as ideology or hegemony. 'Power' is borrowed from Foucault's *History of Sexuality, Volume 1*, London: Penguin, 1981. It refers usually to the relations of domination and resistance which saturate our social, political and cultural relations, but it can also refer to the ways in which power is a productive, even pleasurable, part of our existence. Power in new historicist analysis hovers between being oppressive and being productive, and one of the most elusive aspects of this term is that it seems to emanate from us, and to be applied to us. The discussion of power will appear throughout this volume.

5. Hegemony is Gramsci's term for the way in which a dominant class or group in society makes compromises, forges alliances, exerts moral and intellectual leadership and creates a network of institutions and social relations, in order to create a basis for the consent of the people from all classes and sections of society. Prior to Gramsci's formulation of the term it had usually referred to the domination of one people or group by another, but Gramsci refined it to explain the ways in which the bourgeoisie, the class enemies of the proletariat, acquired and maintained the submission and complicity of the proletariat in their own domination. See Bottomore *et al.* (eds.), *A Dictionary of Marxist Thought*, 229–31.

6. Epistemé is a concept which new historicists borrow from Foucault. Foucault explains the concept in the preface to *The Order of Things* as similar to a period of history, but referring not to historical events but to the character and nature of 'knowledge' at a particular time. According to Foucault, knowledge is defined and organised in various societies and at various times in different ways, so that he is able to identify that the Classical age of knowledge begins in the mid-seventeenth century and the modern age of knowledge begins in the early nineteenth century. Foucault's analysis, and likewise new historicist analysis, consists often of a tracing of the emergence of particular concepts or ideas to a particular epistemé, or period in the history of thought and knowledge.

7. Sinfield examines the position of the Royal Ordnance in Thatcherite Britain, careful to place the Royal Ordnance in the context of its newly privatised status, of its diminished role in post-imperial Britain, and of its subsidiarity to the global strategies of the USA. This is a good example of how cultural materialist critics are engaged both in reading representations, and in situating those representations in material and historical practices.

8. The concept of cultural artefact is borrowed from Clifford Geertz, whose influence on the new historicism is discussed in the next section of this volume.

Part I

The Turn to History

1 Key Contexts and Theorists

so I came to you, you men of the present, and to the land of culture....
Truly, you could wear no better masks than your own faces, you men
of the present! Who could – *recognize* you! Written over with the signs
of the past and these signs overdaubed with new signs: thus you have
hidden yourselves well from all interpreters of signs!

Friedrich Nietzsche, *Thus Spake Zarathustra*

Key contexts

Before embarking on an explanation and exploration of the issues,
debates and the evolution and development of new historicism and
cultural materialism, we need to set these theories in the context of
wider and older debates taking place in the academy and in intellectual discourse. For the most part both new historicism and cultural
materialism share common influences, although to different extents.
Marxism is much more apparent as an influence in cultural materialism than it is in new historicism, whereas the influence of anthropology is more discernible in new historicism than in cultural
materialism. In this chapter of the book I will examine the various
factors and figures influencing new historicists and cultural materialists, but, because these influences differ in degrees between both
theories, my immediate point of departure is the relationship
between new historicism and cultural materialism.

The relationship between new historicism and cultural materialism

In some ways new historicism and cultural materialism are fully inter-
twined, hence the fact that they are considered so compatible for a
book of this nature, and the fact that they have been consistently

placed alongside each other in anthologies and critical books. When Jean Howard attempted to account for the developments of new historicist interpretations in 1986 she referred to Alan Sinfield and Jonathan Dollimore as typical practitioners of new historicism in Britain (Howard 1986, 13–16), although she recognised in a footnote that there were differences between cultural materialism and new historicism which were beginning to become clear. In some cases the relationship has in my view been misunderstood. Cultural materialists are not simply British critics practising new historicism under a different name, as Richard Wilson and Richard Dutton claim in the introduction to *New Historicism and Renaissance Drama*. It is not simply 'the British wing' of new historicism (Wilson and Dutton 1992, xi), and it is not the case that 'Cultural Materialism was the name they adopted in contradistinction to Cultural Poetics' (15). It is clear from Dollimore and Sinfield's preface to *Political Shakespeare* that there were a variety of factors in British culture and in the British academy which led to the separate genesis of cultural materialism, and which placed cultural materialist critics in separate, although not dissimilar, circumstances and interpretive positions. In particular, a strong tradition of literary humanism[1] had insisted on treating Shakespeare and other canonical authors as part of a great English heritage without recognising the ideological function of such a heritage, and this tradition was most entrenched in the British education system.

Where cultural materialist critics have endeavoured to argue that Shakespeare might equally produce images and ideas of dissidence and transgression for twentieth-century readers or audiences than support the moral values of liberal humanism, new historicists have been more interested in Shakespeare's plays as examples of a prominent Renaissance cultural form which makes visible Renaissance power relations, most particularly the encounter between Europe and the New World. For cultural materialists, Raymond Williams had been the first critic to challenge the liberal humanism of F. R. Leavis in English literary studies, and it is from Williams's use of the phrase 'cultural materialism' in *Marxism and Literature* that Dollimore and Sinfield adopted and defined the new critical practice in Britain, and not in opposition to 'Cultural Poetics', which only gained prominence in the late 1980s and early 1990s as an alternative label which Greenblatt began to prefer over new historicism. There has been a degree of confusion over the relationship between cultural materialism and new historicism, and many critics discuss the two practices as if they were one and the same. In this book I have tried to organise discussion of the two theories into separate sections precisely to avoid confusion. But they also have a large number of preoccupations and interpretive strategies in common, and this is what sometimes makes the relationship between them so dynamic, but also contributes to confusion.

Both made a dramatic impact on studies of Renaissance literature in the mid-1980s, and brought a number of important poststructuralist[2] ideas to literary studies. Chief among these was the idea that all human behaviour, practices and knowledge were constructs and inventions, rather than natural or instinctual. Such a realisation leads to the practice of reading texts as participants in the construction of human beliefs and ideologies, a practice which is common to both new historicists and cultural materialists. Because texts are understood as participating in the production of ideology and culture, both new historicists and cultural materialists insist that there is no division between text and context, or between literature and politics. Out of this common belief both critical practices treat literary texts on an equal basis with texts and documents of all kinds, professing not to privilege 'literature' as a form of expression outside the realms of society or politics or history. This common basis makes it difficult to separate the two, and indeed enhances the work of both new historicists and cultural materialists. The differences between them cannot simply be regarded as the product of different national and state institutions, one from Britain, one from the USA, and we ought to pay attention to the possibility that some so-called new historicists in the USA may be more appropriately called cultural materialist, and vice versa. Kiernan Ryan advocates this degree of subtlety when approaching theoretical distinctions of this kind. He looks forward to a situation 'in which American scholars can find themselves more at home with cultural materialist assumptions; in which radical British readings can thrive when transplanted into transatlantic hotbeds of new historicism' (Ryan 1996, xi).

There is a larger area of concern that looms here in how we define a critical practice in the first place. Inevitably the most prominent practitioners of the theories become the first to define what those theories are, and this is no exception with Greenblatt for new historicism and Dollimore and Sinfield for cultural materialism. Editors of anthologies and authors of explanatory essays and books become the next to set out the major assumptions and defining traits of the critical practice.

Those critics who are negative about the critical practice also help to define it, either by defining what it is not, or by provoking an explanatory response from practitioners. But there are always a diversity of interests and goals in the practices of different critics within new historicism and cultural materialism, and all such labels invite the exclusion of those who no longer practice the particular theory, the inclusion of newcomers, the tracing of developments within it, and the subtle differentiation of degrees of conformity to it. But precisely what is the defining norm of the theory and critical practice is always a matter for debate. There is no way of defining a critical practice without basing it on the work of individual practitioners, but any such definition will rely on the reduction of differences between practitioners to find the common denominators, and the accuracy of such common denominators is somewhat uncertain. Critics rarely work to a formula either, thankfully, and this means that it is difficult to discriminate when a critic is 'being' new historicist and when s/he is carrying this practice into new realms or strategies. It seems to me, for example, that there is little to mark the difference between Greenblatt's work as a new historicist and his work as a practitioner of cultural poetics other than his announcement that he preferred the latter label. If this means that changes in literary studies resemble the world of marketing and brand names, then we need to historicise the emergence of new historicism and cultural materialism more stringently in order to examine the circumstances in which they emerged, and the pressures involved in defining and monitoring new critical practices.

If new historicism and cultural materialism are the products of clever marketing and selling strategies in the academic sphere, this may not altogether be something to be frowned upon. We need to recognise that literary studies is not outside the world of sales and marketing, but in fact is an industry in some ways itself. Glance at the acknowledgements, preface page or notes of a good edition of a Shakespeare play and we can see the efforts which have gone into ensuring that Shakespeare is made meaningful for us, whether it is in translating words which bear no significance today, or in rescuing 'lost' histories of people, places, events or customs which are referred to in the manuscripts. Shakespeare is not naturally familiar to readers in the twentieth century, and there are thousands of jobs and careers built on educating us to read Shakespeare. There is therefore a lot at stake in keeping alive the critical industry of reading Shakespeare, and reading literature in general, and what lies at the heart of this is the belief that reading literature is somehow a morally uplifting, civilising pursuit, which will produce people of good character and of high moral and civic principle. It is within, and sometimes against, this industry of producing people of good character, a highly idealised and ideological construct, that literary theories of the latter half of the twentieth century have been working. One of the most radical trends which has been provoked by new historicist and cultural materialist work is the interpretation of Shakespeare, and many other canonical, 'civilised' authors, in ways which go against the grain of this industry. Reading articulations of transgressive sexualities, anti-colonial sentiments, feminist and post-Marxist politics, both new historicism and cultural materialism attempt to find alternatives to the humanist deployments of literature as a vehicle for the production of the moral, law-abiding citizen. Perhaps the most successful way of marking this radical break from humanist tradition is by marketing itself as a new way of approaching literature, open and attentive to alternative perspectives and identities. Marketing a new theory by drawing attention to its common themes and strategies is a way of using the critical industry in literary studies to turn against its more conservative and humanist tendencies. Recognising that literature has been used to construct and reinforce conservative and humanist ideology is an important realisation of Marxist literary and cultural theories, and Marxist thinkers such as Althusser, Benjamin and Lukács have had a wide-ranging influence on new historicism and cultural materialism.

Marxism

On a simple level Marxism fractures the idea that history is singular and universal by positing that all history is rife with class struggle, in which the interests of the dominant economic group are represented as the interests of society in general while the interests of the proletariat, those who sell their labour for wages, are not represented, or are represented as those of a particular minority. One direct consequence of this view is evident in the work of Marxist historians who have revisited conventional accounts of the past with a view to telling stories of how the working or labouring classes lived. E. P. Thompson's *The Making of the English Working Class* is a classic example of this kind of work. Broadly speaking, Marxist thinkers have followed two different interpretations of this idea that, in Marx's words, 'the ruling ideas of each age have ever been the ideas of its ruling class' (Marx and Engels 1991, 50). The first interpretation is that economics is the determining factor in any society or culture, and that the ruling mode of economic production (e.g. capitalism, feudalism) determines the ruling mode of cultural production. According to this view, which tended to dominate the institutional Marxism which came to prominence in the USSR and China among other places, all ideas, beliefs, values and cultural forms belong to and shape the superstructure which is determined by the interests of the economic base. Capitalism, therefore, produces its own ideology. This drove Lenin, and in particularly crude forms, Stalin and Mao, to believe that a change in the economic structure would destroy capitalist ideology and would replace it with the ideas, beliefs, values and cultural forms of a communist society. More sophisticated Marxist thinkers such as Antonio Gramsci, Georg Lukács, Louis Althusser and Raymond Williams have found this view too deterministic and crude, and have overhauled the base-superstructure model in favour of an interpretation which sees economics and ideology in a relationship which is interactive and dialectical.

This forms the basis of the second interpretation, which focuses less on economics as determining factor, and more on the function of cultural representation. For Marx the existence of culture as an autonomous entity devoid of politics was an illusion which concealed the fact that culture functioned as a means of control. The ruling class employed cultural forms to represent its interests as the interests of all humanity:

> Only one must not form the narrow-minded opinion that the petty bourgeoisie, on principle, wishes to enforce an egoistic class interest. Rather, it believes that the *special* conditions of its emancipation are the *general* conditions within which alone modern society can be saved and the class struggle avoided. (Marx and Engels 1991, 114)

Rather than ideology being the product of this dominant class, the petty bourgeoisie, ideology also plays a vital part in producing the ruling class. It is the 'false consciousness' by which the ruling class come to believe (and by which other classes also come to be convinced), that its interests are the interests of the whole society, and in this way ideology is as much a determining factor in the construction of economic interests as vice versa. In *The Eighteenth Brumaire of Louis Bonaparte*, Marx explains how Napoleon's nephew came to rule in a coup in December 1851 by representing himself in heroic guise as his uncle, and so acquires power through an act of representation rather than a product of economics. Doubtless there are economic factors involved also in his coming to power, but economics is not the only determining factor.

One can trace the influence that this idea has had on new historicist and cultural materialist critics through a line of Marxist thinkers who revise and add to it. Much has been made of the materialism of Marx's thought, and certainly Marx insisted that all cultural and ideological forms were embedded in material practices and institutions, but one can see in the work of Marx and of Marxist thinkers that representation becomes as significant a field of struggle as the world of empirical economic circumstances. It is finally the control of the means of representation which ensures that the peasant class in Louis Bonaparte's France remain exploited and oppressed, as Marx describes the position of the peasants: 'They cannot represent themselves. They must be represented' (Marx 1991, 164). The bourgeois may dominate the peasants by economic means, but their dominance is made plausible and is perpetuated at the level of representation. For Gramsci the task of Marxist criticism is then to engage with capitalism on an ideological level, representing the interests of the working and peasant classes and exposing the contradictions and 'false consciousness' of the bourgeoisie. Indeed the possibility of all social and political change relies upon the outcome of this ideological struggle, as Gramsci explains in his *Prison Notebooks* 'men acquire consciousness of structural conflicts on the level of ideologies' (Gramsci 1971, 365). According to the view which sees economics as the sole determining factor, ideology is a delusion which conceals the real, and therefore need only be dismissed as false while the real task of transferring the means of economic production to the proletariat is conducted. But this is to miss the point that bourgeois ideology succeeds in holding the captive attention and support of all classes. Gramsci referred to this condition as hegemony.

Both Gramsci and Lukács were struggling to understand the events that had taken place in Western Europe after the First World War. In their respective countries, Italy and Hungary, conditions for the revolution had reached a crucial point for Marxists who saw economics as the determinant. The bourgeois economy had entered a severe crisis, an optimum moment for the proletariat to recognise its true destiny in obtaining the means of production for itself. No such revolution occurred, and in Italy Gramsci witnessed instead the emergence of an extreme right-wing system which adhered all the more rigorously to bourgeois ideology. Despite the virtual collapse of the capitalist economic system the structure of bourgeois civil society remained intact. Clearly the prediction that an economic crisis would automatically precipitate a socialist revolution had failed. Lukács and Gramsci were instrumental in searching for a Marxist interpretation of why the revolution had failed. Lukács posited the notion that although material circumstances determined the position of the proletariat, and although material circumstances also determined that capitalism would enter into a crisis which would provide the opportunity for change, there was no inevitability about the proletariat coming to a sudden consciousness of their historical destiny. The problem for Marxism was not one of economics but of consciousness and the ideological factors which exerted pressures on consciousness. Gramsci argued that the relationship between economics and ideology was not one of a base which determined a superstructure but was rather of an economic structure which acted in mutual exchange with an ideological structure, thus while economics determined the position of the proletariat, ideology determined the consciousness of the proletariat. Ideology was not simply some grand delusion, therefore, but existed through a vast material mechanism of schools, churches, the media, the army, the parish and town civil organisations, political parties and the law courts. The whole system of social, political and cultural organisation was implicated in representing society to itself according to the interests of the ruling class but in the name of the general good of society, and because the proletariat lived, worked, were reared and educated within these material institutions and apparatus they were also fully implicated in those representations, and unconsciously subscribed to them.

We are getting close to the point of saying, then, that the choices, goals and ideas of the proletariat, as of all classes of society, were already inscribed within the system of ideological representations. Gramsci looked for a thorough examination of how the institutions which acted as extensions of the state could succeed in winning the hegemonic consensus of the people. Louis Althusser conducted this examination in *Lenin and Philosophy* and, in particular, in the essay 'Ideology and the Ideological State Apparatus'. In this essay, he describes the operations of the state as divided into the Repressive State Apparatus (RSA) and the Ideological State Apparatus (ISA). The former relies on the use or threat of violence to maintain order, through the police and army. The latter relies on the construction of social norms and parameters through the material institutions of education, religion, politics, and so on. It is through the ISAs, Althusser says, that the actions and ideas of a society are determined. Althusser at this point goes further than Lukács or Gramsci in positing that no such thing as free will or choice exists for the proletariat (or the bourgeois, for that matter), and that all individuals are 'subjects' whose subjectivity is constructed through ISAs:

> Ideas have disappeared as such (insofar as they are endowed with an ideal or spiritual existence), to the precise extent that it has emerged that their existence is inscribed in the actions of practices governed by rituals defined in the last instance by an ideological apparatus. It therefore appears that the subject acts insofar as he is acted by the following system (set out in the order of its real determination): ideology existing in a material ideological apparatus, prescribing material practices governed by a material ritual, which practices exist in the material actions of a subject acting in all consciousness according to his belief. (Althusser 1984, 43–4)

The implicit pessimism of this view, effectively arguing that all actions and ideas are already prescribed in the material ideological apparatus, anticipates the dismal conclusion of new historicist critics that subversion is precipitated by power in order to be contained, thereby precluding the possibility of radical transformation. Gramsci, Althusser and Raymond Williams all come to the conclusion that power operates in society according to a hegemonic logic which penetrates deep into social and cultural codes and conventions. Williams argues this view best when he says that if ideology were simply an imposed set of ideas and assumptions, 'the result of specific manipulation, of a kind of overt training which might be simply ended or withdrawn', radical change would be much easier to achieve than it ever is (Williams 1980, 37). Instead ideology is always the invisible, invidious force which unconsciously determines the limits and norms of thought and action through its material institutions, penetrating society and culture to the extent that it operates as unexamined common sense, the most rudimentary assumptions of that society and culture. Ideological hegemony, according to Williams, is a complex system with a myriad of internal structures, contradictions and processes of change, that works on a fundamental level 'deeply saturating the consciousness of a society' (Williams 1980, 37). Pinning down the individual or groups 'behind' it is a fruitless exercise precisely because its structures and processes are embedded in the material practices pervading our society, and is therefore not a set of instruments or tools to be wielded like weapons by the bourgeoisie over the proletariat. Rather, ideology is a self-perpetuating force, and becomes known in new historicism as 'power', borrowing from Foucault.

Marxist thought, particularly the more sophisticated strands which I've been discussing above, is a crucial context for understanding the development of new historicism and cultural materialism. Both new historicist and cultural materialist critics seek to examine the existence of an ideological system by reading its material practices, customs and rituals. In this way both draw heavily from the work of Althusser in delineating the forms which the ideological state apparatus takes. Where new historicism and cultural materialism differ most radically can also be seen in the context of the Marxist debate. New historicism tends to favour the route taken by Foucault and Althusser in examining the textual form taken by material practices and institutions, and exposing the transformations, contradictions, and the production of subversion in order to recuperate power. Its practice is therefore more to do with the description of processes and forces. Cultural materialism, on the other hand, favours Walter Benjamin's approach. Like Benjamin's 'historical materialist', the cultural materialist 'regards it as his task to brush history against the grain' (Benjamin 1992, 248), which is to say that the cultural materialist shares the new historicist method of describing the processes and forces of ideological hegemony, but also attempts to activate the dissidence and subversion which the cultural materialist believes lies dormant in any textual manifestation of ideology. Both new historicism and cultural materialism, as Catherine Gallagher says, 'possess a remarkable continuity with certain cultural assumptions of the New Left' (Gallagher in Veeser 1989, 43):

> We have tended to insist that power cannot be equated with economic or state power, that its sites of activity, and hence of resistance, are also in the micro-politics of daily life. The traditionally important economic and political agents and events have been displaced or supplemented by people and phenomena that once

seemed wholly insignificant, indeed outside of history: women, crim-
inals, the insane, sexual practices and discourses, fairs, festivals, plays
of all kinds. Just as in the 1960s, the effort in the 1980s has been to
question and destabilize the distinctions between sign systems and
things, the representation and the represented, history and text.
(Gallagher in Veeser 1989, 43)

Marxism, by drawing attention to the conflict and contradiction at the
heart of 'history' and 'representation', opened the way for a full-scale
examination and challenge of the processes and forces of ideology or
power, and this is the task of new historicism and cultural materialism.

Historicism

In some ways Marxism and historicism were already imbricated in
one another's discourse before new historicists developed Marxist
thought on ideology and hegemony. For Marx investigations of the
means by which the past acted on the ideas and actions of the present
was crucial to understanding the possibility for future action and
transformation:

> Men make their own history, but they do not make it just as they
> please; they do not make it under circumstances chosen by them·
> selves, but under circumstances directly encountered, given and
> transmitted from the past. The tradition of all the dead generations
> weighs like a nightmare on the brain of the living. (Marx and Engels
> 1991, 93)

Marx is essentially making a historicist point here, that the past structures and organises the present, and is an immensely powerful deter·
minant of possibilities for action and thought in the present.
Historicists are best understood as historians and intellectuals,
mainly in the nineteenth century, who became suspicious of the practice of history as the objective description of a knowable past or as the
empathetic recreation of that past. According to historicists, then, the
practice of history could never be separated from the interests of the
individuals or groups practising history in the present, nor ought it to
be the vain glorification of a romantic view of past traditions. The
history practised by historicists was as suspicious of its own position
in the present as it was of the stories that people of the past told of
themselves. Historicists deciphered the present as much as they deci-

phered the past, precisely because they believed that the kind of history which we constructed in the present represented as much a view of ourselves in the present as of those in the past.

Historicism is a complication of enlightenment[3] versions of historical practice in that its suspicion that the stories we tell of the past reflect the stories we want to tell of the present exposes the degree of ideological investment a society puts into stories of the past. Since the eighteenth-century enlightenment, Western capitalist democracy has told stories of itself which blended pride in the virtuous traditions and glorious successes of its past with a firm belief that it is constantly making advances and progress in the present. The examples, of monuments and institutions commemorating and perpetuating legendary victories and figures, are abundant, as are technologically driven advances in drug therapy, car speed, communication accessibility and production capacity. Behind these stories is a complex value system which influences and determines the way in which the historians of the present scan and write about the past, often constructing a narrative which reflects or inadvertently indicates the continuity of certain traditions into the present, the conditions of life in the past which have been improved since, and the crises and turmoil which society has endured in order to reach the triumphs of the present. Contemporary historians may even tell stories of decline and loss in the present which imply that the people of the present have strayed from the proper course of continuing enlightenment and progress. Historicism regards such stories with a great deal of scepticism while simultaneously recognising that they themselves are not outside that value system and must acknowledge the ideological interests at stake in their own interpretations of the past.

For the major philosophers of historicism – Vico, Schleiermacher and Dilthey – the past did not consist of a set of objective facts which could be discovered, related to other facts and used together to tell the story of what had taken place in the past. Instead, the past was expressive rather than objective, expressive in the same way that a literary text is expressive. Historicists understand the past as a narrative, and accordingly they narrativise the past. For historicists, the past constitutes many possibilities for meaning, and the task of the historian is not simply to 'find' the facts but also to interpret and examine critically the way in which a society constructs its records, documents and histories. More recent historicist philosophers, such as Hans Georg Gadamer, would argue that because the records of the past are expressive rather than objective, the best way to understand our relationship to the past is as a conversation rather than a laboratory dissection. In this view, the historian is much more of a literary critic, constructing a dialogue between text and text, and between text and critic. Typical of historicism also is the complexity of this dialogue. As the novelist L. P. Hartley notes at the beginning of *The Go-Between*, 'the past is a foreign country' (Hartley 1958, 7), and this idea produces two immediate points. The first is that historians must investigate and interpret the past only by first attempting to reconstruct imaginatively a series of half-available relations and structures, recovering whatever possible of the lost ideologies, belief-systems and values of past societies. The second is that historians approach the past as a strange territory, as another culture effectively, and therefore are particularly susceptible to recognising familiar explanations in the unfamiliar signs produced by past records and texts. This partly explains the interest which new historicist critics have shown in Renaissance accounts of encountering the New World, as these encounters between Europeans and alien cultures resemble the distance from which historians approach the alien pasts, without sufficient knowledge of the sign systems, possibilities and parameters for meaning, customs and rituals of the past.

New historicism tends to distance itself from historicism on the grounds that historicist critics often viewed the past in terms of epochal trends and orders, and that the Renaissance period, or the Reformation period, for example, was characterised by a single dominating system of explanation and belief; whereas new historicist critics, on the other hand, tend to view the past as consisting of very diverse configurations of beliefs, values and trends, often coming into conflict and contradiction with each other. New historicism might be understood as a refinement of the previous historicism, then, but it is also difficult to separate the modes of understanding the relationship between the past and the present elaborated by historicist thinkers from the critical practice of new historicism. Both new historicism and cultural materialism share a willingness to question and examine the assumptions behind their own interests in the past, and ground their practices of historical interpretation in explanations of political pressures in the present. So, too, they share the suspicion which historicism exercised on the stories which past societies told of themselves, and share the belief that the past is a complex and distant culture which requires sensitive reconstruction and an attention to the unfamiliarity and inscrutability of past practices. In many cases, new historicist and cultural materialist critics were only able to approach this task of historicising the texts and records of the past when historians in Europe and America had begun to tell previously hidden histories of the past, and when work in anthropology and ethnology added a new mode of analysis to the literary interpretation of historical texts.

Anthropology and history

For new historicists, approaching the sign systems of the past was analogous with anthropologists approaching the sign systems of another culture. In one way, new historicism attempts to conduct anthropological studies as well as historical or literary studies, in the sense that its practitioners are more usually interested in the encounter between one culture and another, as well as being aware of their own cultural distance from the past. This is particularly evident in a work like Stephen Greenblatt's *Marvelous Possessions*, for example, in which Greenblatt examines the phenomenon of 'wonder' in the responses to the New World of European 'discoverers'. Greenblatt recounts in the introduction to that work his own sense of wonder when travelling through Bali at a group of Balinese villagers who had assimilated Western TV and VCR technology into their own culture, using it to show their own rituals and village dances. His wonder is produced by the fact that the villagers have completely gone against his expectations of finding a Balinese culture dominated by Western technology, representations and culture. The anecdote about his own travels and the wonder which they have produced allows Greenblatt to forge an anthropological metaphor for the sense of wonder which he finds in the writings of Columbus, Mandeville, Díaz and others encountering strange cultures. The sense of wonder in all cases is a product of the distance between the one who arrives with the aim of studying, knowing about, an other culture, and the sign systems, customs and practices of that culture.

A cultural distance lies between the observer and his objects of study, and this distance for new historicists must be accounted for and negotiated rather than evaded or ignored. Partly this is the lesson learned from Edward Said's *Orientalism*, a rudimentary work in post-colonial studies, one aspect of which is the point that anthropologists, scientists, historians and writers of all kinds were complicit in forming and perpetuating the discourse of imperial domination. It was precisely by reducing other cultures to a form of knowledge to be consumed and used by the imperial powers that intellectuals and academics played a vital role in preparing the way for more repressive means of domination. In the light of this study, which employed the lessons of Foucault's work, which also had a decisive impact on the new historicists, the practitioners of new historicism were already better placed to reflect on their own sensitivity to the power relations between them as interpreters and historians not only of past times, but also of other cultures in the past. It was also the work of anthropologists which directly influenced new historicists like Greenblatt and Montrose. Clifford Geertz brought anthropology closer to the practices of literary studies when he asserted that human beings are 'cultural artifacts' (Geertz 1993, 51). He argued that contrary to popular anthropological assumption, culture had been a central ingredient in forming human beings, rather than being an addition to human life which had been developed after a biological essence. Human beings actually required cultural symbols and signs in order to function at all, and according to Geertz, 'there is no such thing as a human nature independent of culture' (Geertz 1993, 49):

> By submitting himself to governance by symbolically mediated programmes for producing artifacts, organizing social life, or expressing emotions, man determined, if unwittingly, the culminating stages of his own biological destiny. Quite literally, though quite inadvertently, he created himself. (Geertz 1993, 48)

It is not difficult to see the range of possibilities that such thinking brings for cultural studies, a discipline in which new historicists are situated comfortably, and which indeed they have in many ways expanded. Man creates himself, hence, perhaps, the title of Greenblatt's *Renaissance Self-Fashioning*. Geertz, unwittingly, appropriates the historical evolution of humankind for cultural studies, rather than biology and scientific ethnology.

In Geertz we have a theoretical context for the way in which new historicists examine how a particular period or culture fashions itself, manufactures itself. The point with new historicists is not whether or not this self-fashioning is 'true' – all we have to make such a judgement is the textual and artefactual remains of their self-fashioning, anyway – but how and why an individual or a people fashion themselves in a particular way. Neither is it the practice of new historicists

to generalise specific examples of self-fashioning into the fashioning
or imagination of an age or nation. Geertz insists on paying attention
to detail and difference in the study of cultural forms and symbols,
respecting the diversity at work in cultural systems, and pushing
through generalising labels:

> We must, in short, descend into detail, past the misleading tags, past
> the metaphysical types, past the empty similarities to grasp firmly the
> essential character of not only the various cultures but the various
> sorts of individuals within each culture, if we wish to encounter
> humanity face to face. In this area, the road to the general, to the
> revelatory simplicities of science, lies through a concern with the
> particular, the circumstantial, the concrete, but a concern organized
> and directed in terms of the sort of theoretical analyses that I have
> touched upon – analyses of physical evolution, of the functioning of
> the nervous system, of social organization, of psychological process,
> of cultural patterning, and so on – and, most especially, in terms of
> the interplay among them. That is to say, the road lies, like any
> genuine Quest, through a terrifying complexity. (Geertz 1993, 53–4)

The interpretive or analytic practice that Geertz is describing here is
known as 'thick description', a practice that has become a feature of
new historicism. The new historicist critic must 'descend into detail',
constructing meaningful exchanges between texts of diverse forms
and orientations, in order to get closer to the linguistic, cultural and
social fabric of the past. Geertz's description above could indeed be a
description of new historicist critical practice, with some slight alter-
ations. New historicists seek to understand the operation of power
within and through human culture, rather than seeking to 'encounter
humanity face to face'. Where Geertz is obviously interested in following up physiological and biological arguments, new historicists are
more interested in the scientific and pseudo-scientific discourses in
which such arguments take place. We will come across the practice of
'thick description' again later in the volume, but it is an important
dimension of new historicism that this concept and practice comes
first from the discipline of anthropology and that new historicists
have put the disciplines of literary studies and anthropology into a
mutually beneficial exchange.

   If anthropology had to open new avenues of investigation before
triggering new forms of investigation in the study of culture within
and through the discipline of literary studies, so too did the discipline

of history undergo sweeping changes before becoming an influence on the 'return to history' in literary studies. That is to say that the forms of history and anthropology which influenced and encouraged the emergence of new historicism in the early 1980s were themselves recent developments. It was in the 1960s and 1970s that the discipline of history in Europe and the USA expanded into new areas, and, as Simon During says, 'professional historians ceased to be mainly interested in restricted-code political and state history' (During 1991, 175). The new subdisciplines of social and cultural history emerged and enjoyed considerable expansion during this period, and in some university departments are now the dominant forms of historical enquiry practised. By shifting attention away from the major battles, lines of monarchical succession and honoured heroes and leaders, and focusing on the histories of marriage, religious belief, rural labourers, child labourers, entertainment rituals and customs, motherhood, gambling or the slave trade, social and cultural historians reconstructed the everyday lives of vast sections of the population whose stories had been neglected in traditional history. Initial efforts in literary studies to dovetail with the new histories were geared towards seeing those same neglected stories reflected in literary texts. This gave way to new historicism and cultural materialism which have attempted to analyse the social and cultural processes by which the lives and cultures of whole sections and classes of people were neglected and marginalised. Opening up these hidden histories has focused the energies of new historicist and cultural materialist critics on the lives of women, cultural minorities, the insane, the underprivileged and the criminalised. Of course in the discipline of history new avenues for rescuing the stories of women, the colonised and the oppressed have been opened too, but while the function of these new histories has been primarily to tell the hidden histories, new historicism and cultural materialism have sought to understand how they became hidden in the first place, and what forces are at work in hiding and revealing them in the present.

Key theorists

Although new historicism and cultural materialism both emerged in the light of new directions in Marxism, historicism, anthropology and history, the work of two scholars in particular must be emphasised as decisive to the formation of both critical practices: Raymond Williams and Michel Foucault. Williams was Professor of Drama at Jesus College, Cambridge from 1974 to 1983, and taught there until he died in 1990. Working within Marxist literary and cultural studies – indeed, he was instrumental in creating this genre of studies in Britain – he influenced Sinfield and Dollimore, and contributed to the *Political Shakespeare* anthology which could be said to have launched cultural materialism. He also taught Stephen Greenblatt while Greenblatt studied in Britain on a scholarship in the mid-1970s, but Greenblatt is more closely linked with the French social scientist and historian of ideas, Michel Foucault. Foucault came to prominence in the humanities as a brilliant historian of madness, sexuality and discipline. His histories are more a combination of philosophical inquiry into the meaning and function of these phenomena, and their discursive manifestations, in human society with genealogies[4] of how they change through different eras, always altering according to the needs and demands of a self-regulating system of power in society. Foucault gave lectures at Berkeley, University of California, in the late 1970s which Greenblatt attended, and at which university a number of new historicist critics were employed. It was Foucault's achievements in tracing the structures and forms of power which have led Greenblatt to attempt similar projects, and Foucault's influence is discernible also in the work of Louis Montrose, Jonathan Goldberg and to a lesser extent, Catherine Gallagher. This section of the book discusses the significance of Foucault and Williams for literature and history in general, and in particular as precursors of the emergence of new historicism and cultural materialism.

Raymond Williams

In retrospect, two critics dominate literary studies in 1950s Britain and to a large extent since then – Raymond Williams, who published *Culture and Society 1780 to 1950* in 1958, and F. R. Leavis, who had made his mark on literary criticism since the 1930s, and who published *The Great Tradition* in 1948 and *The Common Pursuit* in 1952. Williams was a much younger man than Leavis, a more junior academic when Leavis was at the height of his academic career, but the two critics retrospectively represent two traditions of literary criticism which have had a considerable impact on the emergence of cultural materialist practice. Leavis was the leading advocate of humanist criticism which posited that literature's primary function was to examine and reveal the intricacies of human nature, and that the trained literary critic could classify literature according to how complex was the portrait of morality, feeling and life. So, in *The Great Tradition*, Leavis argues that Jane Austen is a great novelist because of her 'intense moral preoccupation' (Leavis 1962, 16), whereas he dismisses the work of Arnold Bennett: 'Bennett seems to me never to have been disturbed enough by life to come anywhere near greatness' (16). Williams, on the other hand, became one of the chief pioneers of Marxist literary and cultural studies, and examined literature as a mode of cultural production. Literature for Williams was not the highest expression of human nature, but, rather, was a changing social practice which produced language in a specialised, seemingly privileged way. Literature represented the social and cultural values of certain sections of people, and not, as in humanist criticism, the great universal truths of human nature.

Both Leavis and Williams were founders of the professionalised discipline of literary studies as we know it today. Leavis argued that literary critics were not just devoted readers and commentators of literature, but were highly trained readers, with an acquired appreciation of the subtleties and complexities of language. In *The Common Pursuit*, for example, in dealing with the relationship between literature and society, he insisted that literature could be a vital source of education about political and social matters, but 'only if it is approached as literature' (Leavis 1984, 193). Williams certainly worked on the same professional approach to literature as Leavis. Where they can be seen to differ widely is the uses to which they put literary texts. Leavis sees literature as a hierarchy of writers, from the great who 'add' something to literary tradition by the intuition of their genius, to the popular or low who debase literature by pandering to popular taste. Leavis's critical practice is basically a matter of examining 'great' writers as to the reasons for their greatness, usually finding that literary greatness resides in promoting an 'awareness of the possibilities of life' (Leavis 1962, 10), in the 'subtleties of the artist's use of language and ... complexities of his organizations' (Leavis 1984, 193), or in 'the insight, the wisdom, the revived and re-educated feeling for health' (Leavis 1964, 16). The emphases in Leavis's critical practice are on the intelligence and genius of a writer and the way that a writer synthesises artistic form and human nature. The criteria for his critical judgements, however, are largely a matter of taste. Clearly, what is insight and wisdom to some will be common sense or stupidity to others. Subtlety may be read as vagueness, complexity as confu-, sion, and the humanist pinnacle – 'awareness of the possibilities of life' – may, according to one's taste, be found not in Jane Austen or Henry James but in a comic book or a Mills and Boon novel. Despite Leavis's attempts to delineate a hierarchy of judgement and taste in literary studies, the criteria for this hierarchy ultimately resided in the dictates of his own taste.

Williams, on the other hand, is genuinely interested in literature not as a privileged form for the expression of genius, nor as a league table of achievements in subtlety and complexity of language, but rather as one form of social experience and practice. In *Culture and Society 1780–1950*, Williams criticised Leavis for promoting literature as the exclusive possession of a privileged élite of trained intellectuals, as the domain responsible for 'controlling the whole range of personal and social experience' (Williams 1961, 249). In doing so, Williams argued, Leavis was neglecting vast areas of human experience, knowledge and practice:

> I agree with Leavis ... that a society is poor indeed if it has nothing to live by but its own immediate and contemporary experience. But the ways in which we can draw on other experience are more various than literature alone. For experience that is formally recorded we go, not only to the rich source of literature, but also to history, building, painting, music, philosophy, theology, political and social theory, the physical and natural sciences, anthropology, and indeed the whole body of learning. We go also, if we are wise, to the experience that is otherwise recorded: in institutions, manners, customs, family memories. (Williams 1961, 248)

In criticising Leavis here, Williams reveals much about his own interests and practice. Williams shares Leavis's interest in human experience, but sees literature as only one form of the material expression of human experience. The combined forms of expressing human experience are what Williams called 'culture', and his analysis of these forms is what he referred to in 1977 as 'cultural materialism'. His critical practice, if we take the above passage as a description of it, anticipates the social histories that were to follow in the 1960s and 1970s, and anticipated the wide range of cultural reference found in new historicist and cultural material practices which followed in the 1980s.

In *Culture and Society 1780–1950* Williams began by sketching a history of the key words 'industry', 'democracy', 'class', 'art' and 'culture', an idea which was more fully explored in his *Keywords: A Vocabulary of Culture and Society*. In the changing meanings of these words from the eighteenth to the twentieth centuries he saw a reflection of a changing society, more specifically the reflection of an emerging, powerful array of institutions in economics, politics and society. That these institutional transformations were embodied in language indicates the level at which Williams believes that language (and its constituent modes of social and cultural expression) is fully implicated in material practice. Language changes just as the material practices, objects and institutions to which it refers change, and likewise, it is only possible for us to conceive of these material changes when concepts for the new forms already exist in language. In this way, culture and society are mutually interactive, and we may recall at this point that this idea is typically Marxist in its insistence on the dialectical[5] relationship between base and superstructure, economics and ideology, or society and culture.

Williams differs from Leavis, then, in two important respects. First, he sees literature not as the highest form of human expression but as one of many forms of expression, and as part of a system of culture which is constantly shifting, rather than a self-perpetuating 'great' tradition. Second, he assigns responsibility for shifts and changes in literature not to the insight or wisdom of an individual genius but to shifting economic, political, social and cultural conditions in general, and therefore takes literary studies out of the domain of judging the relative merits of one writer over another (judgements dependent on taste) and into the domain of describing and analysing the specific cultural conditions in which literary texts are produced and received. Williams marked a radical break from humanist conceptions of literature and was crucial to the development of a critical practice which would analyse the way in which culture both reflected and acted upon the society of which it was a part. His theoretical assumptions and defences have become the bases of contemporary cultural materialist practice. So, too, cultural materialists have been influenced by Williams's attention to the wider cultural spheres of education, the press, communications and social spaces in works like *The Long Revolution, Communications,* and *The Country and the City*. This range of reference is combined with an anthropological focus on the social and cultural practices of modern society, and this has endorsed cultural materialist attempts to construct narratives of literature as a practice embedded in material institutions such as education, the media and the theatre.

Perhaps even more significant for cultural materialists, however, is Williams's outlining of a Marxist conception of power relations in *Marxism and Literature*. Williams argues in this work that a cultural system must not be defined solely by its dominant features. He has in mind the way in which bourgeois culture may be dominant in our 'modern' era (which we might loosely define as 1700 or 1750 onwards), but is not the general and exhaustive condition of human existence in this period. Here, Williams is taking us back to Marx's idea that the bourgeois class believes that the special conditions in which it is emancipated are the general conditions for all humankind. Williams invites us to distinguish between the dominant features of a cultural system, which are determined by the dominant social group, and the movements and tendencies of the whole cultural system, which do not belong necessarily to the dominant social group. There may be elements of a previous dominant system residing in the current one – feudal tendencies in bourgeois culture, for example. Or, indeed, there may be emergent tendencies of a new cultural system at work in the current dominant system. So, Williams's classic model of cultural systems involves three main elements: the dominant, the residual and the emergent.

Williams cites three examples of 'residual' elements within the cultural system, and by residual he means some social or cultural practice which has been effectively formed in another epoch but which plays a significant role within contemporary culture. The first is organised religion, which he says has been partly incorporated into the dominant culture in the form of 'official morality, or the social order of which the other-worldly is a separated neutralizing or ratifying component' (Williams 1977, 122). Where it has been incorporated it is not effectively distinguished from the dominant. Only unincorporated 'remainders' – Williams suggests 'absolute brotherhood, service to others without reward' as ideas based in organised religion which have not been incorporated – have the potential to act in an oppositional manner towards the dominant culture, where these ideas come into conflict with the dominant ideology. Williams gives rural communities and the monarchy as two further examples of residual elements within the British cultural system, although he argues that the idea of the rural community has almost completely been incorporated as the fetishised leisure facility of the dominant order, while the monarchy is incorporated, 'marking the limits as well as the methods of a form of capitalist democracy' (123).

The residual is relatively easy to detect, given its longer history and previous social and cultural forms. Much more difficult to detect for Williams is the emergent. The chief difficulty lies in distinguishing 'between those which are really elements of some new phase of the dominant culture ... and those which are substantially alternative or oppositional to it' (123). Williams discusses the formation of a new social class as an example of what he means by emergent forms. Perhaps even more so than residual elements, the emergent is particularly subject to incorporation within the dominant culture. Williams describes the emergence of the working class in Britain as a process constantly incorporated through the simultaneous emergence of the popular press, advertising, and popular writing. Immediately new working-class cultural forms emerge they are incorporated within bourgeois interests, precisely by being accepted within predefined cultural norms and conventions. Working-class writing, for example, conforms to predefined literary norms in order to gain acceptance as literature, yet by this very action also gains acceptance as a bourgeois form. Even if emergent forms do succeed in projecting oppositional or alternative positions it is substantially more difficult for these to be recognised with any accuracy than residual forms. For the literary critic, or more specifically the cultural materialist critic working in the aftermath of Williams's ideas, this difficulty of recognising genuinely oppositional or alternative positions has incited the kinds of cultural analysis which attempt to work 'against the grain' of incorporation. Much of the labour of cultural materialist criticism has gone into producing oppositional readings of dominant forms, and also into recognising where and in what conditions incorporation has taken place.

If cultural materialist critics are more positive about the potential for subversion and dissidence than new historicists, as I believe is the case, the bases for such optimism can be found in Williams's *Marxism and Literature* too. Williams, despite his insistence on the difficulty of residual or emergent forms achieving genuine opposition to the dominant culture, emphasises that the dominant culture is not omnipotent:

> no mode of production and therefore no dominant social order and therefore no dominant culture ever in reality includes or exhausts all

human practice, human energy and human intention. This is not merely a negative proposition, allowing us to account for significant things which happen outside or against the dominant mode. On the contrary it is a fact about the modes of domination, that they select from and consequently exclude the full range of human practice. (Williams 1977, 125)

The cultural materialist practice which has emerged from Williams's ideas does not seek to reconstitute the 'whole picture', as it were, of human culture, recovering those excluded practices suggested by Williams above. Rather, cultural materialists have been primarily interested in examining the processes of inclusion and exclusion, incorporation and marginalisation, acceptance and opposition which are characteristic of the dominant culture. Williams has been a central influence in the work of critics such as Sinfield, Dollimore and Belsey because of the central role he has had in describing the interrelations of powerful elements within the cultural system, and because of his empathy for critical attempts to locate and foreground oppositional or alternative positions as well as ideological conflicts in this cultural system. For this reason, although his critical practice is quite different from cultural materialism, his descriptions of the cultural system and its component material elements and functions make him the first and foremost theorist of cultural materialism.

Michel Foucault

Michel Foucault is the most notable and most pervasive influence on new historicism, but his work is not without its old historicist precedents, particularly in the writings of Friedrich Nietzsche. Foucault's recognition that the structures of knowledge, information and decision-making in modern Western society are predicated on claims to power echoes Nietzsche's argument that all claims to truth are in reality claims to power. This is obviously similar to the arguments made by Marx, Benjamin and Althusser as discussed above, that 'the truth' was simply a version of events preferred, indeed imposed, by the dominant or ruling group in society. Outside political contest and competing wills to power there was no such thing as truth, only different versions of events. Nietzsche's late work *The Genealogy of Morals* follows this argument in examining the evolution of the concepts, and the etymologies of the words, 'good' and 'bad', the current terms used to describe degrees of moral or immoral behaviour. In a typical historicist gesture, he has contemporary moral issues at heart when he retraces these concepts through language and history. Nietzsche finds that 'good' and 'bad' (in German, *gut* and *schlecht*) derive not from any intrinsically moral or theological distinction, but instead from an intensely social and political one. Good signified noble blood, or fine breeding, in feudal Germany, and bad was equated with simple, rustic, or low. The basis of this moral distinction was then a class distinction, and Nietzsche traces the roots of morals to one class dominating and distinguishing itself from another. The will to power which is evident in this class hierarchy is hidden behind a moral façade.

This begins to sound like a Marxist exercise in exposing class struggle. Nietzsche, however, is very far from a Marxist position. He uses this genealogy which he has traced to extol the virtues of the noble class, particularly as he links nobility to a set of racial features. Nietzsche argues that at some point the 'low' classes and races have appropriated 'good' to mean weak, humble and pitiable, and that these classes and races – he attacks Jewish people viciously in this essay – now overshadow the noble and the fine. It is not surprising that Nietzsche was a favoured philosopher of the Nazis with his predilection for racial strength and nobility. He seems in fact to be in awe of strength and power, hence perhaps his will to trace the history of its mastery, and to warn of its downfall in the face of pity, humility and weakness. The first essay of *The Genealogy of Morals* acts as a call for the revival of a strong – i.e. noble – morality. There are two things worth following up here in relation to the work of Michel Foucault. The first is the idea of philosophical genealogies of concepts and social practices, which I want to argue is akin to Foucault's 'archaeologies' and 'genealogies'. The second is the awe in which Nietzsche held the history of power and mastery, the dominance of the nobility over the weak and oppressed, a sense of admiration which I want to argue is present in Foucault's work, although it is in a very different form. Furthermore, these philosophical connections between Foucault and Nietzsche are important contexts in which to place new historicism's relationship to Foucault.

Foucault discusses Nietzsche's genealogies in his essay 'Nietzsche, Genealogy, History', an essay which attempts to advocate the Nietzschean idea of genealogy as much as defining the historical practice which emerges from it. For both Foucault and Nietzsche, genealogy as a method is distinct from history in that it does not pursue 'origins' or patterns of evolution. Rather, genealogy searches for hidden structures of regulation and association, a method of tracing etymological, psychological and ideological ancestors of modern social, cultural or political practices 'in the most unpromising places', as Foucault says (Foucault 1977, 139). Above all, according to Foucault, 'it must record the singularity of events outside of any monotonous finality' (139), and so must attend to discontinuities, differences and disparities in these hidden structures as much as it attends to continuities. It is all too easy to construct a narrative of historical continuities in order to represent disparate events as parts of the same evolutionary pattern. This is 'the historian's history', in Foucault's terms, crafted to seem like a neutral, unbiased narrative of events, but in fact based on an impossible position, outside space and time, 'an apocalyptic objectivity' (152). The fact that no interpreter of the past can speak from a point in time and space which is not affected by its own cultural conditions is something which applies to Foucault's and Nietzsche's genealogist too. But at least the genealogist, in true historicist fashion, is cognisant of the provisional nature of her/his own subject position, and the specific contemporary conditions from which s/he is interpreting the past.

Nietzschean genealogies are from the beginning, then, opposed to the 'historian's history' as well as to the impossible objectivity of scientific discourse. Moreover, Foucault claims that such genealogies are the '*positive unconscious* of knowledge' (Foucault 1974, xi) in the English edition of *The Order of Things*.[6] By this he means that where scientific and historical discourses have emphasised their objective and verifiable nature and have denigrated the unreliability of discourses dealing with living experience and thought, they have remained unconscious of the common structures of thought in which a whole series of disciplines and modes of knowledge collude:

> unknown to themselves, the naturalists, economists, and grammarians employed the same rules to define the objects proper to their own study, to form their concepts, to build their theories. It is these rules of formation, which were never formulated in their own right, but are to be found only in widely differing theories, concepts and objects of study, that I have tried to reveal, by isolating, as their specific locus, a level that I have called, somewhat arbitrarily perhaps, archaeological. Taking as an example the period covered in this book, I have tried to determine the basis or archaeological system common

to a whole series of scientific 'representations' or 'products' dispersed throughout the natural history, economics, and philosophy of the Classical period. (Foucault 1974, xi–xii).

Foucault substitutes 'archaeology' here, however arbitrarily, for genealogy. They are almost one and the same idea, almost because archaeology suggests more of the sense of seeking out origins, whereas genealogy may involve only the tracing of historical transformations and not concern itself with origins. Foucault poses the possibility that a series of different disciplines and modes of thought employ the same basic methods and the same scientific assumptions, collaborating in a self-regulating system of representations. This system is not closed to change, but neither is it evolutionary. It operates according to a dominant structure of regulation which, when it transforms, transforms as an order, however gradually. Foucault sees science, history, literature, language, economics, and so on, as discourses which have their own rules, conscious and unconscious, and whose practitioners behave within distinct parameters and methodological assumptions. That these discourses and practitioners share common assumptions and systems of thought signifies that something of an ideological order exists: 'what if empirical knowledge, at a given time and in a given culture, *did* possess a well-defined regularity? If the very possibility of recording facts, of allowing oneself to be convinced by them, of distorting them in traditions or of making purely speculative use of them, if even this was not at the mercy of chance?' (Foucault 1974, ix). These questions, Foucault explains, are the beginnings of his 'archaeological' explorations into the structures of regulation. Far from being the result of chance, the associations and connections between these discourses reveal an order regulated by powerful ideological conditions.

Both Foucault and Nietzsche acknowledge that they are working in neglected, even original, areas of study. The questions they ask about the history of certain discourses are not of the same character as conventional history. Nietzsche describes his project in *The Genealogy of Morals* as:

> 'Under what conditions did man construct the value judgements *good* and *evil*?' And what is their intrinsic worth? Have they thus far benefited or retarded mankind? Do they betoken misery, curtailment, degeneracy or, on the contrary, power, fullness of being, energy,

courage in the face of life, and confidence in the future? A great
variety of answers suggested themselves. I began to distinguish
among periods, nations, individuals; I narrowed the problem down;
the answers grew into new questions, investigations, suppositions,
probabilities, until I had staked off at last my own domain, a whole
hidden, growing and blooming world. (Nietzsche 1956, 155–6)

Nietzsche's investigations bear with them the impending sense of
new discoveries, a world of ideas and connections without intellectual
precedent. The world which he lays bare is not that of causal links
between one event and another, or between an economic trend and a
political tradition, not a world, that is, of continuities and progres-
sions as in conventional history, but rather the one of discontinuity.
Nietzsche starts at the point of definition – 'Under what conditions
did man construct the value judgements *good* and *evil*?' – and therefore at a point of substantial transformation. And because his interest
is not in the evolution of a modern sense of morality but in the different forms that it took in different instances and epochs, his analysis
rests on defining moments of discontinuity and rupture.

  Both Foucault and new historicism belong to this Nietzschean
school of history, combining the philosophical interest in the definition of concepts and ideologies with the historical-anthropological
interest in the social and cultural practices in which such concepts
and ideologies are manifest. In the 'Introduction' to *The Archaeology
of Knowledge*, Foucault begins to define what he calls 'the new
history', which he argues is emerging from the history of ideas, history
of science, of philosophy, of thought, of literature, and not from
history proper, which 'appears to be abandoning the irruption of
events in favour of stable structures' (Foucault 1972, 6). In contrast to
this, the new history is concerned with discontinuity and rupture, the
moments of transformation and difference:

> the problem is no longer one of tradition, of tracing a line, but one of
> division, of limits; it is no longer one of lasting foundations, but one
> of transformations that serve as new foundations, the rebuilding of
> foundations. What one is seeing, then, is the emergence of a whole
> field of questions, some of which are already familiar, by which this
> new form of history is trying to develop its own theory: how is one to
> specify the different concepts that enable us to conceive of disconti-
> nuity (threshold, rupture, break, mutation, transformation)? By what
> criteria is one to isolate the unities with which one is dealing; what is

a science? What is an *œuvre*? What is *a* theory? What is *a* concept? What is *a* text? (Foucault 1972, 5)

Foucault's work focuses on epistemological breaks, the points at which a theory emerges into definition, the point where a new discourse[7] becomes dominant, or when a new social practice enters into public representation. This is evident in his 'histories', like *Madness and Civilisation*, dealing with the epistemological emergence of modern categories of insanity, like *The Birth of the Clinic*, dealing with the emergence of modern ideas of medical care, health and the care of 'the self', and like *Discipline and Punish*, dealing with the emergence of modern methods of penal correction and punishment. It is not difficult to see the importance of Foucault's methods for new historicists. Greenblatt's *Renaissance Self-Fashioning* aims to show that 'in the sixteenth century there appears to be an increased self-consciousness about the fashioning of human identity as a manipulable, artful process' (Greenblatt 1980, 2). In his *Marvelous Possessions*, Greenblatt argues not only that 'wonder ... is the central figure in the initial European response to the New World' (Greenblatt 1991, 14), but that a shift can be seen in the European experience of 'wonder' from a medieval wonder which was a sign of dispossession to a Renaissance wonder 'as an agent of appropriation' (24). Louis Montrose, in his essay 'Eliza, Queene of Shepheardes', argues that the pastoral form in the Elizabethan period was characterised by the symbolic mediation of state power and ideology. In each case, more clearly with Greenblatt than Montrose, what is at work is the tracing of an epistemological rupture, a break with tradition and the foundation of a new mode of power. New historicists are particularly prone to this type of historical focus, depicting the emergence and operation of new orders of thought and regulation, and this, as I've argued above, has its precedents in Nietzschean genealogies and Foucauldian archaeologies.

The second connection between Nietzsche and Foucault which has a direct bearing on new historicist critics is the awe and admiration with which Nietzsche holds the phenomenon of 'power' or mastery. Nietzsche's constant aim in his work was to work out a 'godless theology' by which he would expose the fact that God was dead and elevate man to a stature capable of replacing God. Man would therefore be the object of admiration, and his feats and achievements would be celebrated. It is for this reason that Nietzsche champions the 'superman', or *Übermensch*, which, as R. J. Hollingdale points out in his introduction to Nietzsche's *Thus Spake Zarathustra*,[8] does not mean a very strong, very intelligent or very powerful man, but refers to a self-fashioning man, a man who has 'overcome' himself and has determined a new self. Nietzsche finds that the basic drive behind all human existence is the will to overcome others or to overcome oneself. This, he explains, is a will to power, and in Zarathustra's speech to 'you wisest men' he says: 'You want to create the world before which you can kneel: this is your ultimate hope and intoxication' (Nietzsche 1961, 136). The death of God leaves a nihilistic void in its wake, and this is what Nietzsche observes in modern European society. The only salvation from this void is to enter a new phase of humanity, a phase in which man overcomes himself and becomes a new order. For this reason Nietzsche sees the exercise of the will to overcome, the will to power, as triumphs. His admiration for the nobility in *The Genealogy of Morals* is a good example of this, in which he argues that the characteristic difference between the nobility and the weak masses is that the true nobility 'have in them an excess of plastic curative power, and also a power of oblivion' (Nietzsche 1956, 173). In other words, the nobility have the capacity to overcome, to cure themselves of poisonous emotions or misfortunes, to rise above the circumstances determined for them and to fashion their own circumstances.

Whereas in Nietzsche this admiration for the will to power and its exercise centres on a particular class or particular individuals, Foucault recognises that power is not at the control of individual subjects or groups but instead is a general force which is only visible in particular events and actions. To a certain extent this is true of Nietzsche also, in that Zarathustra says 'Where I found a living creature, there I found will to power' (Nietzsche 1961, 137), and so recognises that the will to power operates everywhere, but Nietzsche celebrates the direct mastery of the will to power in specific individuals and groups, denigrating the plebeian uses of power. Foucault, on the other hand, insists that power operates in a structural and systematic way, and is not an instrument mastered by individuals or groups. There is no sense of man triumphantly overcoming a set of determined circumstances and creating a new order, but the structures and modes of power certainly do transform and create new orders. Power for Foucault is a force which passes through, rather than emanates from, every possible relationship.

In *The History of Sexuality, Volume 1,* first published in 1976, Foucault argues that in taking sexuality as an object of study, and in particular addressing the repression or censoring of sexuality which is associated with the Victorian period, our questions ought not to be about who repressed sexuality, or what laws or institutions were instrumental in the censorship of sexuality. It is not, in other words, a question of who is specifically responsible for changes in the social norms for sexuality. Instead Foucault asks us to conceive of the whole discourse of sexuality becoming prominent in a particular form as a result of power relations. Sexuality, he argues, only becomes a prominent discourse 'because relations of power had established it as a possible object; and conversely, if power was able to take it as a target, this was because techniques of knowledge and procedures of discourse were capable of investigating it' (Foucault 1981, 98). If this is the case our questions ought to be about the specific local power relations and the formation of a knowledge of sexuality, how this knowledge might have been used to support power relations, and how this power and knowledge nexus manifests itself in specific forms and places (Foucault's examples are 'around the child's body, apropos of women's sex, in connection with practices restricting births', 97). Foucault's analysis of power relations is distinctly different from a Marxist model, then, in which we might say that certain repressions in society are conducted in the interests of the bourgeois order. For Foucault no one individual, group, class or sex is responsible for these repressions, and nor are they outside or immune from them. Power, instead, is 'the name that one attributes to a complex, strategical situation in a particular society' (93), a series of forces at work in every social relationship, or to put it in Foucault's much quoted phrase: 'Power is everywhere; not because it embraces everything, but because it comes from everywhere' (93).

For some critics this notion that power enjoys a ubiquitous status in society is problematic. Frank Lentricchia sees Foucault's account of the genealogy or archaeology of power as a 'totalitarian narrative' with a 'depressing message' (Lentricchia in Veeser 1989, 235). The ideas that power is everywhere, power is ineluctable, and that power produces and co-opts subversion as an effect of its own operations have been contentious for both Foucault and new historicist critics in general. Greenblatt has equally been criticised for his dismal view of the possibilities of effective resistance and genuine opposition to power. For Lentricchia the work of Stephen Greenblatt seems to be a continuation of Foucault's 'totalitarian narrative'. Certainly new historicists have followed Foucault's fascination for the Renaissance period as the turn from the classical epistemé to the modern epistemé, and have, as noted above, followed both Foucault's conceptions of power and his analyses of critical transformations in Western discourse. What Lentricchia finds most alarming is Foucault's failure to define or locate power to a finite source, and this, he argues, has left its depressing legacy in new historicism:

> Greenblatt's [*Renaissance Self-Fashioning*] announces to liberal optimists ... Foucault's depressing message, and his description of power endorses Foucault's theory of power, preserving not only the master's repeated insistence on the concrete institutional character of power, its palpability, as it were, but also his glide into a conception of power that is elusively and literally undefinable – not finally anchored but diffused from nowhere to everywhere, and saturating all social relations to the point that all conflicts and 'jostlings' among social groups become a mere show of political dissension, a prearranged theater of struggle set upon the substratum of a monolithic agency which produces 'opposition' as one of its delusive political effects. (Lentricchia in Veeser 1989, 235)

Power, according to Lentricchia, has become an elusive, undefined paradigm for Foucault, a determinist, omnipresent and omnipotent force, the new god. A glance at *Madness and Civilisation, Discipline and Punish* or *A History of Sexuality* will establish that Foucault takes for granted that there is some undefinable force behind the emergence of the institutionalisation of insanity, the emergence of disciplinary prison regimes or the emergence of prudish attitudes to sexuality. Because this unseen force is taken for granted, Foucault seems to accept without reservation or criticism its operations, functions and effects. Indeed, we might even say that he implicitly endorses 'power' in all its manifestations.

Although this endorsement is hardly articulated as such by Foucault, he clearly has a fascination for the technologies and systems of power. In *Discipline and Punish*, for example, Foucault spends some time describing the layers of labour, administration, surveillance and discipline which were established at the prison of Mettray opened in 1840. Inmates were organised into 'families', 'armies', 'workshops' and 'schools' and were treated under an internal judiciary system, all with the aim of training, engineering, the inmates into model regimes. Foucault marvels in the complex mesh of power and knowledge in the extensive collection of information amassed through the interrogation, surveillance and training of each inmate: 'a body of knowledge was being constantly built up from the everyday behavior of the inmates; it was organized as an instrument of perpetual assessment' (Foucault 1979, 294). The analysis which Foucault pursues in this work does not single out the prison as a unique instrument by which power engineers the conduct and personality of an individual – the prison is simply the most visible, tangible example of how various technologies of power are brought to bear on the individual. For Foucault these technologies – surveillance, training, assessment, information-gathering – are brought to bear on all individuals, on every aspect of society, and through these technologies fundamental power relations are established. The sheer complexity and enormity of the power–knowledge nexus seems to be attractive and marvellous to Foucault, a source for admiration as much as for dread.

This is a point which Foucault makes himself in an interview in 1977, in which he makes it clear that what is at stake in criticisms of his work as depressing or negative is the very definition and conception of power as a force pervading society:

> In defining the effects of power as repression, one adopts a purely juridical conception of such power; one identifies power with a law which says no; power is taken above all as carrying the force of a prohibition. Now I believe that this is a wholly negative, narrow, skeletal conception of power, one which has been curiously widespread. If power were never anything but repressive, if it never did anything but to say no, do you really think one would be brought to obey it? What makes power hold good, what makes it accepted, is simply the fact that it doesn't only weigh on us as a force that says no, but that it traverses and produces things, it induces pleasure, forms knowledge, produces discourse. It needs to be considered as a productive network which runs throughout the whole social body. (Foucault 1980, 119)

Perhaps it is the repressive connotations of the term 'power' which have been the cause of Foucault's critics describing him as cynical, depressing and totalitarian. Power tends to be associated with visions of a *Nineteen Eighty-Four*-like police state, whereas Foucault sees power as 'a productive network', that does indeed induce pleasure. In a review of the collection in which Lentricchia's essay appears,

Geoffrey Galt Harpham criticises Lentricchia for failing to recognise that power cannot wholly be negative: 'Lentricchia ... insists on regarding "opposition" and "power" as structurally at odds, with all value, as well as all the pleasure and freedom, on the side of the former' (Harpham 1991, 370). Certainly the force which Foucault calls 'power' produces incarceration, repression, the containment and exclusion of marginal peoples, inhibitions and punishments, and maintains a vast array of technologies and weapons in its support. But it is not something outside us to which we must show defiance, which we must overthrow – it is in fact the name of our own repressions, inhibitions, and incarcerations, it is our own self-fashioning and self-policing force. It produces our loyalty and obedience, our conformity and unconscious submission in the process of producing us.

In this sense it is perhaps wrong to make the comparison between Nietzsche's admiration for mastery and nobility and Foucault's admiration for the technologies and structures of power, for power is as productive and progressive a force as it is repressive and punitive. But the comparison stands in equating Nietzsche's admiration for the transformative capacity of human beings as individuals or in groups, the ability to 'overcome' determining historical forces, with Foucault's fascination with the transformative energies of 'power' and the emergence and proliferation of new modes of power in modern Western society. The principal difference lies in the fact that Nietzsche specifies the force which has the potential to overcome in the form of a class or type of people, with certain racial and social distinctions, whereas Foucault merely attributes the word 'power' to 'a complex strategical situation in a particular society' (Foucault, 1981, 93).

Foucault's legacy to new historicism is to have imbued new historicist critics with a fascination for the structures and technologies of power relationships at every level of human society, from the feats and methods of colonisation to the roles and functions of entertainment rituals. Foucault has been a major influence on critics like Greenblatt, Montrose and Gallagher, both in terms of his initial support for their work and as a lasting influence on their methods and theoretical assumptions. This legacy has produced some excellent and fruitful analyses of the social and cultural fabric of Western society, but it also has a negative side. Foucault's accounts of past societies did tend towards ascribing a plethora of practices and functions to one overarching, monolithic system, and so were, in a sense, the 'totalitarian narratives' described by Lentricchia. By explaining a wide range of different cultural and social forms as the functions of one single mode of power Foucault imposed a monologic view of power relations on the past, and new historicists are heir to Foucault's faults as much as they are heirs to his innovations.[9] As we witness a huge diversity of texts, events and peoples falling subject to the same mode of power, being explained in the same way again and again, we might question the suitability of Foucauldian or new historicist theories for the task of analysing and interpreting the complexity and diversity of the past. The next three chapters of this volume will examine closely the forms which new historicist and cultural materialist analyses of the past and the present took in emerging from their respective origins and key influences.

Notes

1. Humanism has a long tradition of writing and scholarship dating back to the Renaissance. At that time, humanism represented the shift in scholarly attention from God to Man. Increasingly, Western intellectual discourse focused on celebrating the achievements and genius of human beings. For literary studies in Britain the most prominent example of a humanist critic is F. R. Leavis, who judged literary texts according to their reflection of human values and sensibilities. Leavis's influence was pervasive in literary studies at secondary and tertiary levels of education in Britain, and a similar movement called the new humanism dominated American literary studies during the 1930s and 1940s. See the section on Williams in this part of the book where Leavis is discussed as an influence on Williams's work.

2. Poststructuralism is a blanket term used to refer to a wide range of critical theories which responded to, and reacted against, structuralism. It includes the work of Derrida (often called deconstruction), Foucault, Kristeva, Barthes, Irigaray, Cixous, and a host of other feminist, post-Marxist and postmodern theorists. See some of the other volumes in the Transitions series of books: Julian Wolfreys, *Deconstruction • Derrida*, Mark Currie's book on narratology, and Moyra Haslett, *Marxist Literary and Cultural Theory*, all forthcoming, London: Macmillan, 1998.

3. In the eighteenth century in Europe a new philosophical tradition emerged which came to be known as enlightenment philosophy. It celebrated reason and empirical modes of knowledge, and gave birth to

the modern discourse of science, technology and empiricism. In part, historicism was a reaction against the enlightenment in that it rejected the claims of empirical history to analyse the past from the objectivity of the present. But historicists slipped into the error of narrating the past from the point of view that the present represented progress and more enlightened attitudes. Historicism shared some assumptions with enlightenment rationality, then. Poststructuralist thinkers like J.-F. Lyotard, Jacques Derrida and Michel Foucault represent a turn against the enlightenment, and the idea of modernity which the enlightenment tradition fosters, and attempt to critique its theoretical assumptions.

4.　Genealogy is a concept which Foucault is adapting from Nietzsche. I explain Foucault's adaptations, and the meaning of the concept for Nietzsche, later in this chapter.

5.　In Marxist terminology, dialectics refers to the struggle between opposing historical forces, both as a logical opposition, and as the dynamo of a process of historical change. So, for example, proletariat and the bourgeoisie are in dialectical struggle because their interests are logically opposed, and each needs the other in order to shape their own historical conditions. Similarly, Marx sees dialectics in the relationship between economic base and ideological superstructure because they are both logically opposed and interdependent.

6.　*The Order of Things* was first published as *Les Mots et les Choses*, Paris: Editions Gallimard, 1966. Foucault's foreword to the English edition is useful in defining his 'archaeological' methods, and also for his request not to be labelled a 'structuralist'.

7.　Discourse in Foucault's work refers to systems of statements and texts which define the conditions of possibility for an object of study, and which form a kind of official language. Psychiatry is an official language, or discourse, in the sense that it consists of a network of texts, statements, relationships and authorities, all of which work together to form the system of psychiatric practice and study. The texts which form this discourse are not confined only to psychiatric textbooks or case studies. The language and discourse of psychiatry may be formed from any number of different genres and disciplines – literature, scientific, legal, penal, medical, and so on. What defines the discourse as a discourse is the extent of their regularity and dispersion through society.

8.　*Thus Spake Zarathustra* was written between 1883 and 1885. The edition used here was published by Penguin in 1961, introduced and translated by R. J. Hollingdale.

9.　See Chapter 10 in Part III of this book, in which I argue that new historicists have not lived up to the potential of Foucault's ideas and strategies.

New Historicism, Cultural Poetics and Cultural Materialism

Jacques: All the world's a stage,
And all the men and women merely players
Shakespeare, *As You Like It*

Each of the critical movements discussed below – new historicism, cultural poetics and cultural materialism – began in a sense with the recognition that 'all the world's a stage', that Renaissance society and politics were deeply theatrical, and that there was therefore something more historical, more 'real', at stake in examining Renaissance theatre than entertainment or the aesthetic principles of drama. Indeed, one of the critical forerunners of new historicist critics, Stephen Orgel, argued in 1975 that the very real fusion of theatre and politics evident in the courts of both Elizabeth I and James I made Renaissance theatre 'antidramatic', and made the study of Renaissance theatre an investigation of the role of the monarch, of the state hierarchies, and of the cultural systems of which they were a part (Orgel 1975, 36). At their best, the critical practitioners in each of these movements demonstrate the rewards and potential of turning literary and cultural analyses on history and politics, scrutinising the rhetorical construction of every historical action. But we might also ask, like many critics of the 'new histories', what it is exactly in new historicism that is 'new'. What Greenblatt tells us about the politics of theatre and the theatre of politics is already implied in the epigraph from Shakespeare's *As You Like It* quoted above. My aims in this section of the volume are to explain how new historicism, cultural poetics and cultural materialism emerged and developed, to look at their major preoccupations and methods, and to offer critical appraisals and point out vulnerable aspects of those theories.

2 New Historicism: Representations of History and Power

Most critics and anthologists of the new historicism cite the year 1980 as the beginning of new historicism as a theory and critical practice. There is good evidence to support this – namely the publication of Stephen Greenblatt's *Renaissance Self-Fashioning*, and of Louis Montrose's essay 'Eliza, Queene of Shepheardes', both of which are seminal works in the elaboration of new historicist methods of analysis.[1] Both works seem to announce the chief characteristics of new historicism as it would develop and grow in the years following 1980. Where Greenblatt writes in his introduction to *Renaissance Self-Fashioning*: 'the written word is self-consciously embedded in specific communities, life situations, structures of power' (Greenblatt 1980, 7), Montrose demonstrates this point in his examination of the role of the pastoral literary form in mediating power relations, and argues 'that the symbolic mediation of social relationships was a central function of Elizabethan pastoral forms, and that social relationships are, intrinsically, relations of power' (Montrose in Veeser 1994, 88). Both see literature as inseparable from other forms of representation, and that modes of power function 'without regard for a sharp distinction between literature and social life' (Greenblatt 1980, 3). Both critics cite anthropologists as prevalent influences on their work – Greenblatt citing Clifford Geertz and Montrose citing Abner Cohen – and follow the argument that culture fashions the subjectivity of human beings. Greenblatt's project is a broad analysis of instances and modes of self-fashioning, not just individuals fashioning themselves but of how Renaissance culture fashioned itself. Montrose, on the other hand, looks specifically at how Elizabeth fashioned her reign on the symbolic modes of the pastoral, the virgin and the poor. The way in which literary texts or forms can be co-opted to serve as tools in the construction of power is a central focus for new historicist work, and this focus is first evident in a clear and methodical manner in Greenblatt's and Montrose's work in 1980.

There are good reasons for choosing 1980 as the year in which new historicism emerged. But some of the conventions of new historicist analyses can be traced further back. Stephen Orgel's book, published in 1975, *The Illusion of Power*, as mentioned above, certainly contains some of the same theoretical assumptions as the work of Greenblatt and Montrose, and indeed Orgel acknowledges gratitude to Greenblatt among others for discussion and criticism of Orgel's work. Orgel writes about the early modern period, focusing on the reigns of James I and Charles I. In particular he argues that the reigns of both monarchs saw theatre fully incorporated as a device of power, forming an essential component of political will. In the case of Charles I, 'the stage at Whitehall was his truest kingdom, the masque the most accurate expression of his mind' (Orgel 1975, 79). Orgel's argument about the role of the masque in the self-representation of Charles I is similar to Montrose's argument about the role of the pastoral form in Elizabeth's self-image:

> the masque could be seen to provide the monarchy chiefly with an impenetrable insulation against the attitudes of the governed. Year after year designer and poet re-created an ideal commonwealth, all its forces under rational control, its people uniquely happy and endlessly grateful. It is a mistake to think that there was deception in this vision, or cynicism in the king's satisfaction with it – history is not so simple. The vision was a perfectly accurate projection of the way Charles saw his realm. (Orgel 1975, 88)

Compare Orgel's description of the role of the masque in Charles I's monarchic vision with Montrose's description of the pastoral for Elizabeth:

> The 'symbolic formation' of pastoral provided an ideal meeting ground for Queen and subjects, a mediation of her greatness and their lowness; it fostered the illusion that she was approachable and knowable, lovable and loving, to lords and peasants, courtiers and citizens alike. What was ostensibly the most modest and humble of poetic kinds lent itself effortlessly to the most fulsome of royal

encomia. The charisma of Queen Elizabeth was not compromised but rather was enhanced by royal pastoral's awesome intimacy, its sophisticated quaintness. Such pastorals were minor masterpieces of a poetics of power. (Montrose in Veeser 1994, 110–11)

For both Orgel and Montrose, cultural forms participate in the structures and techniques of power. Neither Charles nor Elizabeth can be credited with inventing these techniques of power. It seems that these forms of representation simply coincide with, and, perhaps even unconsciously, collaborate with, the projection of a monarch's vision of her/his reign. In fact these representations create an illusion not just for the subjects of the monarch but form the basis of the monarch's vision of her/him self. To come back to Greenblatt's formulation, such representations provide raw materials for the early modern period to fashion itself.

For Orgel, as for Montrose and Greenblatt, literature or theatre are inseparable from other forms of representation and culture, inseparable from the milieux of social relationships. Symbolic formations are as much a part of religious, political and socio-economic relations as they are part of literary and theatrical modes. As this is a central tenet of new historicist methodology it is possible to argue that Orgel's 1975 book constitutes an origin of new historicism as much as Greenblatt's and Montrose's works in 1980. But there are differences between Orgel's arguments and those of Greenblatt and Montrose. What is missing from Orgel's account of the use of theatre as a device for the function of power is the sense of hegemonic control which it exercises. For Montrose the pastoral form is effective in convincing the public of the illusion that the Queen was a humane ruler, and functions both to co-opt the public's collaboration in a powerful illusion and to provide the Queen with a cogent self-image. For Orgel it is the mechanics of how theatre provides the monarch with an appropriate self-image and how theatre is used to project the political will of the monarch. Orgel does not deal with how successful is the projection of this political will, how the illusion functions for political subjects. Orgel might not fulfil all the criteria which we might associate with new historicism, although how these criteria are defined is very much part of the problem in discerning the origin of the theory, but there are sufficient affinities between the work of Orgel, Greenblatt and Montrose to problematise the idea that new historicism emerges abruptly in 1980.

One could go further with such conjecture and look at the relationship between new historicist critics and the work of E. M. W. Tillyard in the 1940s. In *The Elizabethan World Picture*, published in 1943, Tillyard examines what he calls the 'cosmic order' in the Elizabethan age: 'this idea of cosmic order was one of the genuine ruling ideas of the age' (Tillyard 1963, 7). Admittedly, this is a crude way of describing the phenomenon of power, but Tillyard shares the new historicist idea that a single complex process operates in early modern culture. For Tillyard the idea is a highly detailed and structured hierarchy in which the Elizabethan political and social order is justified as part of a larger cosmic order. For Greenblatt the idea is a process of self-fashioning, by which the subjectivity of each individual is constructed within a heightened awareness of the position of the self within structures of power. Both understand these processes as constitutive of society and culture, both understand that, in Greenblatt's words, 'literary and social identities were formed in this culture' (Greenblatt 1980, 6). Tillyard quotes from the literary texts of Milton, Shakespeare and Spenser, yet he intersperses references to literature with references to juridical, theological, historical and didactic sources. He quotes from these sources in a manner which is akin to Geertz's 'thick description', a means by which Tillyard reaches across the distance between the Elizabethan age and his own time and attempts to re-imagine the social and cultural fabric of the past. In similar fashion, as noted above, new historicists are particularly prone to using a variety of scholarly sources to reconstruct the conversations between all kinds of texts which form the complex fabric of the social and political structure. Tillyard also notes the relevance of treating the Elizabethan order seriously for the events taking place in central Europe in 1943, just as new historicists often note the relevance of the early modern period for recent issues of colonialism, gender, sexuality and Marxism.

As in the case of Orgel, there are also differences at a fundamental theoretical level between Tillyard and the new historicists. One of the principal differences is the treatment of history in relation to literary texts. Greenblatt and Montrose treat literary texts as symbolic formations which differ in no respect ultimately from other symbolic formations, including historical events and trends. For this reason they treat history not as a background context, as one possible frame of reference which might help make the literary text meaningful, but instead they treat history as the very subject and form in which literature is enmeshed. They read literature with all other sources and textual forms in order to read history in the foreground. Not so with Tillyard, for he argues that the Shakespearean chaos which he examines 'is without meaning apart from the proper *background* of cosmic order by which to judge it' (Tillyard 1963, 24 – my emphasis). The variety of non-literary sources are used to construct a background knowledge against which we can judge the proper significance of a literary text. Such a rigid separation of literary and non-literary spheres into foreground and background does not take account of the way in which a literary text like any other text may contribute to the formation and understanding of 'background knowledge'. That is to say that literary texts do not just make sense of the world when examined in historical context, they also serve a particular function in persuading people of a particular view. Tillyard's analysis, then, according to a new historicist's view, would be peculiarly tautological – it would insist that a text's meaning could only be seen in the context of definite historical situations, when in fact that text had already participated in shaping and defining those historical situations. This is an important distinction between Tillyard's work and that of new historicism, for although the relationship between them is close enough to evoke strong theoretical parallels, there is sufficient distance between the way in which they see the relationship between literature and history for us to mark Tillyard as a pre-new historicist. He has more in common with new historicists, certainly, than he has with historicists, but the role of literature in making a view of the world plausible and making power relations acceptable is an important aspect of new historicist thinking, and this is missing from Tillyard's work.

Tillyard and Orgel are the most prominent examples of critics who might have been new historicist before their time. Despite the differences between them and the new historicist critics – differences which in the broadest view may seem no more notable than the differences between new historicist critics themselves – the affinities which we found problematise the sense that new historicism is 'new'. Paul Hamilton even implies that Herodotus, the Greek historian from the fifth century BC, can be usefully traced as an ancestor of new historicism (Hamilton 1996, 11).[2] As a label to describe the work being carried out in the early 1980s by a handful of scholars, mostly in Renaissance studies, 'new historicism' was always controversial. Greenblatt coined the phrase in a special edition of the journal *Genre* which he edited in 1982:

many of the present essays give voice, I think, to what we may call the new historicism, set apart from both the dominant historical scholarship of the past and the formalist criticism that partially displaced this scholarship in the decades after World War Two … . The new historicism erodes the firm ground of both criticism and literature. It tends to ask questions about its own methodological assumptions and those of others … the critical practice represented in this volume challenges the assumptions that guarantee a secure distinction between 'literary foreground' and 'political background' or, more generally, between artistic production and other kinds of social production. (Greenblatt 1982, 5–6)

Greenblatt had already demonstrated this critical practice in *Renaissance Self-Fashioning*, although he referred to it in that work as 'a *poetics of culture*' (Greenblatt 1980, 5), a phrase to which he has returned frequently, and which has significance later in this volume. The first chapter of Greenblatt's book examines the role Thomas More adopted in the court of Henry VIII. Greenblatt considers More's writings, Holbein's painting 'The Ambassadors', Machiavelli's *The Prince*, and, briefly, Erasmus's *In Praise of Folly*, in order to explore More's identity, his representations and constructions of himself. More must be an astute political mover in the court, a genial family man at home. He must embody the repressive, punitive powers of the state in public life, the utopian father and husband in private life. To achieve this More must fashion himself into different beings:

> one consequence of life lived as histrionic improvisation is that the category of the real merges with that of the fictive; the historical More is a narrative fiction. To make a part of one's own, to live one's life as a character thrust into a play, constantly renewing oneself extemporaneously and forever aware of one's own unreality – such was More's condition, such, one might say, his project. (Greenblatt 1980, 31)

One of the central assumptions and arguments of new historicist analyses is that identities are fictions which are formulated and adapted through narratives and performances, and that they are formulated and adapted in response to and as a way of interacting with the prevailing historical conditions. No identities are natural, unchanging or true, in other words, or, at least, as H. Aram Veeser described this point, 'no discourse, imaginative or archival, gives

access to unchanging truths nor expresses inalterable human nature'
(Veeser 1989, xi). Discourse, by which is meant all sign systems and
generators of meaning, is the only material subject of study, and
therefore the only route to the past, to self, to any form of knowledge.
Discourse is also, of course, the system through which we describe
and read, through which More fashioned himself, and through which
we fashion our study of him. This dizzy circularity of representations,
literary and non-literary, textual, visual, architectural, and so on, is
the object (as well as the medium) of new historicist study.
Greenblatt's fascination with More – and at times this seems to border
on admiration for the ingenuity of More's self-fashionings – focuses
on the importance of More's adopted roles in their specific historical
contexts:

> There are periods in which the relations between intellectuals and
> power is redefined, in which the old forms have decayed and new
> forms have yet to be developed. The Renaissance was such a period:
> as intellectuals emerged from the Church into an independent lay
> status, they had to reconceive their relation to power and particularly
> to the increasing power of the royal courts. (Greenblatt 1980, 36)

For Greenblatt, then, More's redefinition and negotiation of his relationship with power takes place within a major epistemic shift for
Western society, and his response is characteristic of intellectuals in
this time. As Greenblatt formulates in later chapters of the book, this
characteristic response is one of 'improvisation'. It is, he claims, the
key to power in the Renaissance state. In the final chapter of
Renaissance Self-Fashioning, entitled 'The Improvisation of Power',
Greenblatt argues that improvisation is 'a crucial Renaissance mode
of behavior' (227), and defines it as 'the ability both to capitalize on
the unforeseen and to transform given materials into one's own
scenario' (227). It plays a key role in the European conquest of the
American natives, according to Greenblatt, and can be found equally
in the works of Shakespeare. It is primarily the mode of behaviour
through which power adapts to the structures and roles of its other in
order to accommodate and appropriate opposition. Greenblatt tells
the story of Spanish colonisers, in need of mineworkers, arriving at
the Lucayan islands. Hearing of the Lucayan belief that death would
bring their souls to a paradise island, the Spanish improvised and
convinced the natives that they came from paradise and would bring

the Lucayans there in their ships. The enterprise proved disastrous as the Lucayans, on discovering the lie, committed suicide or gave up the will to live, but Greenblatt insists that colonisation thrived on such improvisations.

Improvisation is always the instrument of power, but it may not always be in the hands of repression or destruction, however. Greenblatt gives some examples at least of how improvisation was a mode of survival also adopted by heretics or dissidents. In the second chapter of the book Greenblatt tells an anecdote about Sir John Oldcastle, organiser of a fifteenth-century rebellion, who, on being interrogated about his religious beliefs and practices of worship, threw his arms out to make himself into the shape of a cross and so invoked images of himself as Christ on the Cross, his interrogators as Christ's executioners. Greenblatt sees in this gesture a desperate act of improvisation which succeeds in claiming some symbolic victory over his interrogators: 'Oldcastle ... like any individual or group confronting a hostile institution that possesses vastly superior force, has recourse to the weapon of the powerless: the seizure of *symbolic initiative*' (Greenblatt 1980, 78–9). It is an act which is always subsumed by the dominant institution of the Church, which not only puts Oldcastle to death some years later, but also generates its own powerful symbolism. Improvisation is not always destructive, either. It is also capable of being creative, according to Greenblatt, echoing Foucault's argument that power creates pleasure as well as pain.

There are many ways in which *Renaissance Self-Fashioning* conforms to what Greenblatt calls 'the new historicism', then. Chief among these is the way that literary and non-literary texts are examined side by side in order to describe dominant modes of Renaissance behaviour, and the way that different epochs are identified as having characteristic modes of power. Louis Montrose's essay, 'Eliza, Queene of Shepheardes', also first published in 1980, conforms to these principles too. The essay is characteristically new historicist in its insistence on treating literary texts as part of a general social and political discourse, its focus on invisible and insidious forces of power, and its assumption that each period has its own specific and pervasive mode of power. In 1981 Stephen Greenblatt published what has become perhaps the most famous and widely anthologised new historicist essay, 'Invisible Bullets'. It was first published in the journal *Glyph*, and has been revised and abridged several times since then. In 'Invisible Bullets', Greenblatt discusses the possibilities for subversion in Renaissance society and the means by which society contains and neutralises subversion. Greenblatt explains his interest in this process at the beginning of the essay:

> My interest in what follows is in a prior form of restraint – in the process whereby subversive insights are generated in the midst of apparently orthodox texts and simultaneously contained by those texts, containing so efficiently that the society's licensing and policing apparatus is not directly engaged. (Greenblatt 1981, 41)

This is, in short, the central assumption of Greenblatt's work on power and subversion. Subversion is possible, but is always contained by the society's ability to regulate and check deviations from its constructions of reality and normality. It goes further than this. Power depends upon subversive beliefs in order to reinforce its constructions of reality and normality. Greenblatt recounts anecdotes of instances of Renaissance culture in which the interests of power – the colonial enterprise, for example – are served by subversive tendencies, and argues that 'subversiveness is the very product of that power and furthers its ends' (48). Power can only define itself in relation to subversion, to what is alien or other, and at the heart of power is therefore the production and subsequent containment of subversion.

Greenblatt takes us through the stories of an Italian miller and heretic Menocchio, the atheist mathematician Thomas Harriot in England's Virginia colony, Shakespeare's *I Henry IV*, and the theatricality of the reign of Elizabeth I. Connecting all these stories apparently is the endless web of power. In Italy, Virginia and London it is supposedly the same force pervading the actions and beliefs and ideologies of each culture, as, for Greenblatt, each instance of convergence between a dominant culture and an alien culture is an encounter between power and its other, and is inevitably an instance in which the subversive potential of the other is contained. In the very different cases of a religious controversy over heresy and a colonial encounter with the alien culture of the native, the result is the same: power is reinforced and the threat of subversion is eradicated. For Greenblatt there is such a thing as a Renaissance mode of power which, in all instances where power is threatened with subversion, recycles and produces itself continually. What Greenblatt says of 'the self-validating, totalizing character of Renaissance political theology' may be true also of his conception of the elusive and omnipresent 'power', namely that it seems to have the 'ability to account for almost every occurrence, even (or above all) apparently perverse or contrary occurrences' (52).

Greenblatt's methodology of moving from one anecdote to another, one site of power struggle to another, and finding the same 'essential mode of power', is questioned and tested rigorously by Carolyn Porter in an article entitled 'Are We Being Historical Yet?' from 1988. In it Porter argues that the new historicism demonstrated in Greenblatt's 'Invisible Bullets' is a method of analysis which avoids historical and cultural specificity altogether in an uncritical acceptance of the thesis that power is omnipotent and ineluctable. She cites the shifting from one culture to another as evidence of the totalising inclination of new historicist critical practice, single-minded in its affirmation of an exhaustive model of power:

> Such a model of power can work to produce a totalized vision of history which, to be sure, is innocent of certain sins of an old histori-cism which wanted to periodize it by reference to world views magis-terially unfolding as a series of tableaux in a film called Progress. On the other hand, this new historicism projects a vision of history as an endless skein of cloth smocked in a complex, overall pattern by the needle and thread of Power. You need only pull the thread at one place to find it connected to another. (Porter 1988, 765)

New historicists may be assured of their distance from the pitfalls and errors of old historicist thinking, but Porter finds that whereas old historicists worshipped the unfolding narrative of Progress, new historicists imitate the same rituals with tales of an ever-present force called Power. What Porter finds particularly unsettling about Greenblatt's argument is that at no point is it possible for resistance to succeed, nor is it possible that 'literature might well – at least occa-sionally – act as an oppositional cultural agent in history' (765). There is a comforting circularity to Greenblatt's argument that power produces the subversion which it then contains, a circularity that seems to rely on neglecting to distinguish between Italian and English culture, between religious clashes and colonial encounters, between one mode of writing and another, between one specific historical moment and another, between one form of power and another. In short, Greenblatt's thesis concerning power rests upon his ability to see in every anecdote or situation a microcosmic image of the same formula and his willingness to abolish all specificity and difference.

The only difference Greenblatt admits is between historical epochs or epistemés. Renaissance culture is most certainly distinguished from Victorian culture, and indeed from 'our' culture, and each epoch, according to Greenblatt, is characterised by its mode of power and its attendant cultural forms. It was the privileged visibility of theatre for the Elizabethans, whereas it was the realist novel, the panopticon model, for the Victorians, and these modes and forms of power characterise the age, and distance our time and culture from theirs. One might question the easy periodisation of history in Greenblatt's schema, constructed as if the complex and shifting tangle of the past could be ordered into neat parcels. Greenblatt's epochal analysis allows him to establish that there is an absolute and impenetrable barrier between 'us' and the past, and that our reading of the past is necessarily conditioned by the power relations in which we live and think. In remarking upon *I Henry IV*, Greenblatt says: 'we are free to locate and pay homage to the play's doubts only because they no longer threaten us' (Greenblatt 1981, 57). Implicit in this view is Greenblatt's extension of a totalising analysis of power to the conditions in his own time and culture which allow him to read subversion in Renaissance texts, thereby allowing Greenblatt to justify the thesis once more that texts can do nothing but produce and reproduce power, while also allowing him to explain the conditions which permit his own exposition on the possibilities for subversion in early modern culture.

Greenblatt's argument in 'Invisible Bullets' might be totalising and self-validating, but this doesn't necessarily mean that all new historicists share these characteristics. If we compare another of Greenblatt's essays with essays by other new historicist critics, all published in the same year, the similarities and differences between them, and hence their common assumptions and practices, may become clearer. In February 1983 Greenblatt, along with Svetlana Alpers and an editorial board of thirteen scholars, all based at the University of California in Berkeley, launched the journal *Representations*, which was to become the flagship publication of new scholarship and analyses from new historicist practitioners. In the first issue of the journal Greenblatt published an essay entitled 'Murdering Peasants: Status, Genre and the Representation of Rebellion', which examines cultural works from 1525 through to the

Elizabethan period. In that same issue D. A. Miller published an essay called 'Discipline in Different Voices: Bureaucracy, Police, Family and *Bleak House*', focusing obviously on Dickens's novel from 1853. In the next issue Louis Montrose published his essay '"Shaping Fantasies": Figurations of Gender and Power in Elizabethan Culture', dealing with Shakespeare's *A Midsummer Night's Dream*. In the same year Jonathan Goldberg published his second book, *James I and the Politics of Literature*, dealing with the literature during the reign of James I. In these four works we have examples of the critical practice of four prominent new historicists, published in the same year, and covering a diversity of literary periods (although three of them analyse works by Shakespeare).

Three of these four works are focused on the early modern period, itself indicative of the close relationship between new historicism and the Renaissance. This relationship owes as much to the lure of revising the reputation of a canonical, apolitical Shakespeare, as it owes to the view that the Renaissance is the beginning of the modern world. This explains why new historicists are as determined to politicise Shakespeare as they are to tell stories about 'our' society and culture through the vehicle of studies of the Renaissance. To begin with Greenblatt's essay, 'Murdering Peasants', he analyses four texts primarily: Dürer's designs for civic monuments in the *Painter's Manual* (c.1525), Sidney's *Arcadia* (1581), Spenser's *The Faerie Queene* (1596), and Shakespeare's *2 Henry VI* (1592). Greenblatt begins the essay with the analysis of how Dürer was playing with the conventions of civic monuments and their commemoration of victories and heroism when he designed monuments to mark the suppression of the peasant's rebellion in 1525. Dürer depicted a monument made from the spoils of the victory, peasant's tools, wares and products, crowned with a statue of a peasant slumped on a chair with a sword piercing his back and protruding through his chest. This, Greenblatt argues, creates a genre problem, that a monument to commemorate victory in fact represents the anti-heroism and brutality of putting down a peasant rebellion. What links Dürer's designs to the works of Sidney, Spenser and Shakespeare, according to Greenblatt, is the problem of representing rebellion, and Greenblatt argues that for Dürer, Sidney and Spenser the problem remains essentially the same, whereas for Shakespeare the problem has been removed by shifting genres to the history play. Now, on considering this essay I suggest that there are four characteristics which we might think of as criteria for examining the other essays. First, although it is less problematic (because less reductive), in 'Murdering Peasants' Greenblatt employs the same method of examining widely different texts contributing to the same idea of the relationship between power and subversion as he employs in 'Invisible Bullets'. Second, he treats literary texts as inseparable from other texts and forms, and inseparable from the social and political contexts in which they are embedded. Third, this essay is as much concerned with arguing that subversion is contained within texts or genres as is the case in 'Invisible Bullets'. Fourth, it is also clear in this essay that Dürer, Sidney, Spenser and Shakespeare belong to the same epoch, and that each epoch in Greenblatt's eyes has its own mode of power. Hence he argues that 'in response to the art of the past, we inevitably register, whether we wish to or not, the shifts in value and interest that are produced in the struggles of social and political life' (Greenblatt 1983, 14), that our epoch recognises certain shifts of power in their epoch, thereby marking the distance between early modern culture and our own.

D. A. Miller's essay, 'Discipline in Different Voices', takes up Foucault's interest in the carceral and looks at the way in which Dickens's *Bleak House* represents and makes visible the carceral in mid-nineteenth-century England.[3] Miller's emphasis is on one novel, and therefore is not interested, as Greenblatt's essay obviously is, in tracing the shift in power relations or in the mode of representation of power through widely different texts and contexts. The essay is, then, more of an application of a Foucauldian idea to a literary text than a genealogy of power. Miller resembles Greenblatt in the sense that he treats literary texts as inseparable from their contexts, and indeed, the very idea that *Bleak House* acts as a vehicle for the carceral in Victorian Britain demonstrates his belief that literary texts are embedded in social and political discourses. According to Miller the novel has a precise function within these discourses:

> The topic of the carceral in Dickens – better, the carceral as topic – thus worked to secure the effect of difference between, on the one hand, a confined, institutional space in which power is violently exercised on collectivized subjects, and on the other, a space of "liberal society", generally determined as a free, private and individual domain and practically specified as the family. (Miller 1983, 59)

Although Miller makes no explicit comment on the possibilities of subversion in this society, it is implicit in his argument that power works through the medium of cultural forms like Dickens's novel in order to secure its own interests against subversion. *Bleak House*, he argues, serves to remind its readers and their families that outside the comfort and security of home awaits the violence of the prison, the workhouse and the mental hospital, and therefore warns against any disruption of the cosy economy and values of the home and the family. It is also clear in the essay that the relationship between the novel and the carceral is a product of the particular forms which both took in the Victorian period, and that this Victorian period therefore has its own particular mode of power. With the exception of the first of our criteria, Miller's essay broadly shares the characteristics of Greenblatt's critical practice, and perhaps the most important similarity is that both regard literary texts, all texts, as vehicles of power.

Louis Montrose's essay, "'Shaping Fantasies'", appeared in the second issue of *Representations*. The subject of this essay is the construction of a powerful mythical identity for Elizabeth I through narratives and dramas which played out the 'shaping fantasies' of Elizabethan culture. Montrose examines two texts principally, a dream recounted in the autobiography of Simon Forman, and Shakespeare's *A Midsummer Night's Dream*, but he also looks at travel tales of the Amazon. So, here are our widely different texts which have a common function in Montrose's analysis, which is to explain how the persona of Elizabeth I was invented and disseminated. It is also evident in this essay that literary texts and other texts are interdependent, and that they are not only produced by social and political discourse, but are also in fact the makers of this discourse, as Montrose sees *A Midsummer Night's Dream*, for example, playing a vital role in shaping the cult of Elizabeth. Montrose's conception of the relationship between power and subversion may be different. As he constantly reminds us in the essay, Elizabeth was precariously placed as a woman at the head of a strongly patriarchal society, and her power was then a series of contradictions and complications which had to be manipulated and managed, both on a bureaucratical and a symbolical level, in order to secure her interests as a flawless head of state. It is notable, of course, that the only possibility of subversion mentioned in the essay is one raised in Simon Forman's dream, itself suggestive of effective containment. Nevertheless, Montrose entertains a more complex and inherently unstable notion of power than does Greenblatt or Miller. On our final criterion, that

each epoch is characterised by its own mode of power, this is doubtless true of Montrose's argument since the subject of his analysis is
the specific modes and media of power which shape the reign of
Elizabeth I.

   The final text in this comparison, an extract from Jonathan
Goldberg's *James I and the Politics of Literature* in which the author
discusses Shakespeare's *Measure for Measure* (reprinted in Ryan 1996,
117–25), takes as its theme the issue of representation as the common
ground of literature and politics. Perhaps unfairly for our comparison
with other essays on the grounds of use and variety of texts, this
extract was selected in the first place for its focus on one text. But in
Goldberg's book, he does make use of other texts, and emphasises
their relationship to *Measure for Measure* and its representations of
power, although the relationship between texts in his case is not so
clearly interdependent and woven into the fabric of other texts as is
the case with Greenblatt and Montrose. For Goldberg, however, literature and politics are rooted in language where they are 'endlessly
reduplicative, endlessly re-presenting' (Ryan 1996, 124), and where
'Shakespearean improvisation partakes of the royal mode; it achieves
the show of transparency, the heart of inscrutability, to which the
king's double language aspired' (117). Goldberg's practice of reading
literature as interchangeable with other discourses is not as wide-
ranging as Greenblatt's, who is prepared to use several different
genres or disciplines of writing as source material. Goldberg is more
narrowly focused on the relationship between the theatrical or literary
text and regal behaviour. Goldberg's argument implicitly conforms to
our third criteria, that subversion is contained within a text. He argues
that 'the dominant trope in *Measure for Measure* is the unfolding of
government, the revelation of the politicization of the body, of the
single cloth that links public and private spheres' (124), and claims
that Shakespeare's contribution to the Jacobean period is to recognise
the shared language of literature and royal power. This argument
suggests that Shakespeare knew but was trapped within the language
and economy of power, able to recognise and to 'unfold' that power,
but never to subvert or elude it. This may be a different emphasis to
Greenblatt's, who prefers the argument that the Elizabethans were
trapped within their own modes and networks of power while we can
see those mechanics and their corresponding subversions, safely
distant from the effects of Elizabethan power, but Goldberg obviously
shares the preoccupation with power and the possibility of subverting

it. Finally, like Montrose, Goldberg seems to concentrate on modes of power that are specific to the reign of James I, and therefore adhere in a sense to the idea that different epochs have their own modes of power.

It is already clear from the comparison of these four new historicist works that even our basic criteria, although broadly supported, could only be generally upheld as the common assumptions of a new historicist critical practice. To be more detailed about those criteria would inevitably require qualifications, exemptions and justifications to take account of the differences between the practices and principles of new historicist practitioners. The fact that these criteria are broadly acceptable suggests that there is such a thing as a new historicist critical practice, but its variety and relative indeterminacy ought to caution us about regarding the new historicism as a uniform, coherent body of criticism.

By 1983, then, there was a recognisable practice to which various literary critics, art critics, historians and anthropologists were contributing essays and books, and which Greenblatt had named 'new historicism'. It made up a significant portion of work on Renaissance studies, had been consolidated as a practice with a journal devoted to publishing its newest essays, and was fostered by a group of professors at the University of California, Berkeley, one of the most prominent campuses in the USA.[4] It had succeeded in drawing attention to a turn towards history in literary studies, and, although many of its practitioners were not always comfortable with the label 'new historicism', they shared some common theoretical assumptions which made them identifiable loosely as a group. In his anthology of essays on the new historicism in 1989, H. Aram Veeser summarised these common assumptions as follows:

1. that every expressive act is embedded in a network of material practices;
2. that every act of unmasking, critique, and opposition uses the tools it condemns and risks falling prey to the practice it exposes;
3. that literary and non-literary "texts" circulate inseparably;
4. that no discourse, imaginative or archival, gives access to unchanging truths, nor expresses inalterable human nature;
5. finally ... that a critical method and a language adequate to describe culture under capitalism participate in the economy they describe.

(Veeser 1989, xi)

Like the common characteristics of new historicist essays which I've listed above in relation to four texts from 1983, Veeser's list of common theoretical assumptions is general enough, which is to say non-specific enough, to allow for the wide range of differences in new historicist ideas, practices and applications. The list could describe correctly the assumptions behind the essays by Stephen Greenblatt and by David Miller discussed above, despite the fact that the essays are also very different from each other – Greenblatt discussing early modern culture and society using an anthropological methodology, Miller discussing one Victorian novel using a Foucauldian model.

In between the launch of *Representations* in 1983 and Veeser's anthology of commentaries and criticisms of the new historicism in 1989, new historicism proved that it could bring a wealth of insights to other periods of literary history besides the Renaissance, and it was consolidated by, and was the subject of, a number of metacritical essays describing and theorising its rise to prominence in literary studies. These two developments highlight the growing confidence of the new historicism as an established body of theoretical standpoint and critical practice. With confidence also comes complacency, and both Jean Howard and Louis Montrose were concerned in 1986 that new historicism was in danger of becoming an orthodoxy.[5] New historicism had been identified as a group of critics sharing common assumptions and critical characteristics, strikingly similar in their ideas of power, textuality, history and the nature of being human. The problem was that by 1986 it was already clichéd in its ideas and its practice. Many of the metacritical essays which dealt with the emergence and growth of new historicism also raised some important criticisms of it.

There is a distinction I want to make at this point between the metacritical essays which deal with new historicism, and which I'm going to discuss below, and the numerous essays and articles which were published to attack and repudiate the ideas and analyses which new historicism produced. As with most successful and burgeoning schools of thought, new historicism had its backlash, its staunch enemies and its detractors, and these attacks have not just come from arch-formalists or from anti-theory scholars but also from important critics in the theorisation of literature and history. Stanley Fish, Hayden White, Gayatri Spivak, J. Hillis Miller and Frank Lentricchia have all launched serious and often ferocious attacks on new historicism, and on issues to which new historicists are vulnerable or have no reply. We shall come back to their criticisms later, but more importantly at this point, the metacritical essays written by new historicist critics and commentators to describe and celebrate the emergence of new historicist ideas and practices also reveal anxieties and concerns about its development.

One of the first and most important of these essays is Jean Howard's 'The New Historicism in Renaissance Studies', published in 1986, which begins by announcing the prevalence of new historicism:

> A new kind of activity is gaining prominence in Renaissance studies: a sustained attempt to read literary texts of the English Renaissance in relationship to other aspects of the social formation in the sixteenth and early seventeenth centuries. (Howard 1986, 13)

At its most basic level, of course, new historicism can be understood, and indeed was understood, as the project of reading literature in relation to history, society and politics. The turn to history was most remarkable in Renaissance studies where it was not only a group of American critics at Berkeley who were looking at this period with fresh insights but a growing number of critics across the USA, Britain and Australia. Two critics based at the University of Sussex in England, Alan Sinfield and Jonathan Dollimore, had edited a collection of essays entitled *Political Shakespeare* in 1985, and, although they professed to be working in a mode of analysis called cultural materialism, there were very clear similarities between their work and the work of American new historicists. In Dollimore's introduction to the volume it is implicit that new historicism and cultural materialism are the same both in theory and practice, distinguished only by being on opposite sides of the Atlantic Ocean. He defines the general concerns of new historicism in Renaissance studies as 'the interaction in this period between State power and cultural forms and, more specifically, with those genre and practices where State and culture most visibly merge' (Dollimore and Sinfield 1985, 3). As I have argued in the chapter above on the relationship between new historicism and cultural materialism, the differences between the two are more numerous and more important than Dollimore acknowledges in 1985, but he was not alone. Jean Howard included Sinfield, Dollimore, and a number of other cultural materialists in her list of exemplary practitioners of new historicism, and singled out Dollimore as a particularly interesting and subtle new historicist critic. My point here is not that

Howard and Dollimore are wrong to see new historicism and cultural materialism as indistinguishable, but that it is much clearer with hindsight and with all the work which has emerged since 1986 that the two differ significantly on a number of issues and theoretical assumptions. In 1986, with both critical practices still relatively new but increasingly prominent, it was perhaps inevitable, perhaps even desirable, to see the two as virtually synonymous.

Howard goes on to suggest some common assumptions of the new historicism, assumptions which Howard argues haven't been made at all explicit and have not been explained in relation to the methodologies adopted by new historicist critics, and they are as follows:

> (1) the notion that man is a construct, not a human essence; (2) that the historical investigator is likewise a product of his history and never able to recognize otherness in its pure form, but always in part through the framework of the present. This last point leads one to what is perhaps the crux of any 'new' historical criticism, and that is the issue of what one conceives history to be: a realm of retrievable fact or a *construct* made up of textualized traces assembled in various configurations by the historian/interpreter. (Howard 1986, 23–4)

At the heart of these assumptions is a question of definition. It is clear to Howard that these assumptions underwrite every new historicist essay and book, but what is not provided in these works is a philosophical explanation and justification for their understanding of human subjectivity and of history. In the case of human subjectivity perhaps definition is not required simply because every major theorist of literature since the 1960s has maintained that the self is a construction, a site of masques, roles and adopted personas beneath which is not some true, natural self, but instead hollowness, nothingness. The self is constructed in relation to society and is fashioned in the interaction between social norms and self-invention. Only humanist dinosaurs would argue that there is an inalterable, eternal human nature, or a true self impervious to history or ideology, and this is partly why the new historicist assumption that the self is a social construct has never been controversial enough to require a sustained theoretical defence.

Its assumptions concerning history are another matter. There are a number of problems with how new historicists conceive of history. Although it is undoubtedly the case that, as Howard puts it, 'literature is an agent in constructing a culture's sense of reality' (25), it would be difficult for many historians to accept that the plays of Shakespeare expressed a world-view which was representative of Elizabethan society's world-view. Indeed even to argue that there was such a phenomenon as a single Elizabethan world-view is problematic, and implies that there is, consciously or unconsciously, a grand design at work in every minute action. In making every local anecdote and occurrence subordinate to a grand narrative of Elizabethan power, new historicists tend to eliminate or ignore historical differences. Howard is suspicious of new historicism for its lack of explanation of such assumptions:

> My main reservation about much of this work is its failure to reflect on itself. Taking the form of the reading, a good deal of this criticism suppresses any distinction of its own methodology and assumptions. It assumes answers to the very questions that should be open to debate: questions such as why a particular context should have privilege over another in discussing a text, whether a work of art merely reflects or in some fundamental sense reworks, remakes, or even produces the ideologies and social texts it supposedly represents, and whether the social contexts used to approach literary texts have themselves more than the status of fictions. (Howard 1986, 31)

It is fairly evident that what remains of the past in the realm of arte-facts and written texts are signs which we must learn to read and piece together, and that on some level all of our knowledge about the past is dependent on modes of interpreting signs. This is a very useful and timely challenge to empiricist historians who might claim to know the past objectively and almost definitively. But it is still an assumption which needs to be explored theoretically and argued philosophically. To reduce all manner of different discourses and disciplines to the level of texts and narratives may after all ignore important distinctions, between fact and fiction, between evidence and fantasy, between critical analysis and hollow propaganda. H. Aram Veeser poses such a dilemma when these kinds of distinctions are blurred:

> Progressives can accept ... one New Historicist's fabrication of a ficti-tious Oxbridge graduate's British Honduras diary as an illuminating way to open his study of Colonial encounters in *The Tempest* ... . But cannot such methods, they ask, at the same time justify specious

propaganda masquerading as scholarship, such as Joan Peters' *From Time Immemorial*, where fabricated data 'proves' that Palestinians are a 'fairy tale'? Or Clifford Irving's biography of Howard Hughes? Or French neofascist tomes revealing that the Jewish Holocaust never occurred? ... Hayden White concedes that the New Historicism leaves intact no theoretical basis on which to call into account even the most spurious historical revisions. (Veeser 1989, x)

There is, then, an ethical problem for the new historicist conception of history. By reducing our knowledge of the past to speculation on the designs and operations of power discernible in texts of all kinds, and by treating all texts as equally susceptible to ideological manoeuvres, history might just as well be called conspiracy. New historicists do not attempt to identify a source of conspiracy, even conspirators, but any historical event, trend, incident or document is inevitably for new historicists complicit in a powerful myth. When this is used to argue that Shakespeare's plays are instrumental in bolstering Elizabeth's public image or in justifying horrific violence in the pursuit of colonies, new historicism seems to be rightly meting out poetic justice against the humanist and new critical insistence that Shakespeare is autonomous from all the dirt and blood of politics and imperialism. But when the same methodology has no defences against an interpretation of texts or artefacts which argues that the Holocaust was a powerful myth, we may worry justifiably about what Hayden White calls the 'textualist fallacy' of new historicism (White in Veeser 1989, 294).

There are similar ethical dimensions to the new historicist insistence that subversion is always already co-opted by power. Lee Patterson argues, for example, that new historicist critics are responsible for perpetuating the interests of power by the very fact that they draw attention away from subversion, the effect of which is to 'silence dissent' (Patterson in Ryan 1996, 95):

At the most basic level, the Foucauldian account of cultural formation that the New Historicists have adopted, by depoliticizing power, calls into question the efficacy of local and contingent political action: since all of life is always already inscribed within and predetermined by structures of dominance and subordination, the powers that be will always be the powers-that-be. At a more local level, New Historicism typically focuses its attention not on the subversive and suppressed elements of society but on the dominant structures – and largely without criticism. (Patterson in Ryan 1996, 98)

Patterson describes in the above passage the curious tautology of new historicist thinking: new historicist critics examine the operations of power, specifically at how power co-opts seemingly subversive elements, and find that power is successful in co-opting subversion. Patterson is suggesting, in other words, that power is everywhere simply because power is the only thing that new historicists are looking for: 'There is no space outside power because power is the only term in the analyst's arsenal' (96). This implies that new historicists are responsible for silencing dissent and for cementing our submission to an ineluctable force, and that the successful co-option of subversive elements is only inevitable in new historicist analyses and not in the cultures which they analyse.

One example of where this criticism of new historicism might be borne out is Leonard Tennenhouse's book, *Power on Display: The Politics of Shakespeare's Genres*. Tennenhouse argues that Shakespeare's plays are political throughout and serve political functions: 'I regard the plays as a series of semiotic events, the staging of cultural materials, the mobilization of political representations' (Tennenhouse 1986, 13). Plays, or indeed any form of public expression, can mobilise political representation in one or both of two ways – to conform to state ideology and power or to oppose it. A Shakespeare play might be oppositional in some ways, and conform in others. It might articulate doubts about powerful symbols and formations, or it might seem to conform while simultaneously maintaining a certain ironic stance towards power. Its mobilisation of political representations might take many forms, but Tennenhouse entertains and pursues only one, that Shakespeare's plays are a means of social control. Tennenhouse concludes his book on a depressing note:

> Like the scaffold or the feast table ... the stage was a place for disseminating an iconography of state. It is not difficult to imagine, then, why there were voices that wanted to rid England of this place. Renaissance drama always assumed the pure community was one and the same as a political body. The aristocracy's power was never really in question on the stage, and any time the theater debated the matter of how one gained access to that power, the desirability of the

pure community was only confirmed. Indeed, when the argument concerning the access to aristocratic power concluded, Renaissance theater came to an end. (Tennenhouse 1986, 186)

Tennenhouse's argument here is similar to Greenblatt's argument in 'Murdering Peasants'. Both contend that as soon as a genre of representations begins to ask troubling questions, power finds a new genre in which to represent its interests. Power always wins the game, even when (perhaps especially when) questions are being asked and doubts introduced, and this is the dismal message of Tennenhouse and Greenblatt, and of new historicism in general. But neither Tennenhouse nor Greenblatt look for successful counter-representations or for radical and dissident subcultures, and, inevitably, they do not find any. Patterson is not alone in arguing that new historicism is responsible for inculcating the politics of apathy. Frank Lentricchia refers to the new historicist ideas on power as 'a paranoid fantasy' which is necessary 'to the sustaining, in ostensibly democratic contexts, of the illusion of totalitarianism', and Lentricchia seems to deplore most the fact that 'none of this seems ever to give Greenblatt, Foucault, or other new historicists pause' (Lentricchia in Veeser 1989, 242). To some commentators, then, new historicism in its eager confirmation of, and relentless focus on, Renaissance modes of power, has succeeded more fully in propagating and reinforcing power in the late twentieth century. Lentricchia seems to attribute the depressing message of new historicism to the disillusionment of left-liberal intellectuals in 1980s America, recognising that a vast majority of liberal Americans voted in, and seemed to believe in, the Reagan administration which embodied the entrenchment of right-wing ideologies under the guise of democracy. The fact that Reagan was an actor turned president seemed to mirror the new historicist interest in the theatricality of power. The fact that the Reagan administration succeeded in being exceedingly reactionary and yet instigated a social and political revolution mirrors the new historicist suspicion of power masking itself as subversion. And the fact that Reagan commanded the support of working-class and liberal America can only have confirmed the disillusionment and apathy already implicit in new historicist thinking. In some ways, then, new historicist analyses seem to be affirming the structures and forms of state ideology of 1980s America, an ironic twist to their own tale.

To assert that these criticisms are valid about all new historicist critics is to believe that all new historicists are the same, use the same methods and come to the same conclusions, and this is largely untrue. As discussed above, there are common assumptions shared by all or most new historicist critics, but they are by no means homogenous in their ideas and methods. There are substantial differences between the work of Joel Fineman and Stephen Greenblatt, for example, despite the fact that both were involved in *Representations* and both gave their support to the modes of analyses known as new historicism. Fineman's essay in *Representations* 20, entitled 'Shakespeare's *Will*: The Temporality of Rape', is very close to adopting Derridean thinking in its play on naming, signature and the letter, and has little or nothing to do with analysing modes of power. There is certainly a characteristic new historicist interest in the institutionalisation of Shakespeare, in the interrelationship of textuality and subjectivity, and the issue of power relationships is raised through the topic of rape, but Fineman's modes of analysis and his interpretative strategies are very different to any of the works discussed above.

So, too, a comparison of Greenblatt, Montrose, Miller or Gallagher with the historical critics Marjorie Levinson, Jerome McGann or Kelvin Everest reveals substantial differences in approach and modes of analysis. Virtually none of the characteristics I identified above of new historicist essays and books can be applied with any accuracy to the writings of these critics, all of whom work on the literature of the Romantic period. Although they have been called new historicists, often they have acquired this label as a result of their interest in the relationship between literature and historical context. Nevertheless, their importance as new historicist critics (however erroneous the application of this label to their work may be) has led many commentators to regard Levinson's essay on Wordsworth's 'Tintern Abbey' as a paradigm of new historicist analysis (Levinson 1986). But Levinson's essay works in very different ways to the more prominent examples of new historicist analyses in Renaissance studies. It aims to recover the original historical context of a literary text rather than using literary texts as a source of access to representations of power in the past. The effect of McGann's work as well as Levinson's is to demythologise Romantic literature, working counter to what McGann calls the Romantic ideology, and this is wholly a different project to the new historicist attempt to revisit a culture's construction of its own symbolic representations (McGann 1983).

Quite apart from these distinctions, there is also a wide gap

between the work of Victorianists and Renaissance critics in new
historicism. New historicism is more usually identified with
Renaissance studies, and this is the period of study for many of the
most prominent new historicist critics such as Greenblatt, Montrose,
Goldberg, Fineman and Tennenhouse. There have been important
studies of Victorian literature from new historicist perspectives, and
the critics Catherine Gallagher and D. A. Miller are probably the most
prominent new historicist Victorian scholars. The difference between
Victorianists and Renaissance critics in new historicism tends to lie in
the degree of Foucauldian influence. For Greenblatt, the influence of
Foucault is implicit in the assumptions guiding his work, and as
Lentricchia has noted, explicit references to Foucault are largely
consigned to footnotes (Lentricchia in Veeser 1989, 242). In the work
of Victorianists Foucauldian thinking is often applied directly to a
literary text or cultural artefact in order to reveal the structure of
power in Victorian society. Miller's essay on *Bleak House*, discussed
above, clearly fits this model. Often Victorianists follow Foucauldian
themes of sexuality, madness and incarceration much more conspic-
uously than Renaissance scholars, and this is, in a sense, because
Foucault was writing about the Victorian and modern periods. We
ought to bear in mind, then, the differences between various new
historicist critics, and to qualify our definitions of new historicism.
There is no one true new historicist theory to be applied unequivo-
cally. But there are, as described above, some common assumptions
and characteristics which we can label new historicist, and they will
form the basis of the readings demonstrated and performed in the
second section of this book.

If the most powerful impetus behind the emergence of new historicism was to oppose formalist approaches to the study of literature,
the new historicism has been successful in opening new avenues in
thinking about literature in relation to history and politics. Most
periods of English literature have been laid open to new historicist
interpretations and readings, and these readings have revealed not
only interesting aspects of the interrelationship between literature
and the characteristics of the period, but have revealed also the benefits of interdisciplinary readings of literature in its historical contexts.
Perhaps the most striking achievement of new historicism as a
distinct method is its adoption of Geertz's anthropological technique
of 'thick description' for the purposes of literary study, and by doing
so, proving the usefulness – better, the necessity – of demystifying the

privileged autonomy of the literary text, and of placing literature in circulation with texts of all kinds. To a certain extent, new historicism has succeeded in breaking down distinctions between academic disciplines, the boundaries of which seemed more bent on keeping a discipline mystical and self-authorising. Reading literature as one source among many for reading the past, and reading the power relations of past societies and cultures, is the common focus of new historicist analyses. New historicists have succeeded also in being controversial, and in particular have provoked debates over the politics of their interpretations. The new historicist refusal to see effective oppositional and subversive agents in literature has challenged the Marxist or leftist orthodoxy in relation to the politics of literature, and simultaneously, new historicism has been successful in replacing the right-wing formalist orthodoxy with a historicising and politicising agenda in literary studies. Above all, new historicists have made the study of literature in relation to history less a matter of supplying incontrovertible historical facts as background information to illuminate the themes, forms and contents of literary texts, and more a matter of addressing the role that discourse, including literature, plays in negotiating and making manifest the power relations and structures of a culture. The fundamental change that new historicism has brought to the relationship between literature and history is to have shifted the methodology from a simple application of historical facts to literary texts to a complex understanding of levels of discursive participation in constructing and maintaining power structures. The next chapter looks at how new historicism underwent changes in the late 1980s and early 1990s, when Greenblatt announced his preference for the term cultural poetics rather than new historicism to describe his work. Whether this was a theoretical and methodological shift, or whether it was a cosmetic change only, is the subject of the chapter on 'Cultural Poetics'.

Notes

1. See Mark Currie's discussion of Stephen Greenblatt's work in the context of narrative theory, in his volume of the Transitions series, *Postmodern Narrative Theory*.
2. Joel Fineman traces Thucydides as a possible precursor of new histori-

cism in 'The History of the Anecdote: Fiction and Fiction', in H. Aram Veeser, *The New Historicism*, London: Routledge, 1989, 49–76.

3. The version of Miller's essay discussed here was printed in *Representations* in 1983. The essay subsequently formed a chapter in Miller's *The Novel and the Police*, Berkeley, Los Angeles and London: University of California Press, 1988.

4. Of the editorial board of *Representations* in 1983, Greenblatt was Professor of English, Svetlana Alpers was Professor of Art History, R. Howard Bloch was Professor of French Literature, Denis Hollier was Professor of French, Thomas Laqueur was Professor of History and David Miller was Professor of English and Comparative Literature, all at the University of California at Berkeley.

5. Howard suggested this in 'The New Historicism in Renaissance Studies', *English Literary Renaissance*, 16 (1986), 13–43. Montrose raised his anxieties in the same issue of *English Literary Renaissance* in an essay entitled 'Renaissance Literary Studies and the Subject of History', 5–12.

3 Cultural Poetics: After the New Historicism?

In 1988 Greenblatt published *Shakespearean Negotiations*, and in the first chapter declared that his work was 'a poetics of culture' (Greenblatt 1988, 5). This was followed with an essay in Veeser's collection, *The New Historicism* (1989), which Greenblatt entitled 'Towards a Poetics of Culture'. In 1990, in *Learning to Curse*, Greenblatt referred to the essays collected in that book as 'Renaissance cultural poetics' (Greenblatt 1990, 1). It seems, then, that in the late 1980s Greenblatt began to prefer the term 'cultural poetics' to describe his work rather than 'new historicism'. Veeser indeed shares this view that Greenblatt began to prefer 'cultural poetics' (Veeser 1989, ix), as does Louis Montrose in Veeser's collection (Veeser 1989, 17). Montrose endorses Greenblatt's definition of 'cultural poetics' given in *Shakespearean Negotiations* as the 'study of the collective making of distinct cultural practices and inquiry into the relations among these practices' (Greenblatt 1988, 5). We will return to Greenblatt's definitions of the concerns of cultural poetics later. In this chapter I have two main aims. The first is to analyse the critical practice of Greenblatt, Montrose, Tennenhouse and others (in short, those critics who had been associated with new historicism) from 1988 onwards. The aim of this analysis will be to test if the term 'cultural poetics' denotes a change in practice, or if indeed it is merely a more appropriate term for what new historicist critics were always doing anyway. At this point we will return to the definition above and ask whether the same criteria cannot be applied satisfactorily to what was characterised as new historicist practice in the previous chapter. My second aim is to examine the turn in terminology from new historicism to cultural poetics, and to investigate the significance of a preference for 'poetics' over 'historicism' in particular. Given the criticisms recalled in the last chapter about the new historicist use of history and politics, it may be that Greenblatt and others retreated into a less contentious area of study, the more aesthetic or formalist interests implied by the term 'cultural poetics'.

It is difficult to know how widespread was the acceptance of 'cultural poetics' among new historicist critics. Veeser, Montrose, Kiernan Ryan, Richard Wilson and Richard Dutton all recognise Greenblatt's preference for the term over new historicism, and Wilson and Dutton even imply that 'cultural poetics' was a new phase in new historicist practice.[1] But there is hardly any mention of the term among other new historicist critics, who, by and large, do not seem to acknowledge that the practice with which they had been associated had changed its name. Only for Greenblatt is it possible to say that there was a change of taste regarding the name of his critical practice. But equally this did not mean that the most renowned figure in what had been called the new historicism was now deserting his colleagues and friends to embark on a different practice. Greenblatt continued to edit *Representations*, which continued to publish essays examining the historicity of texts and the textuality of history. Leonard Tennenhouse, Nancy Armstrong, Stephen Orgel, Catherine Gallagher, Jonathan Goldberg and various other new historicists continued to engage in fruitful collaborations and exchanges with Greenblatt, and continued to acknowledge his help and advice in their books and essays. We may, at least crudely, conjecture two things from this: either Greenblatt's practice of 'cultural poetics' remained substantially the same as 'new historicism', or the other critics also practised cultural poetics without acknowledging a change of name.

The story is, of course, more complex than this. It was not the case, contrary to what is implied by Wilson and Dutton, that Greenblatt called all his work after 1988 'cultural poetics', and that which had gone before 'new historicism'. As Montrose says, Greenblatt returned to the term 'cultural poetics'. He had used it in *Renaissance Self-Fashioning* in 1980, in which he claimed that the 'proper goal' of his critical practice was '*a poetics of culture*' (Greenblatt 1980, 5). He had used it in the same essay in which he introduced the term 'new historicism', in the introduction to the issue of *Genre* dealing with 'the forms of power', in which he claimed that 'the study of genre is an exploration of the poetics of culture' (Greenblatt 1982, 6). One of the surest signs that new historicism was gaining currency as a term, and indeed was obtaining a certain amount of power in the academy, was the launch of a series of books by University of California Press in 1987 devoted to the critical practice which new historicists had intro-

duced. The General Editor of the series was Greenblatt, and the title
was 'The New Historicism: Studies in Cultural Poetics'. Cultural
poetics, then, had been part of Greenblatt's rhetoric since new historicism was first instituted.

Furthermore, the work which Greenblatt chose to call 'cultural
poetics' in *Shakespearean Negotiations* and *Learning to Curse*
comprised essays which he had written since 1980. 'Invisible Bullets',
originally published in 1981, was published in revised form in
Shakespearean Negotiations. 'Murdering Peasants', which had originally been published in *Representations* in 1983, was published again
in *Learning to Curse*. Greenblatt was clearly using the term 'cultural
poetics' retrospectively, and not just to announce a new label for new
work. It was the author announcing his preference for 'cultural
poetics' over 'new historicism', where the latter term had been
adopted and applied by commentators. It is with a certain degree of
reluctance that Greenblatt himself used 'new historicism', and what
we see from 1988 onwards, perhaps, is Greenblatt trying to label his
form of literary criticism more to his satisfaction. After all, he
concedes in his essay in Veeser's collection that the way in which
'new historicism' as a label and practice gained currency and favour
'makes me quite giddy with amazement' (Veeser 1989, 1). His amazement signals, perhaps, an absence of intention that 'the whole thing',
as he calls it, should have become known as 'new historicism' in the
first place, confessing in the process that he had 'never been very
good at making up advertising phrases of this kind' (1). There is a
sense of detachment and alienation in Greenblatt's discussion of his
part in initiating and promoting new historicist works. It is as if the
terms which he used, the practices which he began to advocate, were
appropriated by some powerful force which made them successful,
leaving Greenblatt 'giddy with amazement'. Montrose voiced similar
worries:

> I wrote merely of a new historical *orientation* in Renaissance literary
> studies, because it seemed to me that those identified with it by
> themselves or by others were actually quite heterogeneous in their
> critical practices and, for the most part, reluctant to theorize those
> practices. The very lack of such explicit articulations was itself symp-
> tomatic of certain eclectic and empiricist tendencies that threatened
> to undermine any attempt to distinguish a new historicism from an
> old one. It may well be that these very ambiguities rendered New

> Historicism less a critique of dominant critical ideology than a
> subject for ideological appropriation, thus contributing to its almost
> sudden installation as the newest academic orthodoxy, to its rapid
> assimilation by the 'interpretive community' of Renaissance literary
> studies ... it remains unclear whether or not the latest 'ism', with its
> appeal to our commodifying cult of the 'new', will have been
> anything more than another passing intellectual fancy in what
> Fredric Jameson would call the academic marketplace under late
> capitalism. (Veeser 1989, 18)

Montrose is evidently quite troubled both by the term 'new historicism' and by its success in the academy. As a critic attuned to watching out for the containment processes at work in any culture,
Montrose seems wary of the success of a critical practice which
threatens to reveal and expose the operations of power in past
cultures. It looks like the success of power having assimilated and
contained any subversive or radical potential in new historicism. It
looks, in fact, as if the conservative and reactionary forces at work in
the academy have appropriated the new historicism. Nothing about
new historicism will have changed the way that the academic market-
place functions. Young academics will have accepted it as the latest
orthodoxy to which they must conform, students will be taught how
to apply it to any literary text as a set of rigid beliefs and principles,
and the people who have written books on it, or from its theoretical
and critical standpoints, will receive a greater degree of influence and
prestige. The immediate economy of power within the academy will
not have altered, and will simply have assimilated and depoliticised
new historicism. With Montrose's worries in mind, we may speculate
that the relabelling of 'new historicism' to 'cultural poetics' was an
attempt to reclaim a discourse which had become detached from
what Greenblatt and Montrose were trying to do. Montrose attributed
the success of the appropriation of new historicism to its own 'eclectic
and empiricist tendencies', its own failure to theorise and formulate
its objectives and assumptions. The result of this recognition may be
the 'hardening' of new historicism into cultural poetics which Wilson
and Dutton observe (Wilson and Dutton 1992, 14). In the sense that
Montrose perceived a weakness in new historicism which rendered
it susceptible to appropriation, it may be that reclaiming the critical
practice involved making it even more rigid in its adherence to
a defined set of critical principles, hence Greenblatt's definition

of characteristics and features of the critical practice of cultural poetics.

Greenblatt certainly defines cultural poetics more clearly and specifically than he had ever done for new historicism, which he had only defined in 1982 as a critical practice which 'challenges the assumptions that guarantee a secure distinction between "literary foreground" and "political background", or, more generally, between artistic production and other kinds of social production' (Greenblatt 1982, 6). This definition is, of course, so general that it is hardly problematic since any reading which treats literature as a form of public representation ought to satisfy the criteria. Arguably, even the work of 'old' historicists conforms to this definition. But Greenblatt's definition of cultural poetics, and his identification of the concerns and questions of cultural poetics, is more detailed. It may be that it will refer to a more limited range of critical essays and books. If we break down the criteria into constituent parts and test them against the work of new historicists after 1988 we may get a clearer picture of how different or influential cultural poetics was.

Cultural poetics is defined as the 'study of the collective making of distinct cultural practices and inquiry into the relations among these practices' (Greenblatt 1988, 5). It would therefore require a practitioner first, to identify 'distinct cultural practices', second, to examine how the specific cultural practice was formed, third, to either argue or imply that the formation of the cultural practice was a collective effort and not the work of just one individual, and fourth, to trace the relationship between one cultural practice and others. It is obviously prudent to check that Greenblatt's own practice conforms to these principles. *Marvelous Possessions* (1991), which is made up of lectures written and delivered in 1988, does match Greenblatt's description of cultural poetics. The cultural practice which the book identifies is the appropriation of symbolic power in the new world by European travel narratives in the early modern period. Greenblatt examines how this practice was formed and developed from the Medieval travel narrative to the Renaissance travel narrative, and demonstrates how each text contributes to the appropriation of symbolic power. That these practices are collectively made is implied in Greenblatt's argument that travel narratives are public representations and that representations are necessarily collective. Finally, Greenblatt links the distinct practice of appropriation in travel narratives to European representations in general, establishing that cultural practices of all kinds form a network of representations. So, Greenblatt for one is certainly performing a critical practice based on the criteria he ascribes to cultural poetics.

The *Representations* journal, which continued to promote the work of new historicist critics, is also a likely sponsor of cultural poetics. I have randomly chosen two essays from the journal after 1988 to test the same criteria. The first is Daniel Boyarin's essay '"Language Inscribed by History on the Bodies of Living Beings": Midrash and Martyrdom' (1989). Boyarin refers to his own reading as an example of cultural poetics, and it is not surprising, then, that his essay conforms to Greenblatt's criteria. The cultural practice which Boyarin identifies is the interpretations of the Midrash commentaries on the Torah. He does examine how those interpretations were formed as a discourse and he does describe the nature of Midrash interpretation. He also argues that the construction of the Midrash commentaries, and the interpretations of Midrash, are collective practices, and are conscious of themselves as being always in dialogue with other texts and readers. Towards the end of the essay he also argues that the cultural practice of Midrash interpretation is intertextual, and is linked to other cultural practices of historiography and the history of ideology.

The second essay from *Representations* is 'The Erotics of Purity: *The Marble Faun* and the Victorian Construction of Sexuality' by T. Walter Herbert Jr. (1991). The cultural practice which interests Herbert in this essay is the Victorian construction of sexual purity, in particular, of course, in Nathaniel Hawthorne's *The Marble Faun*. Herbert analyses how Hawthorne appropriated and transformed Spenserian images of purity, how the Victorians constructed images and icons of sexuality from Spenser's *The Faerie Queene*. He argues that the Hawthorne's construction of sexual purity was part of a collective Victorian construction of sexuality, and is therefore not just the product of an individual. So, too, Herbert's essay is an example of cultural poetics in that it discusses the relationship between sexuality and other forms of cultural practice, like expressions of middle-class identity.

As a final test of how close new historicist essays and books are to Greenblatt's definition of cultural poetics, let us examine how Greenblatt's criteria might be applied to a book from the series on 'The New Historicism: Studies in Cultural Poetics', in this case *The Imaginary Puritan*, by Nancy Armstrong and Leonard Tennenhouse, published in 1992. The phenomenon of authorship in the late seventeenth and early eighteenth centuries is the distinct cultural practice which Armstrong and Tennenhouse examine, and indeed, they examine how authorship was constructed as a myth, and indeed how the whole idea of an individual distinct from family, distinct from community, was fashioned by historical and ideological forces in this period. Since Armstrong and Tennenhouse see the whole construction of individuality and the author as creative individual genius as a fallacy, it is not surprising that they also see the process of making these myths as a collective process, one which involves the various contributions of collective class, national and sexual identities. Finally, the interest in the distinct cultural practice is part of an inquiry into the wider discursive practices which go to form personal and collective identities, and the relationship between the notion of author and other aspects of discursive formations is a major focus of *The Imaginary Puritan*. The critical practice of Armstrong and Tennenhouse in this book, then, seems to fit Greenblatt's definition of cultural poetics. Greenblatt's list of the major concerns and questions of cultural poetics are equally applicable to the essays and books treated above. Greenblatt further identifies the concerns and questions of cultural poetics as the following:

> we can ask how collective beliefs and experiences were shaped, moved from one medium to another, concentrated in manageable aesthetic form, offered for consumption. We can examine how the boundaries were marked between cultural practices understood to be art forms and other, contiguous, forms of expression. We can attempt to determine how these specially demarcated zones were invested with the power to confer pleasure or excite interest or generate anxiety. (Greenblatt 1988, 5)[2]

The common theme running through each of these concerns is the way in which the materials and beliefs of everyday culture, politics and society, are transformed into specialised cultural practices called art, theatre, literature, and so on. Greenblatt is interested in discovering how everyday beliefs and experiences are selected for artistic rendering, and how these specialised cultural practices are formed to begin with. How did the practice of writing, criticising and teaching literature come about? In what form did Renaissance society organise and define its theatres? What social and political factors influenced the formation of distinct cultural practices? These are the kinds of questions that a practitioner of cultural poetics might ask. Moreover, Greenblatt is interested in the function of these cultural practices. Art has the power to entertain, to stimulate or to confound, and these functions are licensed and approved by a powerful amalgamation of the state, the artistic producers, and a consenting, and consuming, public. Artistic cultural practices are part of the network of social relations and functions, and therefore ought to be treated in relation to wider cultural and social practices. A close examination of critical works discussed above – Greenblatt, Boyarin, Herbert, and Armstrong and Tennenhouse – will reveal that they share also the questions and concerns set out by Greenblatt as the defining features of cultural poetics.

Cultural poetics as Greenblatt defines and describes it, then, is an influential and common practice among other critics besides Greenblatt, and since the definitions and concerns set out above could equally be applied satisfactorily to new historicist practice before 1988 we know now that we are not dealing with a fundamental change in practice. There are wide differences in how each of the critics go about practising these principles. Boyarin's essay relies heavily on close reading of a single textual passage, whereas Armstrong and Tennenhouse are more interested in describing and interpreting a network of literary and historical relations. But they all seem to conform to the same basic principles of the critical practice outlined by Greenblatt. It is important also to state that these critics are not following a model dictated by Greenblatt. Greenblatt has proved to be remarkably adept, as has Montrose, at describing the common characteristics of a critical practice which he and a number of friends, colleagues and other scholars promote and perform.

It seems the case, then, that rather than arguing that cultural poetics is a new phase in new historicist criticism, markedly different from previous new historicist criticism, we might argue more easily that cultural poetics was simply Greenblatt's preference as a label to describe his work. As a result we must ask why Greenblatt moved away from the label of new historicism and began to prefer cultural poetics. What does such a shift indicate? The term 'new historicism' indicates a will to revise and update the old historicism, and, if in practice the new historicist critics refer only to literary critics like Dover Wilson and Tillyard as old historicists, the term itself invites commentators, particularly historians, to consider the new historicism as a challenge to some forms of historiography. It is as a reading and investigation of history that new historicism has been particularly vulnerable to criticism, and that has situated new historicism polemically in relation to historiography. By calling the practice of historicising texts, and reading all kinds of texts as historically situated representations of power relations, the new historicism, Greenblatt drew attention to the importance of this critical practice for the pursuit of history.

The shift from 'new historicism' to 'cultural poetics' denotes a withdrawal of the claim to historicise texts, and emphasises a more formalist approach to the study of culture, or, as Kiernan Ryan claims, this shift 'exchanges a stress on the historicity of texts for a concern with the textuality of culture' (Ryan 1996, xiv). The critical practice, whether it is called new historicism or cultural poetics, remains the same, but the change in name makes the practice less polemical. The claim that new historicists are 'doing' history is withdrawn by Greenblatt from 1988 onwards. For some, like Richard Strier below, this was a positive move, removing the 'polemics' inappropriate to an academic discourse:

> New Historicism seems to me best as a certain kind of critical praxis, a praxis which does not need to be theorized to be effective, and that does not need to indulge in polemics of any kind. One of the reasons Greenblatt prefers 'cultural poetics' to 'new historicism' is that it is not only wittier, more obscure, and more descriptive than the latter but also less polemical. The profession, however, has fixed on 'New Historicism' as the name of the 'movement' with which Greenblatt is associated because in the current atmosphere polemics are strongly encouraged. (Strier 1995, 68)

New historicism is a polemical label. It suggests a replacement of something old, and it suggests a renewed interest in, and attention to, reading history. In Strier's view Greenblatt abandons this claim and adopts a less polemical term to describe his work. For those who saw in Greenblatt's work a bold approach to historicising texts, and indeed to reading literature as just one among many different forms of representing history, the less polemical tone of the new label, and its more reserved claims upon the attention of academic scholars, sounds the retreat. Indeed, if new historicism was launched with the claim that it was opposed ardently to both the old historicism and the new criticism, some critics have seen in Greenblatt's retreat to 'cultural poetics' the signs of these ghosts of criticism past lurking behind the new label. Strier likens cultural poetics to new criticism:

> To do a 'cultural poetics' is to 'read' a culture in something like the way in which the New Critics read a poem, as a thematically unified whole in which all of what are taken to be the salient parts are 'organically' or functionally related. (Strier 1995, 71)

New criticism had dominated the American literary academy since the 1940s as a critical practice which insisted that the study of a literary text should not be concerned with history, biography, sociology or politics, that a piece of literature should be read as a linguistic structure, the proper practice of which was 'Close Reading'.

Whereas Greenblatt constructed new historicism in opposition to the formalism and insularity of new criticism, Strier sees cultural poetics as simply an extension of new critical methods from a poem to a culture. New critics saw the literary text as an autonomous system, self-contained and complete, and the implication is that the same insular properties are evident in the practice of studying culture as a system. Wilson and Dutton also regard cultural poetics as 'a formalist refinement' of new historicism, which 'tends to view cultures anthropologically, as self-regulating sign systems, distinct in their difference from the present' (Wilson and Dutton 1992, 228). This implies a distinct difference in practice between the new historicism and cultural poetics. Kiernan Ryan sees the two as fundamentally different to each other:

> As a watchword, 'cultural poetics'... marks the posthumous expansion of new criticism to embrace not merely the detached canonical work but the entire cultural formation, to which the resources of close textual analysis can now be applied. The term 'poetics' recalls too the structuralist endeavour to grasp its object synchronically and spatially as a system of relations, suppressing its diachronic involvement in the process of historical change. (Ryan 1996, xiv)

Here we must remember from the analysis above that there is no fundamental difference between the new historicism practised prior to 1988 and the cultural poetics practised after 1988. The difference between seeing new historicism as a practice which opens up disciplinary boundaries, and opens up the relationship between the past and the present, and seeing cultural poetics as a practice which applies the literary technique of close reading to a self-contained cultural system relies upon the change in title and nothing more.

It is possible that the label of new historicism invited literary critics and other academics to see in its practice a claim to be doing more than practising a form of literary criticism, whereas the label of cultural poetics suggests to the same critics and academics the limited scope of such a critical practice. The turn to the label of cultural poetics has signified to many the influence of Geertz's concept of the cultural system on the work of Greenblatt, Montrose and others, and this has perhaps triggered off the idea that the new label is a retreat into a more hermetic position in relation to literature than was evident in the same critical practice under the rubric of new historicism. The use of the term 'poetics', in particular, is striking in its formalist connotations, rendering 'cultural poetics' to mean the study of the formal properties of a cultural system. The change of a label describing a critical practice may be of no significance for how the practice is conducted, but it does provide an opportunity for practitioners and commentators to review the properties, functions and implications of that practice. It is in this regard that commentators see new historicism in a new light, not as a practice which historicises literature and textualises history, but as a practice which hermeticises culture as a self-contained sign system and which consider any notion of reality or history as an effect of this sign system and determined entirely by representations.

Notes

1.   H. Aram Veeser and Louis Montrose in Veeser's *The New Historicism*, as cited above, Kiernan Ryan in *New Historicism and Cultural Materialism: A Reader*, London: Arnold, 1996, xiv, Richard Wilson and Richard Dutton in *New Historicism and Renaissance Drama*, Harlow: Longman, 1992, 4–15.
2.   Montrose endorses these definitions in his essay in Veeser's *The New Historicism*, 1989, where he quotes them in a footnote (32).

4 Cultural Materialism: Literature and Dissident Politics

On a very basic level, cultural materialism has been equated with new historicism because both practices interpret literary texts as historical and cultural artefacts. Cultural materialism, as Jonathan Dollimore and Alan Sinfield described it in *Political Shakespeare* in 1985, 'studies the implication of literary texts in history' (Dollimore and Sinfield 1985, viii), and it is therefore an historical or historicist approach to literature. As I argued in Chapter 1, cultural materialism owes much to British Marxism, particularly to the Welsh critic Raymond Williams, but it is also related to the 'Sociology of Literature' conferences held at Essex University from 1976 to 1984, and to the journal *Literature and History*, founded in 1975, and edited at Thames Polytechnic from 1975 to 1988. Both the Essex conferences and *Literature and History* were significant developments in formulating and fashioning new historical approaches to literature in Britain, and made way for cultural materialism primarily by emphasising the importance of history as a shaping force of literary texts, and the importance of literary texts in shaping history. The Essex conferences historicised the discipline of English literature, and questioned its various self-images, its theoretical commonplaces and its disciplinary boundaries, whereas *Literature and History* extended Williams's historical and materialist approaches to culture, 'popular' as well as 'high' culture. Both the conferences and the journal promoted and spawned new work in a variety of theoretical guises, which, as Dollimore and Sinfield explain, formed very important contexts for the emergence of cultural materialism:

> The break-up of consensus in British political life during the 1970s was accompanied by the break-up of traditional assumptions about

the values and goals of literary criticism. Initially at specialised conferences and in committed journals, but increasingly in the main stream of intellectual life, literary texts were related to the new and challenging discourses of Marxism, feminism, structuralism, psycho-analysis and poststructuralism. It is widely admitted that all this has brought a new rigour and excitement to literary discussions. At the same time, it has raised profound questions about the status of liter-ary texts, both as linguistic entities and as ideological forces in our society. (Dollimore and Sinfield 1985, vii)

Out of this milieu of 'new and challenging discourses' came a materi-alist[1] approach to the study of culture. 'Culture' as a word and a concept keenly interested Raymond Williams, who debated its mean-ings, its applications and the history of its composition in *Culture and Society, Keywords, Marxism and Literature,* and *Materialism and Culture,* and it informed all his scholarly work. Although Williams recognised that 'culture' referred to intellectual development and to the arts in general, in his own practice it tended to have the more anthropological sense of the way of life of a people. It involved their collective practices, beliefs, social customs, political values and forms of expression, and is akin to the cultural system which new historicists took as their object of study. A materialist approach to culture, then, examined how culture was produced, technologically, practically and ideologically.

Williams was by no means alone in conducting materialist analyses of culture in post-war Britain. Since the 1950s Richard Hoggart and E. P. Thompson, as well as Raymond Williams, had engineered major shifts in the directions taken by the academic disciplines of literary studies and history. Thompson was a major pioneer of social history, and his book, *The Making of the English Working Class,* brought a materialist conception of class identity to bear on the study of history. Williams and Hoggart were responsible for creating cultural studies, a discipline formed from literary studies, anthropology and sociology, and were also responsible for making culture as much the object of literary study as literature. Williams argued that literature was not autonomous: 'we cannot separate literature and art from other kinds of social practice, in such a way as to make them subject to quite special and distinct laws' (Williams 1980, 43). While Williams, Hoggart and Thompson had been the founders of these new directions in liter-ature and history, Stuart Hall, Terry Eagleton, Tony Bennett, Peter

Widdowson and Francis Barker were the next generation of materialists. Andrew Milner examines the work of all of the above critics,
particularly Williams, as forms of cultural materialism. Milner argues
that cultural materialism engages in a project of studying the
construction and function of culture within the material fabric of
society, and which elaborates its analysis into a form of political struggle with conservative tendencies in that society. More specifically,
cultural materialism for Milner seems to have as its goal the achievement of 'an emancipatory politics' (Milner 1993, 114). Broadly speaking, the critics which Milner discusses are cultural materialists in that
they study culture from materialist perspectives, but cultural materialism took a more specific, more defined and more self-conscious
form in the work of literary critics such as Alan Sinfield, Jonathan
Dollimore and Catherine Belsey. Indeed, Sinfield and Dollimore
published what amounted to a manifesto of cultural materialism in
1985 with their edited collection of essays, *Political Shakespeare*. They
acknowledged a debt to Williams for the label, however, which he had
applied to his own work in the late 1970s:

> It is a position which can be briefly described as cultural materialism:
> a theory of the specificities of material cultural and literary produc
> tion within historical materialism ... it is, in my view, a Marxist theory,
> and indeed ... part of what I at least see as the central thinking of
> Marxism. (Williams 1977, 5–6)

Some critics, such as Tony Bennett, have disputed the claim that
cultural materialism is necessarily a Marxist theory, but the practitioners of cultural materialism have operated broadly within the parameters of Marxist conceptions of struggle and history. Dollimore and
Sinfield set out the key principles of cultural materialism in the foreword to *Political Shakespeare*:

> our belief is that a combination of historical context, theoretical
> method, political commitment and textual analysis offers the
> strongest challenge and has already contributed substantial work.
> Historical context undermines the transcendent significance tradi
> tionally accorded to the literary text and allows us to recover its histo
> ries; theoretical method detaches the text from immanent criticism
> which seeks only to reproduce it in its own terms; socialist and femi
> nist commitment confronts the conservative categories in which
> most criticism has hitherto been conducted; textual analysis locates

the critique of traditional approaches where it cannot be ignored. We call this 'cultural materialism'. (Dollimore and Sinfield 1985, vii)

The four key principles in this statement are not particularly descriptive of the method or critical practice of cultural materialism, but they are general indications of the conditions in which cultural materialists see themselves operating. Like new historicists, the cultural materialists saw themselves in opposition to the formalist criticism which had prevailed in literary studies prior to the 1980s, preferring instead to historicise, theorise and politicise literary texts. Where cultural materialists are very different from new historicists is that the former advocate political commitment, specifically to socialist and feminist readings, whereas the latter claimed to have no political agenda. Cultural materialists registered a new phase of political and ideological conflict, in which literary criticism could not remain neutral. While the liberal political beliefs and practices of post-war Britain, realised in the form of the welfare state, the NHS, scholarships, nationalised industries and local government, were steadily, often swiftly, eroded by the new right-wing ideologies of Thatcherism,[2] literary critics like Dollimore, Sinfield, Belsey, Barker and Holderness scrutinised how literary texts played their part in sustaining and perpetuating conservative ideologies. Sinfield, for example, has shown how Shakespeare has been pressed into service to teach reactionary social norms, to justify imperialist ideology, even to sell military weapons, but in reply Sinfield has offered dissident readings of Shakespeare's texts which challenge traditional conservative and humanist readings. I will come back to these dissident readings later in this chapter.

In *Political Shakespeare*, Dollimore and Sinfield brought together the work of new historicist critics like Tennenhouse and Greenblatt and the work of cultural materialists, largely, although not exclusively, represented by themselves.[3] The title is polemical to begin with, advertising the commitment to politicising literature which has become characteristic of cultural materialism. In the foreword the editors articulated their dislike of criticism which disguises its political agenda, and which pretends to be politically neutral:

> Cultural materialism does not, like much established literary criticism, attempt to mystify its perspective as the natural, obvious or right interpretation of an allegedly given textual fact. On the contrary, it registers its commitment to the transformation of a social order

which exploits people on grounds of race, gender and class. (Dollimore and Sinfield 1985, viii)

This is quite different to the work of new historicism, almost invariably focused on the past as belonging to a different epoch, ideologically and politically, to our own. Cultural materialists are committed to interpretations and investigations which have overt political ends in the contemporary world. This is not to say that they ignore history, or fail to take account of the 'original' historical context of a text. One of the most important aspects of cultural materialist practice is the examination of historical context, but invariably they are interested in history as a way of dislodging conservative ideologies of the present. Dollimore gives a good example of how this use of historical investigations is focused on the present in his explanation of feminist cultural materialism:

> A materialist feminism, rather than simply co-opting or writing off Shakespeare, follows the unstable constructions of, for example, gender and patriarchy back to the contradictions of their historical moment. Only thus can the authority of the patriarchal bard be understood and effectively challenged. (Dollimore and Sinfield 1985, 11)

The purpose of tracing the critical constructions of a patriarchal Shakespeare back through history is not to replace myth with truth. Cultural materialism does not seek to dislodge a patriarchal Shakespeare in order to impose a feminist Shakespeare. Rather, cultural materialists are engaged in a struggle to contest the idea that Shakespeare's texts have one, and only one, meaning and significance, and they do this by producing through interpretation and historical investigation a multiplicity of 'alternative Shakespeares'. Such a project has two main purposes. First, it emphasises the fact that texts can be mobilised and used for political and ideological ends, and that the 'traditional' views of Shakespeare are in themselves ideological constructs. Second, it seeks to contest the conservative adoptions of Shakespeare's texts by demonstrating ways in which Shakespeare can be appropriated subversively in the present by more radical subcultures and oppositional groups. New historicism may share the first part of this practice as it does expose representations of the past as ideological constructions, but cultural materialism can be

seen to take the project further, contesting these ideological constructions in the present.

In some cases cultural materialism achieves its political ends by
interpreting literary texts from the standpoint of oppositional or dissident subcultures. Dollimore's *Radical Tragedy* and Catherine Belsey's
The Subject of Tragedy are pertinent to this strand of cultural materialism as both interpret Renaissance drama from dissident perspectives.
We shall come back to these books later in the chapter. In other cases,
however, cultural materialism takes the form of an investigation of the
material circumstances in which conservative ideologies function and
are perpetuated. One of Sinfield's essays in *Political Shakespeare*, for
example, explores the role of Shakespeare in contemporary British
education, and details the ideological functions of teaching
Shakespeare to secondary-level students, and indeed researching and
studying Shakespeare at university level:

> In education Shakespeare has been made to speak mainly for the
> right; that is the tendency which this book seeks to alter. His
> construction in English culture generally as the great National Poet
> whose plays embody universal truths has led to his being used to
> underwrite established practices in literary criticism and, conse-
> quently, in examinations. For literary criticism, Shakespeare is the
> keystone which guarantees the ultimate stability and rightness of the
> category 'Literature'. (Sinfield and Dollimore 1985, 135)

Sinfield explains precisely what is at stake in contemporary Britain for
the interpretation of Shakespeare's texts. Shakespeare's plays are not
hugely popular, not bestsellers. They are not deeply expressive of
English cultural identity *per se*, not, that is, of natural appeal to
anyone born in the political entity of England. They are not easily
read, or easily equated with modern life in England. It is difficult to
see the reason for insisting that Shakespeare ought to be a compul-
sory part of English education, given that his plays seem to be neither
popular nor particularly pertinent.[4] Sinfield argues that what is at
stake in the debates concerning Shakespeare in English education are
the values and norms which the education system is geared towards
producing in the hearts and minds of young English people, and
indeed which the education system uses to test the suitability of
students for mental or manual labour. Failure to recognise or
empathise with the coherent identity and critical interpretation of the

text being peddled within the curriculum may have dire consequences for the educational achievement attained by the student. By
systematising interpretation, English education eradicates difference
and diversity, allowing examiners to discriminate between those who
can reproduce the ideological assumptions and values offered to
them, and therefore suitable for positions of intellectual and moral
responsibility, and those who cannot, more likely to fail the system
with all the attendant implications which failure carries.

Sinfield's material analysis of the English education system and its
use of Shakespeare is one example of a type of cultural materialism
which attends to the material circumstances of the present. This is
where the cultural materialism of Hall, Thompson and Bennett
becomes confused with the more specific form usually taken by
Dollimore and Sinfield, for Sinfield's material analyses are as anthropological as they are literary critical. Another side to his work, perhaps
more common, is his dissident readings of literary texts. Before
Dollimore and Sinfield published *Political Shakespeare* they had
written books which were cultural materialist in their interpretative
strategies and methods. Sinfield had edited a collection of essays on
the historical contexts of post-war British culture (*Society and
Literature 1945–1970*, 1983), and had written books on Tennyson's *In
Memoriam* (1971) and Renaissance literature (*Literature in Protestant
England 1560–1660*, 1982), all of which were written from cultural
materialist perspectives. Dollimore had written *Radical Tragedy*, in
which he also engaged with Renaissance literary culture from materialist perspectives. In the second edition of *Radical Tragedy*, Dollimore
described what he terms 'materialist criticism':

> Materialist criticism relates both the literary canon and changing
> interpretations of it to the cultural formations which produce(d)
> them, and which those interpretations in turn reproduce, or help to
> change. In the process it attends to non-canonical texts and offers
> different conceptions of (for instance) human identity, cultural,
> social and historical process, as well as the activity of criticism itself.
> (Dollimore 1989, xv)

The purpose of Dollimore's criticism of prevailing interpretations of
Renaissance drama is not simply to replace them with more updated,
theoretically informed or politically committed readings. It is also to
challenge the cultural values and beliefs which informed traditional

and humanist literary interpretations, and to challenge the way in which literary critics not only policed a literary canon, and policed interpretations of that canon, but policed a set of deeply conservative social and political norms. As Dollimore argues, there is very little to distinguish a criticism 'ready to reproduce the most tired and oppressive clichés' on matters of gender, sexuality, race, or class, from bigotry (Dollimore 1989, xxxiii). The interpretations which cultural materialists offer are not simply different in the evaluative or aesthetic criteria which they adopt in contradistinction to formalists or humanists, for cultural materialist interpretations are informed by, and indeed prioritise, alternative social and political values.

In his formative study of Renaissance literature, Jonathan Dollimore argues that there is more to the interpretation of Jacobean tragedies than humanist and formalist critics have allowed, and indeed that traditional interpretations have implicitly policed a conservative political orthodoxy by insisting on idealist and essentialist[5] categories of knowledge. Critics such as Bradley, Eliot, T. E. Hulme, F. R. Leavis, and Archer advocated conceptions of human life which were timeless, immutable and natural, conceptions which led to an excessive attention to the study of character, to the study of morality, and to human conditions. In their rigid adherence to unchanging categories of knowledge, Dollimore finds these critical conceptions conservative and dogmatic:

> essentialism, rooted as it is in the concept of centred structure and determining origin, constitutes a residual metaphysic within secularist thought which, though it has not entailed has certainly made possible the classic ideological effect: a specific cultural identity is universalised or naturalised; more specifically, in reaction to social change this residual metaphysic is activated in defence of one cultural formation, one conception of what it is to be truly human, to the corresponding exclusion of others. (Dollimore 1984, 258)

The essentialism promoted within humanist literary criticism, then, tends to reinforce the exclusion of alternative social and political identities, and to police the ideological constructs necessary to maintain the division between the sociopolitical norm and the margins. Dollimore shows that Renaissance literature, specifically Jacobean tragedy, is constantly problematising humanist and essentialist assumptions. Two major ideological constructs come under

Dollimore's scrutiny in *Radical Tragedy*: establishment providentialism (which 'aimed to provide a metaphysical ratification of the existing social order', 87) and the autonomous, essential individual (which
instils into the social order the idea of an unchanging human nature,
posited in each individual soul). To these constructs Dollimore brings
bifocal perspective: one eye on the way in which Jacobean tragedies
challenged the dominant ideological conceptions of their society, the
other eye on the forms which the contest between idealist (humanist)
conceptions and materialist conceptions of human society take in the
present.

Providentialism was the ideology which explained the absolute
monarchy of Renaissance times (and earlier) as the product of God's
will. The monarch was supposedly in an absolute position of power,
and the social hierarchy was supposedly determined in its corresponding order of power, according to the wishes and favour of God.
This ideology neatly explained the powerful union of Church and
State, and of course served to discourage public revolts or criticisms
of either institution. By explaining the privileges and powers of the
monarch, with all the attendant faults and abuses, as the product of
divine will was to severely curtail the potential for subversion or
dissent. A new historicist analysis may be content to signal the ways in
which this order functioned, and how it was underpinned by literary
and cultural representations of divine right and natural order, but a
cultural materialist analysis will seek to explain how despite the ideological pressures and constraints to the contrary, Renaissance literature manages to articulate dissident and subversive perspectives.
Such is the case with Dollimore, as he shows how four tragedies
provoke disquieting and challenging insights into the contradictions,
limits and explicit political manipulations of providentialism.
Marlowe's *Dr Faustus*, Greville's *Mustapha*, Jonson's *Sejanus* and
Tourneur's *The Revenger's Tragedy* all fulfil the roles of demystifying
and challenging the providentialist accounts of Renaissance politics
and society. Moreover, Dollimore makes clear that reading anti-provi-
dentialist perspectives in Jacobean tragedies is not just a displace-
ment of twentieth-century concerns on to Renaissance texts
(although there is a twentieth-century agenda obviously and explicitly
at work in Dollimore's book), but that these readings are evident in
the Jacobean period. In a Jacobean audience, therefore, Dollimore's
readings of sceptical attitudes towards providentialism may plausibly
be thought and voiced:

Those in the middle classes who were upwardly mobile and gaining positions of power – and there were many of them – could be expected to be sceptical of providentialist legitimations of the existing order (though they might also substitute similar legitimations of their own position). (Dollimore 1984, 87–8)

A material basis for Dollimore's reading of Jacobean scepticism towards providentialism exists in the dissident perspectives available during that period. As his remark in parenthesis indicates, the dissident or subversive status of such perspectives may be contingent and ephemeral, but they provide a basis for arguing that the subversion that Dollimore sees in Jacobean tragedies were equally available at the time.

An important part of Dollimore's argument rests on the analysis of other discourses besides literature – particularly philosophical and political tracts – to establish the wider discursive framework within which ideas come to be dominant and contested. In the course of analysing Jacobean tragedies, he discusses the prevalence of ideas concerning ideology, providentialism and 'man' in the writings of Augustine, Aquinas, Francis Bacon, John Calvin, Hobbes, Locke, Machiavelli, Montaigne, and a host of other philosophical and political writers before, during and after the period in question. In particular he follows the development of certain ideas from the Renaissance to the present day. Providentialism was not such a pressing or pertinent concern of the 1980s as it was in the 1600s obviously, but Dollimore's other concerns in *Radical Tragedy*, the critique of ideology and the decentring of man, remain as crucial to materialist criticism of today as they were to Jacobean tragedies. Perhaps the best example of this is Dollimore's comparison of Althusser's concept of ideology with Montaigne's concept of custom to show the many similarities between the two. This is not to say that Dollimore sees an unbroken chain of thought from the Renaissance to the present, or that we face exactly the same political and philosophical problems as did the Jacobeans. Rather, it seems that Dollimore traces the most conservative and reactionary discourses of the late twentieth century to the different historical forms which they began to take in the early seventeenth century, and finds that the earliest moments of the dominance of essentialising notions of ideology and man were also troubled by scepticism, contradiction and opposition. This has the effect not only of radically altering our conception of the Renaissance but also of articulating dissent from the conservative tendencies of the present.

The bifocal perspective characteristic of cultural materialist readings of Renaissance literature is evident in Dollimore's discussion of the decentring of man. He sees in Jacobean tragedy some of the most important concerns of cultural materialism:

> Jacobean tragedy anticipates, and is therefore usefully explored in relation to, a central tenet of materialist analysis, namely that the essentialist concept of 'man' mystifies and obscures the real historical conditions in which the actual identity of people is rooted. (Dollimore 1984, 153)

In this fusion between the concerns of the object studied (Jacobean tragedy) and the concerns of the subject studying (cultural materialism), Dollimore has avoided the conventional imposition of the interests of the subject on the object studied. A central tenet of cultural materialist analysis is already at work in Jacobean tragedy, and indeed Dollimore shows how humanist criticism, by emphasising one aspect of Hegelian philosophy at the cost of another, 'reconciliation rather than dialectical process, "character" rather than history' (261), has been able for so long to ignore the anti-humanist challenges of Jacobean tragedy. Only a materialist criticism, historically aware, theoretically informed and politically committed, can contest the humanist reinforcement of conservative ideological constructs in the present, and, in the words of Benjamin, 'brush history against the grain' (Benjamin 1992, 248).

What is particularly impressive about Dollimore's argument in *Radical Tragedy* is the extent to which he recognises and examines the same pressing need to demystify and denaturalise the concept of man in the very different historical periods of Jacobean England and Thatcherite Britain. In the case of Jacobean tragedy he examines Chapman's *Bussy D'Ambois*, Shakespeare's *King Lear, Antony and Cleopatra* and *Coriolanus* and Webster's *The White Devil*, and how each text decentres and demystifies the human individual, revealing the autonomous individual to be an ideological construct and a vehicle of state power and ideology. In the case of the late twentieth century, he makes poignant critiques of liberal humanism and rightwing individualism, arguing that the naturalising and essentialising discourse of humanism is as strong as ever in bolstering conservative and reactionary tendencies in the present. It is only in the conclusion to *Radical Tragedy* that Dollimore fully explains what is at stake in the interpretations of both Jacobean tragedy and contemporary culture. He concludes by citing Barthes's aim to 'reveal nature itself as an ideological construct', and writes:

> Perhaps this remains the most important objective in the decentring of man, one which helps to make possible an alternative conception of the relations between history, society and subjectivity, and invites that "*affirmation* which *then determines the noncentre otherwise than as loss of the centre*" (Derrida, *Writing and Difference*, p. 292, his italics). It is a radical alternative which, in the context of materialist analysis, helps vindicate certain objectives: not essence but potential, not the human condition but cultural difference, not destiny but collectively defined goals. (Dollimore 1984, 271)

Cultural materialism aims to subvert the tenets of humanist criticism by replacing the appeals to tradition and humanity with a call to the democratic ideals of potential, difference and the collective definition of social and political goals. In this way, cultural materialists see literary and cultural criticism as participating in politics, active in reinforcing, dissenting from, or opposing, conservative orthodoxies. The critical practice of cultural materialism is orientated towards articulating dissident perspectives on contemporary cultural politics, and this often gives its practitioners a sense of political and social mission.

Cultural materialist analyses of the Renaissance, particularly of Shakespeare, came to the fore in 1985 with the publication of *Alternative Shakespeares*, edited by John Drakakis, *Political Shakespeare*, edited by Dollimore and Sinfield, and Belsey's *The Subject of Tragedy*. As Scott Wilson has argued, Belsey seems to adopt a position adjacent to, rather than in the 'mainstream' of, cultural materialist practice (Wilson 1995, 85), but her work shares many of what I will argue are the central tenets of cultural materialism. In *The Subject of Tragedy*, which is a study of the construction of subjectivity[6] in the Renaissance, Belsey shares the practice identified in Dollimore's work of exploring the past while maintaining a close watch on the relevance such explorations have for the present. Like Dollimore, she sets up her analysis of Renaissance constructions of subjectivity in the context of her opposition to the liberal humanist constructions of subjectivity of the present. This is not just a clever theoretical trick in order to politicise cultural analysis, but is, according to Belsey, a practical and methodological necessity:

> We make a narrative out of the available 'documents', the written texts (and maps and buildings and suits of armour) we interpret in order to produce a knowledge of a world which is no longer present. And yet it is always from the present that we produce this knowledge: from the present in the sense that it is only from what is still extant, still available, that we make it; and from the present in the sense that we make it out of an understanding formed by the present. (Belsey 1985, 1)

Belsey engages in an investigation of how identities were understood and represented in the texts, mostly literary, political and philosophical texts, of the Renaissance period. She does so in an attempt to understand the signifying practices and political functions of Renaissance dramas in relation to subjectivity, and her investigation is thereby historical: that is, her investigation focuses on what meanings and ideas a Renaissance drama constructed at the time of its initial production. Belsey does not seek, however, to delude us into believing that her reconstruction of Renaissance society, and its reception of theatrical representations, is anything other than a twentieth-century exploration. All history is as much, if not more, a study of the time in which it is conducted as the time it takes as its object, and Belsey's book makes this explicit.

The Subject of Tragedy is divided into two parts, the first on 'Man', the second on 'Woman'. The aim of this structure is to draw attention to the fissure between the universalising and libertarian language of humanism, which decrees liberty, property and rights upon 'man', and the subjection and marginalisation of difference which takes place within the state, manifested for one instance in the legal, social and cultural denigration of 'woman'. Belsey traces the origin of the modern (male) subject from the position of the individual subjected to the absolute authority of the monarch through to the fabrication in humanist discourse of an individual as the primary mode of political power, labour or capital power, and knowledge. The degree of success within the system of such an individual was highly dependent on the degree of conformity to the existing objects and goals of humanist knowledge and capital. This can be seen very clearly in the case of academic knowledge, where disciplinary boundaries are erected and policed in order to legitimate some objects of study as knowledge and to marginalise other objects of study as irrelevant or unacademic. In this case the individual student or professor is most successful within the system when s/he validates existing disciplinary boundaries. This obviously gears the social system towards perpetuation, or conservatism, and this is what Belsey describes as the price of a system which rewards an individual, and indeed only recognises an individual as having rights, privileges, dues, and so on, when the individual has confirmed the values and goals already cherished in liberal humanism:

> the price of humanist legitimation is precisely the recognition of existing objects of knowledge and participation in existing discourses. It is, in other words, a high degree of conformity to what is already known, already authorized. (Belsey 1985, 86)

The goal of liberal humanism, Belsey argues, is simply self-perpetuation, the conservation and protection of existing systems of order, knowledge and control. There is no clearer example of how this system functions than the cultural and academic relationship to Shakespeare. Shakespeare is a genius, humanist critics profess. Because he is a genius we must read, perform, study and write about his works. What is the proof of his genius? Shakespeare must be a genius *because* we read, perform, study and write about Shakespeare so much and so avidly. This circular logic perpetuates both the notion of Shakespeare's genius and the prevalence of his works in English and Anglophile culture.

Belsey's book, and the work of cultural materialism in general, challenges the conservatism of humanist arguments by interrogating the roles which literary texts play in the political discourses. Cultural materialists have pursued this task rigorously in relation to Shakespeare's reputation and position in contemporary English culture, and they have sought to explain the political function of texts in history. Belsey's chapter on Alice Arden in *The Subject of Tragedy* is a good example of the latter. Alice 'procured and witnessed the murder' of her husband in 1551, in favour of her lover who was also living in the same house as her and her husband. In a time, Belsey argues, when violent crimes were not uncommon, Alice Arden's crime became the focus of attention in many literary and cultural representations, as well as in moral and political tracts. The first point of inter-

est which attracts Belsey's eye here is the prevalence of representations of the crime in the decades which followed, a point which signifies a considerable level of interest in Renaissance society, and
therefore the importance of the crime to the beliefs, ideas and values
of Renaissance society. What interests Belsey next is the relationship
between the crime and its context, the fact that marriage as an institution was in crisis at the time. Belsey pursues the various dramatic
representations of Alice Arden's crime, noting the variations on the
motives, characteristics and values of Alice, her husband and her
lover between the different texts, and drawing out the implications of
these representations for the institution of marriage, the subjectivity
of women, and the public perception of crimes of passion. In particular, Belsey follows the political connotations of Arden's crime, and the
importance of the crime as a depiction of the state of Renaissance
English society:

> Read as an event which troubled the politics of the state, Alice
> Arden's crime was a defiance of absolutism and, in common with the
> constant reproblematization of such crimes in the period, as well as
> the great number of divorces established in the sixteenth century
> without recourse to the civil or ecclesiastical authorities, it consti-
> tutes evidence of the instability of central control at the time. (Belsey
> 1985, 146–7)

In keeping with the bifocal perspective of Dollimore's critical practice,
Belsey here is both exploring the historical possibilities for defiance
open to a woman in the sixteenth century, and contesting the liberal
humanist notion of a seamless, coherent past perpetuated in the
present by demonstrating the instability of certain ideologies, like
marriage, in the past.

It is useful to return again to the distinction between new historicism and cultural materialism to see the significance of Belsey's investigation. New historicists typically examine the functions and
representations of power, and focus on the ways in which power
contains any potential subversion. Cultural materialists, to the
contrary, look for ways in which defiance, subversion, dissidence,
resistance, all forms of political opposition, are articulated, represented and performed. If new historicists aim to describe the operations of power in the past, cultural materialists set out to explore the
historical *and* the contemporary possibilities for subversion. Jonathan

Dollimore has argued that new historicism and cultural materialism have the same focus, but towards different ends: 'If, then, as Jonathan Goldberg has argued, contradictions are the very means by which power achieves its aims, they also generate an instability which can be its undoing' (Dollimore and Sinfield 1985, 14). In this sentence Dollimore has expressed the difference in focus between new historicism and cultural materialism. New historicism examines the 'very means by which power achieves its aims', whereas cultural materialism examines the conditions of 'instability which can be its undoing'. And whereas Stephen Greenblatt concludes 'Invisible Bullets' on the pessimistic note that 'there is subversion, no end of subversion, only not for us' (Greenblatt 1981, 57), Belsey and Dollimore conclude their studies with calls for the need to reinterpret and reorient radically our understanding of power relations in the past and the present. Their calls are imbued with the urgency of a political manifesto, and this heightened engagement with the politics of culture characterises cultural materialism as distinct from the more neutral pretence of new historicism.

By now, some important characteristics of cultural materialism have become clear: the focus on the possibilities of subversion, the bifocal perspective on both the past and the present, the belief that both the objects of their studies and the methods by which they study are forms of dissidence, the view that all forms of representation are engaged in political struggle – these are some of the more prominent characteristics of cultural materialism. Since the early 1980s Alan Sinfield has written cultural materialist analyses of many different aspects of British literature and culture, from the Renaissance to the Victorian, and to the post-war period of contemporary British history. In each case he has focused on the way in which culture functions as an instrument of reactionary ideologies, but also demonstrated where culture contains contradictions, ambiguities and tensions which allow dissident or subversive perspectives to be articulated.

In his book on Tennyson published in 1986, Sinfield argues that, as Poet Laureate, Tennyson performed the task of policing and containing the subversive potential of the margins. In poems like 'Ulysses', 'The Lotus-Eaters' and 'Timbuctoo', Tennyson invokes a sense of the other, of the foreign and exotic, only in order to reinforce the centrality of self, home and England. So too, in poems like *The Princess* and *In Memoriam*, Tennyson threatens to invert sexual stereotypes and gender roles only in order to reinforce them. *In Memoriam*, for example, can be read as a love poem for Arthur Hallam, Tennyson's best friend, and possibly his homosexual partner, and may therefore seem to challenge Victorian sexual stereotypes and moral values. It was published in 1850, the same year in which Tennyson became Poet Laureate, and came to signify not just the poet's sense of private grief, but also mirrored the loss which Queen Victoria endured and mourned when Prince Albert died in 1861. The poem occupies a central place in the canon of Victorian literature, articulates the Victorian belief in ideas of privacy and individualism, reinforces the Christian faith in an age in which science contested and undermined Christian explanations of existence, and seems to define the sense of mourning which dominated Victoria's reign from the 1860s to her death. It is, then, rather remarkable to find the same poem expressing one man's love for another in an age when homosexuality was scandalised and in 1885 became criminalised. But the suggestions of homosexuality are contained and made 'safe', unthreatening, by two factors. For one thing, Queen Victoria edited a later version of the poem and changed the gender in a number of places so that the poem speaks of a husband and wife, rather than two men. Secondly, Tennyson concluded the poem by celebrating the marriage of one of his sisters, so that the poem seems to reinforce the legitimation of heterosexual love as the only natural and therefore legal form of marriage.

Up to this point we could say that Sinfield's book on Tennyson is more characteristic of a new historicist analysis, in that it focuses on how Tennyson's poetry masks the operations of power and reinforces conservative and reactionary discourses. But Sinfield also makes clear that although Tennyson's poetry seems to support the interests of the dominant culture, we can also read the dissident perspectives available there. From a cultural materialist approach power does ultimately contain threatening ideas, identities or strategies, but it is equally important that a literary text yields dissident or subversive readings and that these can be read against the grain of dominant or conservative readings. So, for cultural materialists, and indeed for Sinfield in his book, Tennyson's poems may be read in critique of empire, of dominant constructions of sexuality, of capitalism, even of monarchy, just as surely as they can be read as vehicles of a dominant ideology.[7] Reading for cultural materialists is a political activity. It reflects and shapes the meanings which we as a society assign to texts and cultural practices, and it is therefore also a site of contest between competing political ideologies.

This sense of reading as political conflict can also be seen in Sinfield's *Faultlines*, in which he states that his intention is 'to check the tendency of *Julius Caesar* to add Shakespearean authority to reactionary discourses' (Sinfield 1992, 21). Literary texts acquire and are assigned cultural authority to different degrees and at different times in each society, and can be appropriated and co-opted to speak for one or more political ideologies. The meanings of these texts will always be contested, but what cultural materialists are interested in showing is that where meanings are contested there is almost always more at stake than insular aesthetic or artistic principles. Or rather, even aesthetic and artistic principles are the subject of political conflict. They reflect social, political and moral values and beliefs, and therefore necessarily reproduce the conflicts between competing ideologies. Sinfield summarises his argument in *Faultlines* as the following: 'dissident potential derives ultimately not from essential qualities in individuals (though they have qualities) but from conflict and contradiction that the social order inevitably produces within itself, even as it attempts to sustain itself' (Sinfield 1992, 41). In new historicist accounts of the operations of power, power seems to function as a flawless, perfectly efficient and effective machine. Sinfield disputes this however, and offers a reading of power which reveals its faults, or more correctly, the conflicts and contradictions within power which may reveal dissident perspectives and which Sinfield calls 'faultlines'.

Dissidence is a concept which has considerable importance for cultural materialism. Dissidence is not opposed diametrically to power, not an antithesis which seeks to reverse the values, trends and strategies of power. It is instead close in resemblance to the structures of power and is in fact produced by the internal contradictions of these structures. It does, of course, imply a deviation from some aspect or tenet of the dominant ideology or culture, but it may be that dissidence achieves no reaction from, or redirection of, power:

> dissidence operates, necessarily, with reference to dominant structures. It has to invoke these structures to oppose them, and therefore can always, ipso facto, be discovered reinscribing something that which it proposes to critique. (Sinfield 1992, 47)

The achievement of a subversion of dominant structures is transient, if even successful, and can easily be found bolstering some aspect of

those very same dominant structures. Yet it is also the very proximity
of dissidence to the operations and structures of power which allows
it to achieve limited success:

> a dissident text may derive its leverage, its purchase, precisely from
> its partial implication with the dominant. It may embarrass the domi-
> nant by appropriating its concepts and imagery. (Sinfield 1992, 48)

In the case of Tennyson's *In Memoriam*, for example, we can see the
instability of the operation of power in the attempt to make the poem
'safe' by changing the gender of one of the lovers so as to render it
husband and wife. As Sinfield points out, this change to the poem
may be intended to remove any suggestion of homosexual love, but it
reveals very clearly that the two men in the poem are understood to
share a marriage-bed (Sinfield 1986, 127). In other words, the same
action of changing the gender of one of the lovers can be read as reinforcing dominant constructions of sexuality, but can also be read as
revealing anxieties about homosexuality and attempts to conceal love
between two men. The point is, that despite the best efforts of reactionary discourses we can still read homosexuality in Tennyson's *In
Memoriam*, and this confirms the suspicion of cultural materialist
critics that texts are always open to contesting and contradictory
readings.

Of all the cultural materialist critics, Sinfield has reflected the most
on what entails and makes possible the critical practice of cultural
materialism. In *Faultlines* he argued that the motivation for cultural
materialist readings lay in the conservative and reactionary uses to
which literary texts had been put:

> Conservative criticism has generally deployed three ways of making
> literature politically agreeable: selecting the canon to feature suitable
> texts, interpreting these texts strenuously so that awkward aspects are
> explained away, and insinuating political implications as alleged
> formal properties (such as irony and balance). (Sinfield 1992, 21)

In order to counter these conservative readings, and in order to make
texts politically *dis*agreeable, cultural materialists can adopt the same
strategies, or turn them against traditional or reactionary texts. If, as
cultural materialist critics assert, Shakespeare is a powerful ideological tool in our society, there are ways of reading which can undo and
counter the authority which Shakespeare lends to reactionary

discourses. In an essay published in 1983 Sinfield explained that there were four principal ways of dealing with a reactionary text:

1. Rejection
Simple rejection of a respected text for its reactionary implications can be stimulating, it can shake normally unquestioned assumptions. ...

2. Interpretation
Interpretation has been the dominant means by which criticism in general handles awkward texts: they are 'analysed' so as to yield acceptable meanings... . Such slanted reading is, of course, available to the socialist critic. ...

3. Deflect into Form(alism)
One may sidestep altogether the issue of the version of human relations propounded by the text by shifting attention from its supposed truth to the mechanism of its construction. ...

4. Deflect into History
History affords a better route away from the embarrassment of the text ... [T]he literary text may be understood not as a privileged mode of insight, nor as a privileged formal construction. Initially, it is a project devised within a certain set of practices (the institutions and forms of writing as currently operative), and producing a version of reality which is promulgated as meaningful and persuasive at a certain historical conjuncture. And then, subsequently, it is re–used – reproduced – in terms of other practices and other historical conditions. (Sinfield 1983, 48)

The last method is obviously a preferred method of Sinfield's, and of cultural materialists in general, of putting the text in its contexts, whether the contexts of production or the contexts of reception, so as to expose the process by which it has been rendered in support of the dominant culture. Once this process has been exposed, then the text can be interpreted by dissident critics 'against the grain' of the dominant reading.

Sinfield and Dollimore in particular have worked on a number of ways in which dissidence and subversion can be read in a text. Sinfield's *Faultlines* claims that 'the social order *cannot but produce* faultlines through which its own criteria of plausibility fall into contest and disarray' (Sinfield 1992, 45). The crucial difference between cultural materialism and new historicism is how each approaches the issue of subversion; the latter believes that subversion is always produced to be contained within the text, whereas cultural materialists work from the more positive belief that even where subversion is contained, traces of it remain which enable the dissident critic to articulate this subversion and thereby contest the meaning attributed to it by the dominant culture. In some ways, then, cultural materialism seems to be more open to differences in interpretation, and the different contexts of interpretation, than new historicism which, as I argued above, seems to deny the possibility of effective subversion or change.

We could apply several of the criticisms of new historicism discussed above to cultural materialism, in particular those criticisms which indicate the problems with not defining the nature and specific historical form of 'power', 'dominant ideology' or 'dominant culture', and those which denote the very limited extent to which cultural materialists think that dissidence or subversion can be effective. There is also a problem which historians have with cultural materialism which is the way in which the past is interpreted consciously and unreservedly from the perspective of the present, making cultural materialist readings seem partial, and perhaps even exploitative, in the uses to which the past is then put. This is a problem not just for historians, however. Kiernan Ryan, a critic whose work is generally of a similar genre to that of new historicism and cultural materialism, is also uncomfortable with the extent to which 'they have locked critics into either a past-bound or a modernizing posture' (Ryan 1996, xvii). For Ryan, too much of new historicist and cultural materialist analysis is concerned with a political agenda which is not immediately appropriate or accessible to the literary text. He indicts both theories for being obsessed with the position of a text within political and ideological formations and, perhaps as a consequence of this, failing to engage with the literary text as a complex linguistic form:

> it is astonishing to observe how much new historicist and cultural materialist criticism hardly engages with the verbal detail of texts at all. Even where textual quotations and allusions abound, their purpose is normally to act as broad illustrations or enactments of a conviction which precedes them, rather than as chances to unravel the mysteries of a unique weave of words. Radical historicist criticism is undoubtedly the poorer for its reluctance to meet the complex demands of a text's diction and formal refinements; for in the end

only a precise local knowledge of a literary work, acquired through a 'thick description' of decisive verbal effects, will allow the critic to determine how far the work's complicity with power truly extends, and how far beyond our own horizon it may already have reached. (Ryan 1996, xviii)

Ryan is criticising new historicism and cultural materialism effectively for not conducting close readings of a text. In fairness to cultural materialist critics, much of their work is more attuned to paying close attention to textual details than is new historicism and relies more on the practice of textual interpretation rather than weaving isolated textual details into broad-ranging historical description. But the criticism may apply, albeit with less force, to cultural materialism, since there is still in the work of Sinfield, Dollimore, Belsey and others a need to make many texts tell the same story about the fate of marginal and oppressed groups. It may be that oppression and marginality are so prevalent that every text will add to the story, but the relentless attempt to make texts from the Renaissance through to the contem· porary express the same dissident or reactionary perspectives often has the effect of closing rather than opening avenues of meaning.

Cultural materialism is responsible, then, for exercising some oppressions itself. It certainly limits the possibilities for meaning in a text. It also, however, limits the kinds of texts which receive critical attention. If the focus of your critical practice is on how texts acquire cultural authority and lend that authority to reactionary discourses, the texts which you will analyse and discuss are already powerful, already canonical. Shakespeare is no less, and possibly even more, of a cultural authority in our society because of the attention given to his work by cultural materialists. Now, both conservative *and* radical educationalists write about and teach Shakespeare as a central part of what it means to read or think about literature. And, undoubtedly as a consequence, less writing and criticism is devoted to exploring the writings of marginalised and neglected writers, writers who have a great deal to tell us but who do not have sufficient cultural authority in our society to merit critical attention. We must therefore question the effectiveness of cultural materialism as a critical practice which sets out to challenge the use of literary texts for the purpose of bolstering authority. Scott Wilson in *Cultural Materialism: Theory and Practice* points out the irony that cultural materialism, among other left-wing forms of literary criticism, became prevalent at a time when right-wing politics were dominating British society and culture. We might suppose that the dominance of Thatcherism in fact gave rise to more left-wing criticism. Despite this, however, and despite the claim by cultural materialists that their critical practice was materially based and politically committed, cultural materialism 'singularly failed to arrest or even adequately resist the sustained attacks on higher education during those years' (Wilson 1995, 16). It has become clear since the 1980s that the radical interpretations and dissident readings manoeuvred into place by left-wing critics have failed to have any material effect on the operation of reactionary discourses even in education, regardless of their effect on social and cultural values. The question must be asked, then, how effective cultural materialism can be, or could have been, as a political strategy, and perhaps, more gloomily, what effect any form of cultural criticism can have in countering reactionary tendencies in education.

Despite these reservations, cultural materialism has had a significant effect on the direction of literary studies in Britain so that questions of historical context and political orientation are now routinely asked in the course of encountering and exploring literary texts. Like new historicism, cultural materialism has been successful in displacing traditional humanist and formalist readings of literature with readings which are more in tune with historical and political contexts, and more sensitive to the problems of ensuring the adequate representation of oppressed and marginalised groups in literary and cultural debate. Cultural materialism has showed the extent to which conservative interpretations ignore the problems of race, gender and sexuality in literary texts, and part of its critical practice focuses on relating texts to the problem of representing the 'other'. This emphasis in cultural materialism, and to a certain extent in new historicism too, has supported and promoted criticism which explores representations of women, gay and lesbian sexualities, colonialism and social marginality. In the next chapter I will examine the directions which new historicism and cultural materialism have taken in the last few years, particularly those who have left behind what I have described as typical concerns of both theories for new work in feminist criticism, post-colonial theory and queer studies.

Notes

1. Materialism, at its simplest, is the belief that everything in existence owes its existence to matter. In Marxist terms, materialism came to mean more than this. Marxist materialism involved emphasising the practical and concrete, such as labour, physical life, and human practice, as opposed to emphasising ideas, mental life and human culture. A materialist approach to culture would involve studying how cultural forms are used and deployed in everyday human practice. Cultural Studies is heavily influenced by materialist approaches, and might include studies of, for example, how men and women adopt cultural artefacts in daily life as a way of dressing, eating, living, or how a sport has specific meanings and functions in daily life.
2. In the immediate aftermath of World War Two, the Labour Party came to power and introduced new legislation in the welfare system in Britain. Some provision for welfare had existed prior to this, but the legislation passed in the late 1940s put in place a system of safety nets for the poor through benefits, income support, pensions and sickness provision. In addition, the government created new opportunities in the education system with scholarships, devolved more power to local government, and set up the National Health Service, which provided free health services for people from all classes together. Successive Labour and Conservative governments throughout the post-war period maintained the welfare state, although the 1970s saw some changes to the system, but the rise of the New Right in Britain put an end to the consensus on welfare politics. After Margaret Thatcher became Prime Minister in 1979, her Conservative government applied various financial and legal constraints on the welfare, health, and education services, diminishing the provision of pensions and benefits, forcing the health service to levy charges for an increasing number of its services, and implementing a wave of financial cuts on schools, universities, hospitals and local government. Thatcherism represented for the cultural materialists and Marxists in Britain the final nail in the coffin of consensus politics. What had begun with politicians in the late 1940s promising an end to poverty, ended in the 1980s when the gap between the rich and the poor in Britain widened, and unemployment reached new and dismal heights. Thatcherism is, therefore, the dominant political agenda to which cultural materialists are reacting.
3. In the second edition of *Political Shakespeare* published in 1994, there are thirteen essays, of which three are written by Dollimore and four by Sinfield.
4. Drama, of course, has never been more popular, with the proliferation

of dramas on television in the form of soap opera, drama series and mini-series, screen plays, and so on. Compare the ratings which one episode of *Eastenders, Brookside* or *Coronation Street* receives, and Shakespeare's plays are far from being the most popular dramas of our age.

5. Marxists and materialists often accuse humanist critics of 'essentialism'. Essentialism is the term used to refer to a mode of thought which assumes the prior 'essence' or existence of an unchanging, knowable human nature. Humanists are often accused of using essentialist concepts and criteria to 'force' a view which is actually highly debatable. For instance, Leavis assumes the existence of certain characteristics in human nature, and therefore rejects as unnatural any character or author who does not seem to possess these characteristics. What he does not allow for, then, is the degree to which that character or author differs from Leavis's preconceptions about life, morality, human character, and so on.

6. The term 'subjectivity' refers to the modern critical understanding of what it means to be an individual. Psychoanalysis, feminism, Marxism, structuralism, and poststructuralism all define the individual as an effect of sociohistorical and linguistic forces, and therefore 'subject' to those forces. Hence subjectivity is the experience we have as individuals of believing in our own capacity for freedom, independence and innovation, while at the same time we are subject, and subjected, to ideological, political, discursive and sociohistorical forces, which shape our senses of 'self'-identity.

7. See also Jerome J. McGann's readings of Tennyson's poetry in *The Beauty of Inflections*, 1985, in which McGann explores ways of reading Tennyson in historical, philosophical and critical contexts which lead to reflections on the time of our reading, as well as the time of Tennyson's writing. Similarly, Gerhard Joseph reads Tennyson through and against our critical methods and approaches, and studies in detail the textuality of Tennyson's poetry in his book, *Tennyson and the Text*, 1992.

5 New Historicism and Cultural Materialism Today

Hugh: 'It is not the literal past, the "facts" of history, that shape us, but images of the past embodied in language ... we must never cease renewing those images.'

Brian Friel, *Translations*

New historicism and cultural materialism are engaged in the process of renewing our images of the past, of revisiting the past. They carry out this work to different ends: new historicism aims to show that each era or period has its own conceptual and ideological frameworks, that people of the past did not understand concepts like 'the individual', 'God', 'reality' or 'gender' in the same way that we do now; cultural materialism aims to show that our political and ideological systems manipulate images and texts of the past to serve their own interests, and that these images and texts can be interpreted from alternative and radically different perspectives, often constructed by placing those images or texts in their historical contexts. I want to argue in this chapter that both new historicism and cultural materialism are concerned from the beginning with the concept of 'difference', both historical and cultural difference, and that this concept becomes important in explaining how both critical practices have changed in recent years. In the 1980s both were interested in stressing the extent to which the past differs from contemporary uses of the past, the extent to which the past is alien or 'other' to our own modern epistemé, and, borrowing from Foucault and Geertz, new historicists and cultural materialists were at the same time aware of the structural similarities between this historical difference and the cultural differences being emphasised by postcolonial critics, feminists, gay theorists and race theorists. A shift can be detected in new

historicist and cultural materialist work, then, which began by examining historical difference primarily and has moved closer towards the
examination of differences in race, class, sexuality, gender and
nationality.

This shift is, in one sense, more pronounced in new historicism
than in cultural materialism, in that cultural materialism claimed
from the beginning to have feminist, Marxist and anti-colonial politics on its critical agenda, whereas new historicism, although
acknowledging Marxist 'roots', also steered a course between and
away from overt political positions. In recent times, as I will argue
later, new historicist critics seem to be working in fields of study more
usually known as feminism, postcolonial studies and queer theory.
Here, critics utilise the notion of cultural difference in order to
critique the liberal humanist discourse which employs the rhetoric of
sameness, universality and common sense to conceal the way in
which discriminatory and oppressive power structures are perpetuated and maintained. Jean Howard allows us to see that the recent use
of cultural difference in this way is related to the earlier use of historical difference:

> By and large new historicists produce new readings of canonized
> texts, though in doing so they lay those texts beside a host of 'non-
> literary' texts to show how tightly what we call the literary is bound
> up with common ideologies and discourses of its historical moment
> of production. And one goal of this work is to make a certain kind of
> difference visible: i.e., historical difference, to take texts we have used
> to tell the story of an unchanging human nature and to suggest that
> the story is more complicated, that sexuality, the self, the polis may
> have meant something different then from what they mean now,
> though we can never grasp that difference in an unmediated 'objec-
> tive' fashion. (Howard 1991, 153)

What is made clear in the Nietzschean and Foucauldian analyses
undertaken by new historicist critics is that concepts like 'objectivity',
'universality' and 'common sense' are used to legitimate authority
and power, that all claims to common truth are claims to power. Even
the act of writing a book which explains, criticises and demonstrates a
theory or critical practice is a claim to knowledge which in turn is a
claim to power, a claim to have sufficient mastery of a subject to
warrant a degree of authority. And even the act of reading, learning

from, and going on to practise the lessons of that book involves claiming mastery, claiming power. The power in the case of both the author and reader of this book may be very limited, but this does not take away from the fact that there are power relations involved. The critical practices performed by new historicists and cultural materialists set out to undermine the humanist rhetoric which conceals the power relations immanent in everyday social acts and exchanges, and they do this by exposing the differences between historical periods, and the differences between cultures.

To take once again the example of Shakespeare's plays, it is easy to see, particularly in Britain, where Shakespeare has been on the English syllabus at secondary and tertiary education levels throughout the twentieth century, that they have been used to support humanist claims that moral values and human subjectivity (or individuality) are unchanging and eternal. If we place the emphasis in reading Shakespeare's plays on the notion of character and morality, then they may seem to mirror our beliefs that the individual is a self-sufficient, singular unit of identity, and that there is a basic and unchanging set of moral values to which we must all adhere. But new historicist and cultural materialist critics challenge this use of Shakespeare by arguing that this is to impose our twentieth-century values on Shakespeare's texts, and by reading those same texts in relation to their historical contexts. Thus they expose the historical differences between our culture and Shakespeare's culture, and make visible the power relations implicit in every text or discourse.

While critics like Stephen Greenblatt, Stephen Orgel, Jonathan Goldberg, Jonathan Dollimore and Alan Sinfield have continued to adopt the same critical methods, and maintained their interests in distinctions between the past and the present, the emphases in their studies have moved from general analyses of ideological and power structures to more particular analyses of various subcultural perspectives on, and positions within, those structures. In *Historicism*, Paul Hamilton argues that new historicism is a useful point of departure for post-colonial and feminist perspectives, tending 'to isolate the problems from which those critical efforts take off, and when it goes further, itself mutates into one or the other' (Hamilton 1996, 5).[1] It is the mutation of new historicism into postcolonial, feminist and queer readings that we can discern in the recent work of the critics mentioned above: Greenblatt's *Marvelous Possessions*, Orgel's *Impersonations*, Goldberg's *Sodometries*, Dollimore's *Sexual*

Dissidence and Sinfield's *The Wilde Century.* Each of these books deals with issues of empire, gender and sexuality.

Much of the most recent written work in books, essays and journal articles by new historicist and cultural materialist critics is concerned with the same issues. For new historicists the emphasis on specific identities and political groups is a more recent trend than for cultural materialists. Both Wai-Chee Dimock and Felicity Nussbaum have criticised new historicism for paying too little attention to material relations and cultural differences. Nussbaum writes:

> New historicism, in its alignment with some versions of feminism and Marxism, needs to take more account of the dissonances that emerge from the juxtaposition of strongly held contestatory subject positions through history to consider the mode of production, as well as class, gender, and race relations. The relationships among them cannot be adequately conceptualized if discourse is imagined to float free of lived experience. More exactly, without a notion of the materiality of ideology, new historicism fails to establish a hierarchy of causes and effects and thus displays a relative indifference to these social relations and hierarchies. (Nussbaum 1989, 14)

Nussbaum's study of gender in eighteenth-century autobiographical writing shares some aspects of new historicist practice in that it focuses on the ideological constructions of subjectivity in the eighteenth century, but it differs from earlier new historicist work in that it locates subject positions for women in material practices. It therefore combines the general methodologies of new historicism with the specific political agenda of materialist feminism.

In her essay, 'Feminism, New Historicism, and the Reader', Wai-Chee Dimock surveys the theoretical and critical ground on which a materialist feminism may counter the reductive tendencies of new historicism. Dimock demonstrates, in a reading of Charlotte Perkins Gilman's 'The Yellow Wall-paper', that new historicist readings overlook the complexities of subject positions by interpreting all texts as functioning unproblematically within a power system, and that the act of reading (with the attention to detail and the 'difference' produced between interpretations which 'reading' implies) is what new historicism ignores to its cost. Whereas new historicist practice typically may concentrate on the totalising nature of power, history and representation, so that every text or event reproduces the same effect of power, containing subversion and promoting coherence, materialist criticism insists on the notion that all texts, events, ideologies, systems and representations of power must be mediated by, as indeed they may participate in forming, the individual subject. If subjectivity is fractured, incoherent, rife with contradiction and a sense of difference, then power cannot be total, or fully effective. For Dimock, it is the concept of 'the gendered reader, understood both as a historical figure and as a historied figure' that fractures the unity and coherence of 'power' or 'history' (Dimock 1991, 622).

We can put this another way. If new historicism insists that structures of power determine subject positions, and that representations foreground the structures of power, it fails to take account of the fact that representations must also be 'read' or mediated by the subject, and that when individual subjectivity is understood to be a function of difference (gender, class, race, and so forth), then even individual acts of reading can destabilize power. Difference will be produced endlessly in the process of reading, and it is the inexhaustibility of difference which Dimock argues is necessary to a properly materialist criticism:

> gender, as a principle of unevenness, will be important for any attempt to conceptualize history, not as a homologous or synchronized formation but as a field of endless mutations and permutations, a field where the temporal nonidentity between cause and effect and the structural nonidentity between system and subject quite literally open up a space for alternatives, however visionary and unsustained. History, thus engendered and thus decentred, is anything but a totalizing category. In fact, it is not even over and done with, but a realm of unexhausted and inexhaustible possibility. (Dimock 1991, 622)

The danger behind the new historicist attempts to show that the past is alien to us is that they imply that the past is not continually changing on every occasion we speak of it, and that the past has a coherence and a unity all of its own, which is simply different to the unity and coherence of our own time. In doing so new historicists tend to overlook the fact that every event, every representation or text, is experienced in very different ways by different cultures and peoples, according to gender, class, race, nationality, position, and any amount of other social and cultural factors. The past is rife with contradiction and multiplicity, each version and experience of the past overlapping with and breaking away from the other, and it is these 'faultlines' which may be used to show that power is never totalising, even though it may be represented as such.

Neither new historicism nor cultural materialism have accepted the notion that reading can be a destabilising act, nor have they examined to what extent the mediation of power may in fact distort and impair its effectiveness. But they have both moved closer towards the study of subject positions as constructed by sexual, cultural or racial difference rather than by ideological determinism. The subject is not just an effect of structures of power now for new historicist and cultural materialist practitioners, but is instead mobilised at different times and to varying degrees by different subcultures. Indeed the subject may be an *effect* of various subcultural groups and identities, overlapping or clashing with each other. Steven Mullaney argues that where early new historicism can fairly be regarded as conflicting with feminist and postcolonial studies, because of the neglect of 'difference' in new historicist work on Renaissance subjectivities, it does seem the case in more recent years that new historicism has become 'part of a productive, polyvocal, far from harmonious but necessary dialogue with materialist feminism, cultural materialism and other participants in the broader field of cultural studies' (Mullaney 1996, 34).

New historicist critics in the 1990s have turned their attention to the status of women writers (Gallagher 1994), to the changing forms of sexual identity (Goldberg 1992, 1994), to modes of imperial domination (Greenblatt 1991), and new directions have been taken by critics working at the intersection between feminism and new historicism (Nussbaum 1989, 1995; Straub 1992; Dimock 1991). The attempts to address colonial issues is in general less impressive than the new work from feminist perspectives. Studies like Greenblatt's *Marvelous Possessions* and Jeffrey Knapp's *An Empire Nowhere* focus on the attempts by European colonisers to imagine the new world, and on how Europeans acted and behaved according to their projected imaginings and fantasies. As Paul Hamilton points out, however, postcolonial studies has long moved on from the question of how Europe managed to win the ideological battle over the natives in the 'new world', and is now more interested in effective means by which the colonised may counter and resist the continuing legacy of colonial domination (Hamilton 1996, 171). It may be, in other words, that new historicism is still concerned with modes of domination rather than ways in which the structures of power may be resisted from specific social and cultural positions.

On the other hand, cultural materialist critics have adopted strategies which are more firmly located in material and social practices. In *Sexual Dissidence* Jonathan Dollimore traced the changing forms of a specific kind of resistance to the dominant culture, namely sexual dissidence. Dollimore analyses how the normative construction of sexuality polices differences in sexual taste and assigns negative connotations to 'deviations' from sexual norms. He pursues this further and examines how 'deviant' sexual identities can become sites of resistance to 'the language, ideologies, and cultures of domination' (Dollimore 1991, 21). Dollimore's work has progressively become more concerned with specific forms of dissidence, from his early analyses of the means by which radical perspectives can be articulated, to the forms which radical perspectives take from specific subject positions and in specific social or cultural relations. Alan Sinfield's recent work is even more materially based than Dollimore. Sinfield has been a central figure in the development of queer theory and queer readings in British cultural studies, and has become more and more interested in the strategies which may be adopted by subcultures in the present. In *The Wilde Century*, for example, he ponders which are the best strategies to be adopted by lesbian and gay cultures:

> The ultimate question is this: is homosexuality intolerable? One answer is that actually lesbians and gay men are pretty much like other people, in which case it just needs a few more of us to come out, so that the nervous among our compatriots can see we aren't so dreadful, and then everyone will live and let live; sexuality will become unimportant. The other answer is that homosexuality in fact constitutes a profound challenge to the prevailing values and structures in our kinds of society – in which case the bigots have a point of view and are not acting unreasonably. We cannot expect to settle this question, but the hypothesis we adopt will affect decisively our strategic options. (Sinfield 1994a, 177)

From the rehearsal of set strategic positions to the use of an inclusive 'we', Sinfield's recent work bears all the hallmarks of being engaged productively in an active political and cultural campaign. The aim of his work is to probe the collective identities and roles of lesbian and gay subcultures, to locate present struggles and campaigns within a broader cultural and historical context, and, 'to promote a questioning of the constructions through which we have been living' (Sinfield 1994a, 177). If we can summarise the aim of his earlier work as an attempt to locate the general conditions in which it becomes possible for dissidence to be articulated and to be effective in society, it is clear that his most recent work is not a major departure from this. Rather *The Wilde Century*, his work for the *Gay Times*, and other essays and articles written in the 1990s have built on the foundations of earlier concepts of dissidence, faultlines and deviance by dealing with the specific cases of sexual dissidence, and the dissident strategies of lesbian and gay subcultures.

One possible implication which could be drawn from this analysis of recent trends in new historicism and cultural materialism is that, as a result of the fact that most of the major practitioners (and 'founders') of these critical practices appear to be deserting their ranks and beginning to join queer studies, women's studies and post-colonial studies, they may be in the process of dissolving.[2] But this is not the case. New historicism and cultural materialism have become a central part of the critical repertoire of literary studies, and new work using their approaches is supported by journals like *Representations*, *Textual Practice*, *Literature and History*, *English Literary History*, *American Literary History*, *Social Text* and *News from Nowhere*, and by series of books like *The New Historicism* (California), *Cultural Politics* (Manchester), *Cambridge Studies in Renaissance Literature and Culture* (Cambridge), *New Cultural Studies* (Pennsylvania) and *Literature in History* (Princeton). New historicism and cultural materialism are regularly included on courses on literary or critical theory, and in guides to theory and critical practice, and are largely responsible for the turn towards the study of historical contexts in literary studies. It is safe to say that new historicism and cultural materialism are more active and prevalent than ever, but they have altered to accommodate the need for a wider understanding of the role of cultural and social differences in determining our material practices. It is by no means certain that they have succeeded in addressing the questions of specific subject position and identity which feminists in particular felt were lacking from their analyses. In the next part of the book I will demonstrate some ways in which the critical practices of new historicism and cultural materialism are useful in considering the relationship between literature and history, but also some ways in which they impose constraints on our reading strategies.

Notes

1. Simon During makes a similar point about the emergence of women's studies and ethnic studies from new historicist work towards the end of his article 'New Historicism', *Text and Performance Quarterly*, 11:3 (1991), 171–89.
2. A number of critics have implied the disappearance of the new historicism. Brook Thomas suggests that the new historicism is an old-fashioned topic, and both Carolyn Porter and Steven Mullaney attempt to describe what comes 'after the new historicism'. See Brook Thomas, *The New Historicism and Other Old-Fashioned Topics*, Carolyn Porter, 'History and Literature: After the New Historicism', and Steven Mullaney, 'After the New Historicism' in *Alternative Shakespeares II*.

Part II

Applications and Readings

Applications and Readings of New Historicism and Cultural Materialism

> [H]istory is the work expended on material documentation (books, texts, accounts, registers, acts, buildings, institutions, laws, techniques, objects, customs, etc.) that exists, in every time and place, in every society, either in a spontaneous or in a consciously organized form. The document is not the fortunate tool of a history that is primarily and fundamentally *memory*; history is one way in which a society recognizes and develops a mass of documentation with which it is inextricably linked.
>
> Michel Foucault, *The Archaeology of Knowledge*

Material documentation, in all the forms which Foucault lists above, is the principal vehicle of historical knowledge in Western society. Whereas empirical historians have conventionally regarded documents as the information deposits of a lost time and place, new historicism was a late part of the recognition that a society ordered, arranged and interpreted these documents in such a way as to tell particular stories about itself. In other words, historians do not play a passive role of teasing out and revealing the information contained in a document; they play an active role in arranging those documents into specific sequences, relating documents to others according to specific criteria, forming narratives using those documents as episodes or narrative units, and selecting and interpreting documents to accord with a particular historical thesis. That is not to say that there is some foul play, or ulterior motive, lurking in the mind of the historian, but that history is the social activity of telling a story about our past and the state of our present society, and that historical investigations are 'inextricably linked' to a society's means of identifying and imagining itself.

New historicism and cultural materialism participate in this activity of interpreting and explaining material documentation as the representations which a society produces of itself. Both critical approaches are involved in examining the process by which a society organises and produces its own ideological and material practices through representations embedded in texts of all kinds. All texts, all documents, are representations of the beliefs, values and forms of power circulating in a society at a given time in specific circumstances, and therefore all texts of a given time are in some ways interconnecting and interactive. In the next four chapters what we will examine is the ways in which new historicism and cultural materialism interpret and arrange documents and texts of all kinds, how they read literary texts in relation to other texts, and what uses and what limitations are to be found in new historicist and cultural materialist readings.

There is no one true method or type of reading from a new historicist or cultural materialist approach. That is to say that there are no strict methodologies, rules, axioms or techniques which we are compelled to use or apply when reading texts from new historicist or cultural materialist perspectives. But there are common characteristics which the writings of each critical practice share, characteristics which have been identified and discussed in previous chapters. In the next four chapters we will see how these characteristics may be tested on various texts and documents in order to rehearse how new historicist or cultural materialist ideas and practices might be useful ways of thinking about, and experimenting with, the relationship between literature and history. The aim of these chapters is to demonstrate the potential and the constraints of each critical practice, and to encourage a familiarity and confidence with the peculiar and distinctive features of each practice. The first and second chapters are demonstrations of the characteristics of reading and the theoretical perspectives of new historicism, indicating both its uses and its failings as a critical practice. The third chapter briefly rehearses a cultural materialist reading of some of Tennyson's poetry, before moving on to critique cultural materialist readings. The fourth chapter focuses on a blind spot in new historicist and cultural materialist writings, the process of decolonisation, and attempts to read Yeats's 'Easter 1916' from historical perspectives without repeating the limitations of new historicist and cultural materialist practice.

6 'On the Edge of a Black and Incomprehensible Frenzy': A New Historicist Reading of Joseph Conrad's *Heart of Darkness*

To my taste there is nothing so fascinating as spending a night out in an African forest, or plantation; but I beg you to note I do not advise anyone to follow the practice. Nor indeed do I recommend African forest life to any one. Unless you are interested in it and fall under its charm, it is the most awful life in death imaginable. It is like being shut up in a library whose books you cannot read, all the while tormented, terrified and bored. And if you do fall under its spell, it takes all the colour out of other kinds of living. Still it is good for a man to have an experience of it, whether he likes it or not, for it teaches you how very dependent you have been, during your previous life, on the familiarity of those conditions you have been brought up among, and on your fellow citizens; moreover it takes the conceit out of you pretty thoroughly during the days you spend stupidly stumbling about among your new surroundings.

Mary Kingsley, *Travels in West Africa* (33–4)

One of the methods of beginning a new historicist analysis, preferred by Stephen Greenblatt, is to recount an anecdote which contains a microcosmic image of the power relations which the critic seeks to elaborate in relation to the main texts of discussion. The anecdote has acquired a special place in new historicist analysis because it enables the critic to 'discover' in minute pieces of text the larger structures and operations of power, and to show how power extends its operations from minute anecdotes to the more complex and intricate texts and material practices embedded in a particular society or culture.[1]

The anecdote chosen usually belongs to a genre of documents or practices more firmly grounded in the actual or historical – travel narratives, penal documents, historical testimonies, confessional narratives, etc. – than the fictional or dramatic texts which the critic will proceed to analyse. They serve to base the critical interpretations of literary texts, which will follow later in new historicist analyses, in the discourse of truth. In other words, they serve to remind us that there is more at stake in discussions of Shakespeare or Dickens than the reputation of a writer. New historicists are intimating, in using these historical anecdotes, that history is only that which is written, and that what is at stake in the interpretations of literary texts, in circulation with documents and texts of all kinds, is the nature of history and power.

In her account of her experiences travelling in West Africa, Mary Kingsley explains to her English readers the cultural practices and social customs of the tribes whom she encounters on her journeys. In the extract quoted above, she advises her readers against spending a night in an African forest because to a European the forest, like every-thing else African, is inscrutable, like 'books you cannot read' (Kingsley 1993, 33). The basis for European colonisation of Africa lies in this absolute difference between the civilised European and the savage, inscrutable African. But Kingsley also seems to subvert the predicates of colonisation by falling under 'the charm' of the African forest, and finding it to her taste. Kingsley's account of West African tribes is unusual in its sensitivity to local differences between tribes and in its evident fascination with the customs and practices of differ-ent tribes. It is unusual also in its apparent disinterest in moralising on the cannibalism, polygamy or violence of the African tribes (although it does not fail to describe and make conspicuous these practices). Kingsley seems to be celebrating the joys of life in Africa, relishing her role as roving observer of African culture. But implicit in this description of her fascination with Africa is also the binary oppo-sition of colonialism between European master and African slave. Kingsley celebrates Africa, the forest experience in particular, as an experience which 'teaches you how very dependent you have been ... on the familiarity of those conditions you have been brought up among, and on your fellow citizens' (33–4). Africa is the cure for European decadence, dependency and cosiness. Africa becomes the one place where the European can roam freely, if (or perhaps because) less comfortably. Africa is pressed into service in the

European colonial psyche as the site of original, primeval freedom, of primitive simplicity and untarnished beauty and truth. It is the site of the European's confrontation with a mirror of her/his original being, his Adamic other, and hence, Kingsley says, 'takes the conceit out of you pretty thoroughly' (34).

A new historicist reading of this anecdote, then, would point to where there are possibilities for subversion – Kingsley's apparent difference from colonial preconceptions – but also would analyse how the text in question neutralises the possibility for subversion by containing it within a narrative which relies on European domination of the African other. Her narrative offers the possibility of subversion when it attempts to explain some very persuasive practical reasons for the practice of polygamy, or when it insists that there are as many differences between African tribes as there are differences between European countries or regions, but this is always narrated in the context of an academic study which in itself proclaims mastery over the African native. Kingsley explains that her chief motive in travelling to and around West Africa is the study and collection of observations of 'the African form of thought' (160), and this motive betrays the power relations implicit in her own work, the European subject scrutinising and coming to know the African object. In this relationship, the African always remains the object of study, without sufficient knowledge, intelligence and command of language to be anything but an object, while the European narrator or author displays her/his own mastery in the act of disclosing information, knowledge and interpretation of everything from the dietary habits to the military capacity of the African. Kingsley reinforces the absolute difference between the European 'us' and the African 'them' when she advises readers who wish to follow in her footsteps of useful ethnological studies, and of the differences which 'we' can expect to find between 'us' and 'them':

> They are not dreamers, or poets, and you will observe, and I hope observe closely – for to my mind this is the most important difference between their make of mind and our own – that they are notably deficient in all mechanical arts: they have never made, unless under white direction and instruction, a single fourteenth-rate piece of cloth, pottery, a tool or machine, house, road, bridge, picture or statue; that a written language of their own construction they none of them possess. (165)

In this passage the sensitivity to the practices and customs, and local variations and distinctions, of the West African tribes is absent entirely. 'They' are the Africans, and 'you' or 'we' are the whites. The text not only banishes the African from a position of knowledge or mastery over her/his own culture, but excludes all non-white people from the possibility of even reading this narrative. The narrative also insists on the absolute and essential distinction between the mind of the white and the mind of the African, and deems it impossible for the African to advance or become more civilised without the 'direction and instruction' of the European white. It is not just in individual and specific passages that Kingsley's narrative replicates the ideology of colonialism. What becomes blatantly clear when she advises readers of the wealth of ethnological studies which may be consulted on studying the African is that her narrative is backed by a system of representations and academic discourses, the function of which is to know, so as better to control, the native.

New historicism is primarily interested in examining and describing such systems of power as the European colonial discourse as it is found in texts like Kingsley's *Travels in West Africa*. In his essay, 'Invisible Bullets', Greenblatt explains the process which he wishes to analyse: 'My interest in what follows is in a prior form of restraint – in the process whereby subversive insights are generated in the midst of apparently orthodox texts and simultaneously contained by those texts, contained so effectively that the society's licensing and policing apparatus is not directly engaged' (Greenblatt 1981, 41). In Kingsley's travel narrative we see no vast European armies brutalising and repressing the natives, nor do we see the direct effects of discriminatory laws and severe punishments. The native has been dominated, controlled and mastered, not alone by brute force (although this is certainly involved), but in the act of representation, and, more specifically, in the discourse of European representations of the African.

It is in this discourse of European representations of the African that a new historicist analysis may locate Conrad's novel *Heart of Darkness*. Although new historicist critics recognise that a literary text may have a more complex form or structure than other texts, their analyses conventionally place literary texts in circulation with texts of all kinds in order to construct a model of how discourses performed in a particular period of time. Such analyses trace the connections between seemingly disparate texts so as to reveal the presence of a discourse, a discourse which inevitably shapes, as much as it is shaped by, its own society. Kingsley's *Travels in West Africa* can be read with Conrad's *Heart of Darkness* as part of a discourse which represents the African, or even the idea of Africa, in relation to European norms. For the most part, these connections between texts are revealed as surprising correspondences, startling resemblances, which turn out to be a product of being part of the same ideological discourse.

There are indeed some startling resemblances between Kingsley's narrative and Conrad's novel. In both texts the narrators are virtually alone, journeying towards a dark centre in the heart of Africa, and then returning to the safety of home. In both texts the natives are inscrutable, and yet must be scrutinised and 'known'. In both texts colonisation is redeemed by an ideal of order, efficiency and civilisation brought by the white ruler and stamped indelibly on the native. Kurtz is a powerful symbol of that order, efficiency and civilisation to Marlow, powerful because Kurtz is at once the most effective instrument of European colonisation and an enigma which cannot be understood in Europe. As Chief of the Inner Station, Kurtz ensures that the ivory trade for which he is responsible is more productive than in any other region, but his methods are brutal. He stamps his authority through violence on the native population, but Marlow is told that the natives do not want Kurtz to leave. Kurtz corresponds with surprising consistency to Kingsley's description of Mary Slessor in Old Calabar:

> This very wonderful lady has been eighteen years in Calabar; for the last six or seven living entirely alone, as far as white folks go, in a clearing in the forest near to one of the principal villages of the Okÿon district, and ruling as a veritable white chief over the entire Okÿon district. Her great abilities, both physical and intellectual, have given her among the savage tribe an unique position, and won her, from white and black who know her, a profound esteem. Her knowledge of the native, his language, his ways of thought, his diseases, his difficulties, and all that is his, is extraordinary, and the amount of good she has done, no man can fully estimate. Okÿon, when she went there alone – living in the native houses while she built, with the assistance of the natives, her present house – was a district regarded with fear by the Duke and Creek Town natives, and practically unknown to Europeans. It was given, as most of the surrounding districts still are, to killing at funerals, ordeal by poison, and perpetual internecine wars. Many of these evil customs she has stamped out, and Okÿon

rarely gives trouble to its nominal rulers, the Consuls in Old Calabar, and trade passes freely through it down to the sea-ports. (19)

Kurtz also rules like 'a veritable white chief', and seems to have both suppressed the native population and earned their respectful submission. With what methods Mary Slessor has turned an area 'practically unknown' to Europeans into an area over which she has a great deal of control, and, more importantly, inestimable knowledge, Kingsley does not tell us. Precisely how Slessor has stamped out the local customs and wars is not revealed. Just as Kingsley thinks of Slessor as 'wonderful', Marlow comes to admire Kurtz, although his admiration is constructed from the fragments he learns about Kurtz on his journey up the Congo, and like Kingsley too, he never reveals much about Kurtz's methods other than the mention of extermination (87) and of his lack of restraint (97). The shrunken heads of natives on poles at the Inner Station is the evidence of Kurtz's stamp of authority, and are apt reminders that the liberal discourse of civilising the native, instructing him in European ways, is inseparable from the violence used to achieve order, efficiency and civilisation.

Here we might note the presence of a possible subversion of European colonial discourse in *Heart of Darkness*. In England colonialism had been represented as a civilising mission, the gift of white people to the savage natives. In Victorian England, particularly, when evolutionist ideas instilled a fascination with the colonial natives as primitive versions of modern Europeans, Africa became an imaginative space on which English representations projected the fantasy of coming face to face with the primitive origins of civilisation. One of the most pervasive images of this relationship between the modern European and the primitive native, when represented in Europe, was the image of European mother nurturing and protecting her colonial children. William Watson's poem, 'England and her Colonies', written in 1890, is one such representation:

> She stands a thousand wintered tree,
> By countless morns impearled;
> Her broad roots coil beneath the sea,
> Her branches sweep the world;
> Her seeds, by careless winds conveyed,
> Clothe the remotest strand
> With forests from her scatterings made,

New nations fostered in the shade,
And linking land with land.

O ye by wandering tempest sown
'Neath every alien star,
Forget not whence the breath was blown
That wafted you afar!
For ye are still her ancient seed
On younger soil let fall –
Children of Britain's island-breed,
To whom the Mother in her need
Perchance may one day call.

(Watson in Brooks and Faulkner 1996, 275)

This poem deems it a blessing for the natives that Britain has fostered them and that they are now linked 'land with land' to the mother country. The metaphor of seed propagation conveys the idea of colonial expansion as a natural process, and invites the colonies to think of themselves as offshoots or extensions of Britain. Colonialism in this poem is a benevolent, positive process, of taking colonies under the wing of a civilised, educated mother figure, and giving them a family to which they can belong. This is the ideology which Conrad's novel threatens to subvert, for in *Heart of Darkness* colonialism is represented as robbery, savagery and greed.

Kurtz, like Slessor, is an ideal coloniser because he keeps the trade flowing and seems to advocate instructing the natives as well as enslaving them. The company is in the Congo to make money, and the 'civilising' of the natives is a by-product of this capitalist venture. The role of Europeans in educating and 'humanising' the natives justifies their presence in Africa, but Marlow finds that the reality often belies the idea of improving the natives:

> Once a white man in an unbuttoned uniform, camping on the path with an armed escort of lank Zanzibaris, very hospitable and festive – not to say drunk. Was looking after the upkeep of the road, he declared. Can't say I saw any road or any upkeep, unless the body of a middle-aged negro, with a bullet-hole in the forehead, upon which I absolutely stumbled three miles farther on, may be considered as a permanent improvement. (48)

Heart of Darkness reveals the violence and brutality which follows colonialism at every turn, from the French man of war 'firing into a continent' (41) to the sunken heads on poles at Kurtz's station (97). The violence pervades every aspect of the relationship between the coloniser and the native, and Conrad's novel subverts the liberal image of the mother country by revealing this violence. So too, *Heart of Darkness* plays with the image of England itself as a colony, making allusions to the Roman colonisation of Britain, and to London being part of the 'darkness' also. The novel insinuates that far from colonialism being a proud, honourable venture, it is corrupt, shabby, and so pernicious that Marlow must lie to Kurtz's Intended, and must keep the truth of European colonisation of Africa from European ears. It may be tempting to think of *Heart of Darkness* as an anti-colonial novel, as laying bare the brutal realities of colonialism, as subverting the liberal colonial discourse, but a new historicist analysis of this novel will demonstrate that it contains the possibility for subversion by constructing a narrative in which only imperialist European ideas and attitudes are represented, and, more importantly, only Europeans are permitted the ability or power to represent.

New historicist critics analyse a system of representation that is perfectly closed and circular. The subversive potential of the native view of colonialism, for example, is never possible because every time the native appears in that system of representation it is as a projection of the colonising white man. The native is always either the fantasy or the nightmare of the coloniser, and therefore always reflects how the coloniser is feeling and thinking. A system of representation, or discursive formation, is defined by Foucault, a key influence on new historicist practice, as the following:

> That which implies that one can define the general set of rules that govern their objects, the form of dispersion that regularly divides up what they say, the system of their referentials; that which implies that one defines the general set of rules that govern the different modes of enunciation, the possible redistribution of the subjective positions, and the system that defines and prescribes them; that which implies that one defines the set of rules common to all their associated domains, the forms of succession, of simultaneity, of the repetition of which they are capable, and the system that links all these fields of co-existence together; lastly, that which implies that one can define the general set of rules that govern the status of these statements, the way in which they are institutionalized, received, used, re-used,

combined together, the mode according to which they become objects of appropriation, instruments for desire or interest, elements for a strategy. (Foucault 1972, 115)

Foucault is defining here the discursive formation as a system of representations or enunciations which operate according to the same rules when delineating objects, determining subject positions, using modes and genres of representation, making links with other discursive forms, and when being used and defined and gathered together. New historicist critics follow this practice of identifying a number of texts which belong to the same discursive formation, tracing their relationship to one another, charting the transformations which they effect within the system, and charting the regularity with which they replicate the rules of the system. In the course of doing this new historicists also note what the system of representation in question displaces or excludes, and, of course, how the system of representation functions as a system of power by containing subversions within its own structure.

In this chapter, then, what we are doing is, firstly, tracing the relationships between a number of European representations of Africa in order to define to what extent they form a perfectly circular system of representations, and then, secondly, examining *Heart of Darkness* in particular for how it functions within this system. At this point we need to make a clear distinction between a discourse and a genre. Throughout the nineteenth century there had been a proliferation of travel narratives written by intrepid explorers giving accounts of their discoveries of strange lands. The extent of this proliferation was to have almost constituted a genre in itself. We could examine a large number of these travel narratives and find similar characteristics and similar representations, and hence have discovered the defining features of a genre. But when these travel narratives can be linked with texts of very different genres – fiction, science reports, government documents, etc. – and all are found to share common characteristics in how they treat the African as object, how they situate the European narrator or author as objective observer, how they represent the relationship between Europe and Africa, how they adopt the language and enunciative posture of anthropology, and how they can be found dispersed throughout European culture in how they are used and institutionalised, then we may say that we have defined a discourse.

We have traced the links between Kingsley's *Travels in West Africa* and Conrad's *Heart of Darkness*. There are also striking resemblances between Conrad's novel and Henry Stanley's *Through the Dark Continent*. When, in *Heart of Darkness*, Marlow notes that the vast blank spaces on his boyhood maps of Africa had since been filled in with rivers and lakes, it is the work of Stanley and others to which he is referring. Stanley's narrative tells the story of his quest to discover the source of the River Congo, and to map Central Africa more comprehensively. Stanley is Marlow's precursor, drawn to the snake-like Congo River as Marlow is, drawn to the same blank spaces which occupy the place of Central Africa on his maps. He recalls a conversation with his companion in December 1876:

> 'Now look at this, the latest chart which Europeans have drawn of this region. It is a blank, perfectly white ... . I assure you, Frank, this enormous void is about to be filled up. Blank as it is, it has a singular fascination for me. Never has white paper possessed such a charm for me as this has, and I have already mentally peopled it, filled it with most wonderful pictures of towns, villages, rivers, countries, and tribes – all in the imagination – and I am burning to see whether I am correct or not'. (Stanley 1988, II.152)

For Stanley, as for Marlow, Africa is a blank space to be occupied and filled in, and even the present inhabitants and occupiers of that land are imagined, 'mentally peopled', in Europe. The African natives cannot be known in their own presence, as living beings with their own cultures and systems of representations. They must always have been the projection of the European imagination, always contained within the European system of representations. To Stanley, Africa is what must be occupied, simply because the European map of the world denotes Africa as an absence, as a blank space, as an anomalous void which awaits its place in the grand order of civilisation.

Like Marlow, Stanley's Africa is the heart of darkness, represented as 'the dark continent' (I. 54). He too feels himself being sucked up river towards this heart of darkness. Stanley may dream of Africa as a blank space which he mentally peoples, but on his journeys into the heart of the Congo the natives become real enough, attacking his expedition, killing his three white companions and half of his African entourage. We could say that the appearance in his narrative of 'real' natives, repelling his colonial expedition, might be a subversion of the

European image, but, if it is, it is contained effectively within a narrative in which the control of the native through knowledge and representation is the ultimate end. In an encounter with the Mowa people Stanley realises that the Mowa distrust the book in which he continually makes notes. They come to his camp threatening war unless the book is burned before their eyes. Here the system of European knowledge, the supremacy of the written word, is threatened, and the task of 'knowing' the native in order to control him may be jeopardised. But Stanley dupes the natives by handing them a copy of Shakespeare with a cover similar to his notebook, and it is Shakespeare which the natives happily and ceremoniously burn.[2] Stanley saves his representations of the Mowa, and in the process reveals what is at stake in his adventures in the Congo – the power to represent, to control, to dupe and to dominate. From Stanley's dream of blank spaces, to his recognition that his notebook must be saved at all costs for European knowledge, it is the capacity of the European to represent the African which is always maintained.

In *Heart of Darkness* Europe meets Africa, and the possibilities of subverting European modes of ontology and epistemology are numerous. Kurtz may have become the primitive 'other', may have been absorbed in African customs and modes of being. Marlow may have recognised in Africa the futility and incongruity of European colonialism. The violence of colonialism may subvert the liberal image of colonial adventures in Europe. Or there may be simply the recognition that Africa exists autonomous and independent of Europe. But a new historicist analysis will demonstrate that all these possibilities for subversion are contained and made safe by the very fact that Africa is represented always within the discourse of European colonialism. There is nothing outside of the European system of representation. The native – his/her views, life, pain or joy – is always represented by the European, in a European book, or by a European voice. Stanley narrates his daring trick of duping the natives in order to save his notebooks, and, so too, Kurtz ensures that Marlow will save his papers on the suppression of savage customs. In each case it is the representation of Africa which is at stake. The value of European modes of representation is evident when Marlow comes across a book, *An Inquiry into some Points of Seamanship*, in a deserted hut on his journey upriver:

> I handled this amazing antiquity with the greatest possible tender-

ness, lest it should dissolve in my hands. Within, Towson or Towser
was inquiring earnestly into the breaking strain of ship's chains and
tackle, and other such matters. Not a very enthralling book; but at the
first glance you could see there a singleness of intention, an honest
concern for the right way of going to work, which made these humble
pages, thought out so many years ago, luminous with another than a
professional light. The simple old sailor, with his talk of chains and
purchases, made me forget the jungle and the pilgrims in a delicious
sensation of having come upon something unmistakably real. (71)

Marlow here associates the values of honesty, simplicity, single-mind-
edness and exactitude with the book of an English sailor, and notice
how the book makes him forget what must be the illusion, or fiction,
of Africa, while he is absorbed in the unmistakable reality of the book.
The book represents European discourse, and as such is the only
reality. Africa is merely the fictional projection of a European fantasy
in which Europe is the only truth, the only reality. The events and
characters which appear in each of the narratives analysed here are
always the objects of European discourse, and, as such, always
contained within that discourse. We must always bear in mind, then,
that even Marlow's journey into the heart of darkness is being
narrated at a dockside in Gravesend, and Conrad's novel is written for
English readers, that Stanley and Kingsley are writing with English
readers in mind, that the maps of Africa with blank spaces are in
Europe too. The African is never permitted to be outside European
discourse.

As Brook Thomas argues in his essay, 'Preserving and Keeping
Order by Killing Time in *Heart of Darkness*', Conrad's novel is one of
many in the late Victorian age and early twentieth century which
portrays the encounter between Europe and its 'others', and, more
importantly, which depict 'Europe's discovery of "the Other" within
itself' (Thomas 1996, 243). In *Heart of Darkness*, the natives, and the
impenetrable darkness of the Congo, are projections of the European
self. They embody a strangeness and an alterity within the self, and
are fantasies of a European unconscious, or evocations of a forgotten
European past. Marlow casts Africa in the role of prehistoric Europe:

We were wanderers on prehistoric earth, on an earth that wore the
aspect of an unknown planet. We could have fancied ourselves the
first of men taking possession of an accursed inheritance, to be
subdued at the cost of profound anguish and excessive toil. But

suddenly, as we struggled round a bend, there would be a glimpse of rush walls, of peaked grass-roofs, a burst of yells, a whirl of black limbs, a mass of hands clapping, of feet stamping, of bodies swaying, of eyes rolling, under the droop of heavy and motionless foliage. The steamer toiled along slowly on the edge of a black and incomprehensible frenzy. The prehistoric man was cursing us, praying to us, welcoming us – who could tell? We were cut off from the comprehension of our surroundings; we glided past like phantoms, wondering and secretly appalled, as sane men would be before an enthusiastic outbreak in a madhouse. We could not understand because we were too far and could not remember, because we were travelling in the night of first ages, of those ages that are gone, leaving hardly a sign – and no memories. (68–9)

This passage begins with the fantasy that the Congo is prehistoric earth, a world unrecognisable to the European through the distance of time, and in which the pilgrims with Marlow are the Adamic first inhabitants. It is a poignant fantasy of Europeans being the first men, alone at the beginnings of the world, poignant because the narrative belongs to a discourse which is entirely Eurocentric. But Marlow and his fellow travellers are shocked out of this fantasy by the presence of natives near the river. For a moment these natives represent the interruption of European fantasy, the interruption of a Eurocentric notion of original man. For a moment the natives are real, and the shock for Marlow, as he says in the paragraph which follows this passage, is the 'suspicion of their not being inhuman' (69). To recognise the natives as human would be to recognise their difference, their independence, their existence outside the European fantasy of prehistoric man, outside the European system of representations. But the narrative silences this interruption by representing the natives as an inhuman, 'black and incomprehensible frenzy' (68).

In this passage, then, there is the 'sudden' possibility of recognising the African natives on the river bank as 'others' outside of European representations, with their own cultures, histories, languages, beliefs and customs, but the narrative appropriates the native as an image of Europe's historical other, 'prehistoric man'. This figure of prehistoric man is the other within the European self, an incomprehensible past, from which 'we' are cut off. The passage represents the relationship between 'us' and 'them' as that of phantoms and the living, and that of the sane and the insane. Phantoms are the abstracted spiritual beings, omnipresent and omniscient, directly contrary to the living, material beings who are earthy, rooted to the land and to physical work. In such a way might intellectual Europe have envisaged itself in relation to the physicality of the African native, or, as Kurtz writes in his report, we '"must necessarily appear to them [savages] in the nature of supernatural beings – we approach them with the might as of a deity"' (86). So, too, the Europeans are described as being like the sane watching 'an enthusiastic outbreak in a madhouse' (69), and experiencing the fascination, the wonder, of observing a 'frenzy' from the perspective of rationality and sanity. Otherness is a spectacle, a theatre of entertainment, for the European, whether it come in the form of insanity or of cultural difference.

In the final part of this passage the African 'others' are represented as the distant or forgotten selves of Europe. The incomprehensibility of the natives is explained as the result of historical distance and the passing of memory. This explanation contributes to the idea of the European as civilised, enlightened, at a more advanced state of intelligence and ability than the African, since it posits that where 'they' are now, 'we' were in the long-distant past. By turning a cultural distance into a historical distance, Conrad's novel appropriates the African natives for what they tell a European reader about Europe. It also justifies the European discourse of representing the African. If the incomprehensibility of Africa is a result of the failure of memory, then it also signifies the failure of representation. The failure to remember is the failure to re-present, since memory is in its most literal sense the re-presentation of the past. This explains the absence not only of memories, but also of signs, of representations. There are no signs by which the European can re-cognise his own past, i.e. the primitive state of European man represented by the African native. In order to reconnect the European to the past, to his former self, the narrative substitutes memory with a representation, which, in this case, is the representation of the African as prehistoric man. The African, in other words, is appropriated within the European system of representations in order to stand in for the gap between modern European and his prehistoric ancestors. The African becomes a convenient explanation of how the European has reached his advanced state of civilisation, and so becomes an indispensable part of the European narrative of progress.

In *Heart of Darkness*, then, as Greenblatt argues of Renaissance texts, power produces its own subversion only in order to contain it. The same text which pretends to stumble 'suddenly' upon the natives in a form which interrupts the European fantasy of original man also appropriates these natives as the justification for the fantasy of European civilisation and progress. There is caution to be learned from this point, too, because Greenblatt's thesis is one which he claims to be the case in Renaissance texts, yet we can see it applying just as easily to a novel published at the beginning of the twentieth century. We might cast doubt on the claims of new historicism to be historicising literature if its analyses 'discover' the same thesis concerning power relations in all texts, regardless of their historical, cultural, formal or linguistic differences. More usually, new historicists argue that, although the same formula of power relations recurs throughout post-medieval Western history, it takes different forms in each epoch or epistemé. Whereas, according to Greenblatt in *Marvelous Possessions*, the Renaissance experience of Europe encountering the 'other' in the new world was characterised by a recognition of radical difference, and a practising of techniques and technologies 'on' the other, we might surmise from the analyses above that the late nineteenth-century experience of Europe encountering the 'other' in Africa was characterised by appropriation, and a substitution of the African with 'prehistoric man'.

Africa is also experienced by European colonial discourse as the site of European nightmare, as the embodiment of a European unconscious or anti-self. If Europe's encounter with the new world in the sixteenth century was represented as a source of wonder and marvel, the encounter with Africa as 'other' within the European self was represented as a source of dread and horror. A persistent theme in travel narratives, particularly colonial travel narratives, was the dread and fear of cannibalism. The prospect of cannibalism appears in Kingsley's *Travels in West Africa*, when she comes across the hands, toes, eyes and ears of human bodies; in Stanley's *Through the Dark Continent*, when Stanley stumbles upon heads on pikes, and a human forearm near a fire; and in *Heart of Darkness*, when Marlow tells of the crew of his boat as including some cannibals. But it is never anything more than a prospect:

> I don't pretend to say that steamboat floated all the time. More than once she had to wade for a bit, with twenty cannibals splashing around and pushing. We had enlisted some of these chaps on the way for a crew. Fine fellows – cannibals – in their place. They were men one could work with, and I am grateful to them. And, after all, they

did not eat each other before my face: they had brought along a
provision of hippo-meat which went rotten, and made the mystery of
the wilderness stink in my nostrils. (67)

The men who help Marlow to keep his boat afloat on the river are
known not by the name of their tribe, or by their village, or even by
the name of African natives, but are called cannibals. But Marlow has
no way of knowing that they are cannibals, since they have the good
manners not to 'eat each other before my face'. He witnesses not one
instance of humans eating humans in the Congo, and sees no
evidence of this practice at all. Cannibalism is a name without a refer-
ent in *Heart of Darkness*. Although the practice is wholly absent, the
assumption that it exists is widespread. When Marlow's boat has
ground to a halt on a bank and his crew of natives are clearly hungry,
he wonders why they do not attack and eat the five white men on
board. He assumes that they are cannibals, and so interprets their
gestures, looks and murmurs as signs of their cannibalistic intentions.

   Stanley, on the other hand, purports to have found evidence of
cannibalism on his journey up the Congo:

> Evidences of cannibalism were numerous in the human and 'soko'
> skulls that grinned on many poles, and the bones that were freely
> scattered in the neighbourhood, near the village garbage heaps and
> the river banks, where one might suppose hungry canoe-men to have
> enjoyed a cold collation on an ancient matron's arm. As the most
> positive and downright evidence, in my opinion, of this hideous prac-
> tice, was the thin forearm of a person that was picked up near a fire,
> with certain scorched ribs which might have been tossed into the fire
> after being gnawed. It is true that it is but circumstantial evidence, yet
> we accepted them as indubitable proofs. Besides, we had been
> taunted with remarks that we would furnish them with meat supplies
> – for the words *meat* and *to-day* have but slight dialectic difference in
> many languages. (Stanley 1988, II. 213–14)

What Stanley and his companions accept as 'indubitable proofs' of
cannibalism makes for flimsy evidence. Like Kingsley, Stanley discovers human remains which he says 'might have been' thrown to the
fire after being eaten, and bones close to the dump and banks where
'one might suppose' the canoe-men ate some human arm. And if
these conjectures are based, as Stanley admits, on 'circumstantial
evidence', the final proof of cannibalism is that the natives taunted

Stanley and his men with suggestions that they are 'meat'. The possibility that this is simply a taunt, a joke, an error of translation, or a word with double meaning, as he suggests, is ignored, and is taken as proof of cannibalism. Again the assumption is that the natives are cannibals, and so the discovery of human remains and the mention of 'meat' confirms their cannibalism.

In his book, *Colonial Encounters*, Peter Hulme identifies Columbus's *Journal* as the first European text in which the word 'canibales' appears. There the word referred to the Carib people of the Antilles, whom Columbus records in his journal were said to be man-eating, and subsequently the word 'cannibal' came to refer to the practice of eating human flesh. But as Hulme shows, the original reference is slippery, since Columbus does not see cannibalism for himself, but hears of it from the Arawaks, who, in turn, don't seem to have seen the practice for themselves, but have explained the disappearance of their fellows at the hands of the 'canibales' as the result of cannibalism. The appearance of cannibalism in these colonial texts seems to be characterised by fear and suspicion without evidence. Everybody knows that it exists, even abounds, among the savage natives, but nobody actually observes, participates in, or finds concrete evidence of, cannibalism. It seems that cannibals are defined not by the practices and customs which they have been observed performing – not, then, by their own deeds – but by the representations of European travellers and colonists. This indicates the complete circularity of European colonial discourse. African cannibalism is not just discovered by the Europeans, who duly react with horror and dread, but is, in fact, invented and constituted in the texts of European colonial discourse.

The power to represent, and hence to dominate, is what is at issue in these signs, or 'proofs', of cannibalism. Without observing or witnessing a single act of cannibalism, European writings habitually assume the widespread practice of eating human flesh.[3] All that is evident in European texts are signs which are taken to mean, or come to represent, the presence of cannibalism. The sign takes the place of the object. Power invents, and then, as if by surprise, 'discovers' the existence of cannibalism. New historicist analyses may bring us to this point of being able to recognise, in the way in which a series of texts and representations come together to form a discourse (in this case, the discourse of European representations of Africa), that discursive formations do not just define, study and analyse the object, but also constitute and produce the object. Foucault indicates in *The Archaeology of Knowledge* that 'madness' does not exist as an idea or concept until a discourse of madness is formed, and madness is produced as the object of study.[4] In much the same way, cannibalism is invented and constituted by the European discourse of colonialism, and is produced as evidence of the savagery of the natives. Colonial discourse must invent the proofs of cannibalism (or incest, physical abnormality, debauchery, mutilation, barbarity) in order to define the native as savage, and hence to justify the idea of European civilisation, enlightenment and progress. This is not to say that cannibalism does not exist, but that when it appears in the European system of representations it has a very specific and powerful function within that system, and is defined and encountered in terms which are predisposed to favour European colonial needs.

Marlow tries to imagine what it might be like to feel cannibalistic. He imagines himself driven to the depths of 'lingering starvation', pondering what one would or would not do in extreme conditions (76). It is Marlow's attempt to get closer to the mentality and motives of the natives whom he thinks are cannibals, and by doing so he comes to admire their restraint for checking their impulses. But in the process he projects on to them the fantasy of being savage, the fiction of cannibalism. Cannibalism, then, is also part of the European experimentation with the 'other' within the self, fantasising a primitive cannibal hidden beneath the modern veneer of reserve and civilisation. *Heart of Darkness* is not the only text of the late Victorian era to experiment with the idea of a primitive other contained within the self. It shares with Wells's *The Time Machine* and Jefferies's *After London* anxieties about the emergence of primitive disorder out of the civilised order of modern Western society. But making visible these anxieties is a device through which power validates the value of 'civilisation', as the new historicists contend that power secures the value of its order by sanctioning glimpses of disorder. Kelvin Everest thinks that the new historicist insight into how a dominant order or powerful discourse engages binary oppositions is one of its most important contributions to critical and literary theory: 'This tendency to take on the guise of the enemy is exactly the danger about which the new historicism has succeeded in making us so vigilant' (Everest 1991, 5). It is one of the legacies of new historicism, then, to have recognised the ways in which power produces and contains what appears to be its opposite, or what seems to be a radical difference.

New historicism is not simply a way of reading literature in its historical contexts. It is also about power relations, ideological functions, epistemic transformations, modes and systems of representation, transgressions of genre, discursive formations and the production of objects of knowledge. It provides useful insights into how literature interacts with texts of all kinds, produced and shaped by the discursive practices and power relations which those texts in turn produce and shape. Both new historicism and cultural materialism, as Catherine Belsey has argued, produce 'political history from the raw material of literary texts' (Belsey, in Wilson and Dutton 1992, 43). But it is not a political history with which many political historians would be content. It is political in that it focuses on the formation and operation of powerful discourses, while it pays little or no attention to the minutiae of parliaments, dictators, trade unions or any narrowly political details. It is historical in that it focuses on how various texts make connections with other texts in the same epoch, textualising historical changes and shifts, and describing ideological formations and power relations at work in that epoch, while it makes little or no mention of the wars, famines, governments, economic trends and lifestyles associated with particular dates and events. We could have read Conrad's novel in the context of the history of the Congo in the late Victorian era, as Hunt Hawkins suggests:

> duly recounting how Henry Stanley discovered the Congo river in 1875, how King Leopold II of Belgium hired Stanley to stake a claim in the region, how Leopold through shrewd diplomatic maneuvering got the Congo as his private territory (rather than a Belgian colony) at the Berlin Conference of 1885, and how the King then proceeded to turn his African country into a vast slave plantation for extracting ivory and raw rubber until the European powers finally took it away from him in 1908. The only difficulty with all this historical background is that it has no obvious connection with Conrad's story, which does not mention any of it. (Hawkins 1992, 207)

On the other hand, the participation of the novel in the historical formation and operation of colonial power, and in the production and representation of European fantasies of otherness, is available for us to read and to link with other representations. There is nothing of the novel's involvement in the operation of powerful discourses which is not 'present' in the novel or in its relations with other texts and discourses. By implication, of course, the novel is complicit in these discourses. While it is inevitably the product of imperialist discourse, it is also a part of that discourse, shaping and serving imperialism. For new historicists, the nuances of Marlow's relationships to imperialism, the hints and suggestions of criticisms of imperialism, are merely devices with which to work more effectively in the interests of imperialist power. What really matters is that the novel permits no other voice or point of observation than that of the coloniser. As Edward Said writes in *Culture and Imperialism*: '*Heart of Darkness* works so effectively because its politics and aesthetics are, so to speak, imperialist, which in the closing years of the nineteenth century seemed to be at the same time an aesthetic, politics and even epistemology inevitable and unavoidable' (Said 1994, 26).

There is the concern, as I argued earlier in the book, that what new historicism is doing in examining how texts of all kinds form a perfectly circular and closed discourse, and linking imperialist texts with other imperialist texts, is refusing to listen to the voices and representations outside that discourse. By arguing that Conrad's *Heart of Darkness* permits no other perspective than that of the coloniser, in an attempt to rehearse here the arguments and methods of a new historicist reading, I have also constructed a narrative about Africa in which no perspective and no representation other than those of imperialism have been considered, or even quoted. In arguing that power produces and then contains subversion, I have silenced any possible dissent by closing it back within a circular system of Western power relations. There are political implications, then, and indeed dangers, in a new historicist reading which we should bear in mind. But there are also useful insights and analyses which can be gained in reading literary texts from new historicist perspectives, and I shall conclude with some of these.[5]

There are two lessons to be gained from adopting new historicist methods of analysis: the first is a means of relating a text to other texts of the same period – it is, then, a way of practising a kind of intertextual criticism; the second is a means of relating literary texts to history and politics. As a kind of intertextual criticism, new historicism allows us to see ways in which texts which were seemingly unrelated (e.g. Shakespeare's *I Henry IV* and Thomas Harriot's *A Brief and True Report of the New Found Land of Virginia*) are in fact related, and, at certain moments and under specific conditions, intersect with each other to form a discourse. New historicism is also a useful practice for its practice of interdisciplinarity. It tends to blur the distinctions between literature and history, between history and social sciences, between what is assumed to be background information and what is read closely in the foreground. It loosens the constraints imposed on reading practices and expectations by rigid disciplinary boundaries, and accepts that a literary text may be read as a work of history, or an anecdotal report might become a way of explaining the cultural and political logic of its time. New historicism is the most prominent indication of a turn to history and politics in literary studies, and it reveals literary texts as political acts and historical events. It enables us, as Belsey says, quoted above, to construct a political history out of literary texts. It provides a sense of how a text participates in sustaining the social order, and joins with other texts to form a discourse which contains subversion effectively by representing it, and controlling it within a defined and limited system of representation. But, perhaps most importantly of all, it exercises its own political influence by taking a literary text out of the realms of liberal humanism, by refusing to allow literature to signify the transcendence of politics, or the freedom from politics. It reveals the sinister, insidious participation of literature in the murky business of justifying oppression, colonisation, capitalism, domination. By revealing the complicity of literary texts in acts of control, new historicism diminishes the capacity of those texts to continue to produce and represent the interests of power. In this sense, new historicism plays a vital role of situating literary texts in a network of power relations, revealing the political acts and historical functions of those texts.

A new historicist reading of Conrad's *Heart of Darkness* enables us to see how this novel which seems to say very little of the historical catastrophes being wrought upon the Congo by a European despot is in fact participating, and complicit, in the European discourse of colonial control. Although Kurtz seems to imply something of these catastrophes in his muttering 'The Horror! The Horror!', and in his advocation of extermination, the real 'otherness' of Africa – its suffering and pain at the hands of European colonisation – remains outside the European system of representation, and remains therefore unrepresented. It is the truth which the novel itself cannot represent, and which the novel contributes to effacing. A new historicist analysis of *Heart of Darkness* enables us to locate that novel in the complex system of power relations and cultural representations which compose the discourse of colonialism.

Notes

1. See Joel Fineman's considerations of the anecdote, and his analysis of its importance in new historicist essays in 'The History of the Anecdote: Fiction and Fiction', in H. Aram Veeser (ed.), *The New Historicism*, London: Routledge, 1989.

2. Stephen Greenblatt concludes the final chapter of *Shakespearean Negotiations*, Oxford: Oxford University Press, 1988, by recalling this anecdote of Stanley's deployment of Shakespeare as a cunning decoy.

3. An interesting counter-text to this European discourse of cannibalism is Olaudah Equiano's *The Interesting Narrative*, London: Penguin, 1995, in which Equiano narrates the account of his experiences as a slave taken from Africa to South America, and of his freedom in England. Equiano is convinced when he is enslaved that his white captors are cannibals who want to eat him. He notes as he is taken on board a slave ship that the crew keep a 'large furnace of copper boiling' (55), and assumes that its purpose is for cooking human flesh. His master also, he says, would 'tell him jocularly that he would kill and eat me. Sometimes he would say to me – the black people are not good to eat, and would ask me if we did not eat people in my country. I said, No' (65). Here, as with European representations of African cannibalism, the signs of cannibalism seem to proliferate without any reference. There are no visible acts of cannibalism, only representations.

4. See Chapters 2 and 3 of *The Archaeology of Knowledge*, 1972, in particular. Foucault's idea of discourse producing the object which it studies is a key influence, then, on the new historicist idea of power producing its own subversion in order to contain it.

5. There are a number of essays which examine Conrad's *Heart of Darkness* in its historical contexts: Hunt Hawkins, 'Conrad's Heart of Darkness; Politics and History', Hunt Hawkins, 'Joseph Conrad, Roger Casement and the Congo Reform Movement', Ian Glenn, 'Conrad's *Heart of Darkness*: A Sociological Reading', Patrick Brantlinger, '*Heart of Darkness*: Anti-Imperialism, Racism or Impressionism?', and Reynold Humphries, 'The Discourse of Colonialism: Its Meaning and Relevance for Conrad's Fiction'. Full details are given in the bibliography.

7   Producing the Subject: A New Historicist Reading of Charlotte Perkins Gilman's 'The Yellow Wall-paper'

We have yet to write the history of that other form of madness, by which men, in an act of sovereign reason, confine their neighbours, and communicate and recognise each other through the merciless language of non-madness.

Michel Foucault, *Madness and Civilization*

In the work of Stephen Greenblatt, Foucault occupies a curiously marginal position. In *Renaissance Self-Fashioning* Foucault is consigned almost wholly to footnotes. In *Shakespearean Negotiations* he is mentioned three times, two of which are references. In *Learning to Curse* he warrants two mentions, both of which tell merely of his visits to Berkeley in the late 1970s. In *Marvelous Possessions* he has disappeared from view altogether. Yet, in other ways, Foucault is everywhere in Greenblatt's work: the analysis of discourse, the role of discourse in determining subject positions, the relationship between power, knowledge and subversion, the wide dispersion of texts which confirm the existence of powerful discursive formations, the fascination with 'marginal' figures and situations – the insane, the heretic, the criminal, the colonial native. Foucault is pervasive as an influence on the work of new historicists, but his influence takes different forms. D. A. Miller, in *The Novel and the Police*, saw his work as an extension and application of Foucault's writings, rather than the result of Foucault's influence. In the first footnote of *The Novel and the Police*, Miller explains:

> [I]n announcing my project as 'a Foucauldian reading of the Novel', I mean to signal, besides an intellectual debt, an intellectual gamble for which that debt is the capital. For perhaps the most notable reticence in Foucault's work concerns precisely the reading of literary texts and institutions, which, though often and suggestively cited in passing, are never given a role to play within the disciplinary processes under consideration. (Miller 1988, viii n.1)

Miller therefore announces his own work as filling in a gap in Foucault's writings, extending a Foucauldian analysis to the realm of literary texts. This is another version of a new historicist critical practice, then, and in this chapter I will focus on an overtly Foucauldian analysis of Gilman's 'The Yellow Wall-paper'. I will be rehearsing a new historicist analysis of the story, in which the story is shown to participate in the discourse of madness.

There is a danger of leaping to judgements about the narrator of 'The Yellow Wall-paper'. At no point in the story is she described as mad, nor are the conditions of her illness, whatever it may be, fully apparent. It might be hysteria, or it might be simply boredom. What is presented in the story is the narrator's perception of her illness, and her physician husband's views and diagnoses: that she is suffering from 'temporary nervous depression – a slight hysterical tendency' (*YW* 3). The point of a new historicist or Foucauldian analysis will not be to speculate on the illness of Gilman's narrator, but to examine the discourse and social practices which come into play in relation to that illness. There are two questions which ought to be of particular significance in this analysis: firstly, how does the discourse of madness and illness function in the story? And secondly, how does the story participate in a 'general economy' of treating madness and illness? Gilman first published the story in 1892, partly as a repudiation of the attempts made by S. Weir Mitchell to cure Gilman's neurasthenia or hysteria by subjecting her to absolute rest, without any work or stimulation. Gilman proved his diagnosis wrong in curing herself by returning to writing and working, and in 'The Yellow Wall-paper' she represents this experience in the conflict between the anonymous narrator, who continues to write secretly while pretending to submit to rest treatment, and her physician husband, John, who insists on her receiving no guests, getting plenty of air and rest, and on giving up all physical or mental labour. There is, then, an interesting biographical context in which to place this story, and indeed we can see from this context that the story participates directly in the field of psychiatry in signalling resistance to, and disagreement with, a predominant method of treating hysterical illnesses in women. But a Foucauldian analysis will direct us away from biographical context to the function of the text independent of its author, to the text as a constitutive part of a discourse of madness.

How does the narrator's illness function in Gilman's story? What does her illness make possible within the story? It allows us to see, first of all, a conflict between the narrator and her husband, John. John becomes everything opposite to the narrator. Her interest in writing, her superstitions and suspicions, her desire for lively company and creative work, all seem to be directly at odds with his extreme pragmatism, his dismissal of superstition, his insistence on rationality and objectivity. She is intrigued by the 'queerness' of the colonial mansion in which they are staying, believing it be a haunted house, while he is a physician, and 'scoffs openly at any talk of things not to be felt and seen and put down in figures' (YW 3). The narrator even suggests that it is perhaps because John is a physician that she does 'not get well faster' (YW 3). This opposition, then, has much to do with her illness, how it is constituted and how it is treated. From the very beginning, the story is about a power struggle, about claims to authority. Both the narrator's husband and her brother are physicians 'of high standing' (YW 3), and both decide that 'there is really nothing the matter with one but temporary nervous depression' (YW 3). Although the narrator disagrees with their views, in the face of their professional judgement of her condition, she can only ask 'what is one to do?' She is without the authority to 'know' the nature or extent of her illness, since they are the physicians, and without that authority her disagreement is only a 'personal' opinion. The story is, then, a representation of the authority of physician over patient, and her narrative, although it constantly reminds us of her own doubts, suspicions and disagreements, confirms her identity as the patient, as the object of study.

Once this authority has been put in place it enables a system of control to come into practice. The illness of the patient is determined by the medical discourse to which the patient has become subject. The physician deems writing to have a bad effect on the narrator's health, and puts up so much opposition to her writing that she gets ill from 'having to be so sly about it, or else meet with heavy opposition' (YW 4). The physician warns that thinking about her condition will make her ill, and so she confesses that thinking about her condition 'always makes me feel bad' (*YW* 4). She describes herself as getting 'unreasonably angry' with John, and blames this on the 'nervous condition' from which she is suffering (*YW* 4). Here she has accepted her husband's and brother's judgement that it is nervous depression, and accepts what can only be their point of view, that she is 'unreasonable' in contrast to their reason. She accepts, therefore, the subject position which medical discourse determines for her, that of the unreasonable, abnormal, mad other who needs to be treated and corrected, who needs to be returned to a normality and state of reason which are, themselves, determined in medical discourse.

From this point on, she is subjected to the technologies of control which medical discourse mobilises at the site of treatment. The first of these technologies is confinement. The room in which John places his wife is, intentionally or unintentionally, part of an apparatus of confinement:

> It is a big, airy room, the whole floor nearly, with windows that look all ways, and air and sunshine galore. It was nursery first and then playroom and gymnasium, I should judge; for the windows are barred for little children, and there are rings and things in the wall. (*YW* 5)

The nursery, the playroom and the gymnasium are sites of discipline, of control, rooms in which observation and instruction take place, rooms in which, even when children or athletes are seemingly out of control, or most at play, are confined, contained. A discipline is maintained under the careful watch of the instructor, or the nanny. But the narrator's room, whatever its history, bears the hallmarks also of the asylum – the barred windows and the 'rings and things in the wall' (*YW* 5). The bed is bolted to the floor, and, when the narrator complains about the room to her husband, he offers her instead a whitewashed cellar. In confining the narrator, the physician can know and control her movements and her treatment. The room allows for ample air and light, and contains her movement and exercise to a minimum. It is, then, one of the methods or technologies by which the physician intends to treat her, and, more importantly, it marks her out as a patient, confined, subject to restraint, and observable.

As Foucault makes clear in *Madness and Civilization*, confinement was a method necessary to a discourse which conceived of madness as requiring the physical demarcation and means of controlling the excessive passion and force of madness. In the nineteenth century, confinement was supplemented, and in some ways replaced, with surveillance as a means of control. To treat the patient with confinement alone was to appear to the patient as a force, as a physical bar on freedom. But to treat the patient by observation, no force need be encountered whatsoever. The narrator in 'The Yellow Wall-paper' is subject to the surveillance of John, her husband, Jennie, his sister, and their housekeeper, and even when Jennie allows her out to walk, it is enjoyed as a lenient gesture within the regime of surveillance and control. Jennie knows where she is, and allows her to walk. That there is the need for permission confirms that the freedom is part of the system of treatment. The narrator knows too that Jennie is part of a regime of surveillance and knowledge-gathering: 'I heard him [John] ask Jennie a lot of professional questions about me. She had a very good report to give' (*YW* 16). Foucault argues that the control of the patient by surveillance works by confronting the patient not with force but with reason. He tells Tuke's story of a violent patient about to throw a stone who, when approached and commanded by the keeper, submitted to the keeper, dropping his weapon. Here the madman is made to regulate his own madness, discipline himself, recognise in the reason of the keeper the 'unreason' of his own behav-iour:

> The keeper intervenes, without weapons, without instruments of constraint, with observation and language only; he advances upon madness, deprived of all that could protect him or make him seem threatening, risking an immediate confrontation without recourse. In fact, though, it is not as a concrete person that he confronts madness, but as a reasonable being, invested by that very fact, and before any combat takes place, with the authority that is his for not being mad. Reason's victory over unreason was once assured only by material force, and in a sort of real combat. Now the combat was always decided beforehand, unreason's defeat inscribed in advance in the concrete situation where madman and man of reason meet. The absence of constraint in the nineteenth-century asylum is not unreason liberated, but madness long since mastered. (Foucault 1971, 251–2)

Admittedly, the patient in 'The Yellow Wall-paper' is hardly exposed to quite the same level of technologies of surveillance and control as are available in the mass asylum, or in the panopticon prison. But if not to the same scale, she is subject to the same processes of surveillance, leading to judgement, leading to control. Foucault explains that the treatment of madness is not so much the issue as the control or mastery of madness. In that familiar circularity of power, which new historicism never ceases to identify, and seems indeed to revere, this story confirms too that control of the patient is the condition which enables the patient to be observed, recorded, known, judged, and once again controlled.

But doesn't the narrator seem to resist, and even finally overcome, the control exercised over her? By freeing the woman behind bars from the wallpaper, by defying her husband, and by proclaiming at the end of the story 'I've got out at last ... you can't put me back' (*YW* 19), she seems to have gained her own freedom from control. But this is not the case, for her final act in the story is to creep around the floor on her hands and knees, adopting the features of a caged animal. John faints because he is confronted with the animality of madness, with the inhuman submission of the patient to madness. The narrator ends the story (and it is significantly, then, the end of her defiant writing) at a point at which she believes herself tied to the wall, she has locked the door, and refuses to go outside the room. She concludes by confining herself to her room, by submitting herself to madness. She has, therefore, internalised the judgements of a medical discourse which has cast her as the mad, the hysteric, the irrational. The wallpaper has functioned throughout the story as an image of herself as the medical discourse is constructing her. At first, she is to this discourse a bewildering pattern, seemingly without design, and then becomes a woman behind bars, a woman to be controlled, observed. The narrator performs this role of surveillance herself on the woman behind bars, until she has so internalised this image that she becomes the woman herself. The bars were only ever the means by which the woman was observed from outside and kept from escaping. That the narrator has removed these bars does not mean that she has found freedom, but, rather, she has, like Tuke's violent patient, submitted herself to the disciplinary practices of the asylum. All that she has succeeded in doing is confirming the association of defiance with madness. The more defiant she has become, the more attributes of madness she seems to verify.

The apparent madness, or hysteria, of the narrator is nothing, because it is not what is at stake. The issue which is really at stake in the story is the power relationship between medical discourse and the insane, between the physician and his patient. The story begins with a woman submitting herself to the treatment of her husband physician and ends with her consent to, and confirmation of her need of, treatment. The treatment does not work, her madness is not corrected or cured, and all that remains is the same power of the physician over the patient. In the conclusion to the story the narrator accepts for herself an identity which can do nothing but deliver her finally and decisively to the confines of madness, for in her fusion with the wallpaper image she becomes the epitome of reason's idea of madness:

> The act of the reasonable man who, rightly or wrongly, judges an image to be true or false, is beyond this image, transcends and measures it by what is not itself; the act of the madman never oversteps the image presented, but surrenders to its immediacy, and affirms it only insofar as it is enveloped by it. (Foucault 1971, 94)

The physician, the epitome of reason, observes the object of study from outside, is able to mark its contours and watch its behaviour, while all the time, like John in 'The Yellow Wall-paper', seeming to do nothing and to remain invisible. On the contrary, the madman is unable to occupy the outside, and can only be 'enveloped' by the image or object with which he is obsessed, as the narrator does with the woman in the wallpaper. In her inability at the end of the story to remain outside the wallpaper, outside the woman, she condemns herself to the exile of madness, and to the surveillance and judgement of doctors.

The function of madness in 'The Yellow Wall-paper' is, then, to make visible the process by which defiance becomes madness, and by which resistance is contained. It is not, as might be argued, and perhaps even the author intended, the function of madness in the story to expose the power relations at work in the relationship between physician and patient, but rather the story represents the authority of the physician and the effects of the patient's defiance in order to make visible to late nineteenth-century society the more frightening madness which awaits the narrator at the end of the story: the horror of a madness in which there is no outside, no objective view, no reason. What makes this depiction of madness even more effective is that it is written in the words of the madwoman, thereby giving insight into the subjective experience of a mind incapable of

perceiving herself 'rationally'. The physician's narration would have
been a comforting assurance that we could safely remain outside
madness, not comprehending its contents, its structures, the depths
to which it might take us. But the narrator is able to take us calmly to
the place where she is most vulnerable to the loss of self-control, and
the loss of reason. In this way, madness functions in Gilman's 'The
Yellow Wall-paper' to enable the story to police the boundaries
between reason and madness.

How, then, does the story participate in the general economy of
madness, and the power of medical discourse on madness? Before we
can answer this, we ought to recognise that there are two ways in
which Gilman's story has the potential to subvert the power of
medical discourse on madness. First, the story, as Dimock says, is
'told by a mad narrator and therefore one that foregrounds the question of interpretive authority' (Dimock 1991, 606). If the story is part of
the discourse on madness, and therefore fulfils the important function of policing the boundaries between madness and reason, why
does it depend on a narrator who is constituted by this discourse as
unreasonable, mad, unreliable? Second, as Dimock also points out,
the representative of professional medical discourse in the story is the
narrator's physician husband, John, who proves to be such a dreadful
reader of his wife's symptoms, and consistently perceives and diagnoses his wife's condition incorrectly, that he can hardly be taken for
an authority at all (608). We might construct from these two points an
interpretation of the story as the representation of a crisis in professional medical authority, a crisis in the system of representations of
madness and reason.[1]

Gilman's narrator offers us a model of defiance of authority.
The story itself is the product of the narrator's defiance of her
husband's ban on writing. She challenges her husband's judgements,
his professional authority, and seems to liberate herself at the end of
the story from his authority (even if this is by appearing even more
'mad' than before). If the narrator's husband, her brother and her
sister-in-law collude, and come to represent authority, then the
narrator's defiance constructs the idea of a free subjectivity, of an
individual who is able to resist authority, and even subvert it altogether by proving it wrong. And the possibility that authority has
failed here implies that an individual can be right, and can determine
and shape her own life and action outside authority. Such a reading

departs from the assumptions and tenets of new historicism, and indeed Foucault.

A new historicist or Foucauldian reading will confirm the pervasive and insidious presence of power, the ineluctability of authority, and the structural determination of the individual as an effect of discourse. The narrator in Gilman's story has already been determined as mad, has already been made an object of study in medical discourse, and so can not shape her own individual identity and practices. Her defiance of authority *seems* as if it is a product of her freedom, but that freedom itself is an illusion. She defies authority while submitting to it. She may write secretly, and articulate dissent from the opinions of her husband, but she remains an effect of the medical discourse on madness. She is the object of the physician's study, the patient of his treatment, and the madness which confirms his reason. If he thinks she is getting better when she is getting worse, diagnoses her incorrectly, and fails to recognise her symptoms, this just corroborates the fact that it is not the individual physician who determines the health or illness of a patient, but that health and illness are the products of a medical discourse. Whether she is healthy or ill, she is defined and determined by medical discourse, and in turn reinforces its claim to knowledge.

There is no escape from this ubiquitous and omnipotent (but also vague and groundless) power called medical discourse. Her defiance merely delivers her further into the system of madness. Gilman's story performs the function, then, of appropriating the potential subversion of a mad woman's narrative, and co-opting the narrative into a system of powerful representations of madness. As much as the story may be a resistance to, and disagreement with, current psychiatric practice, its engagement with psychiatry places it in the same discourse of mental illness. The story meets and validates psychiatry on its own grounds, disputing a technique of treatment while endorsing the objectification of the patient, the technologies of control which psychiatry mobilises, and the discourse on madness. Gilman's story is an effective instrument of power because it appears to be subverting or contesting power, while all the while it serves the needs and interests of power. The story conforms to the form of psychiatric practice as Foucault defines it:

> What we call psychiatric practice is a certain moral tactic contemporary with the end of the eighteenth century, preserved in the rites of

asylum life, and overlaid by the myths of positivism. (Foucault 1971, 276)

The story does nothing outside, or in resistance against, the structures of psychiatric practice. Even the narrator's defiance of the judgements of her physician husband endorse the technologies and means, even rituals, by which she is confined, observed and judged, and adopt the same positivist methods. She accepts from the beginning the moral system by which she is the madness which is treated by, and subjected to, his reason. Her narrative is written, indeed, not in the language of the mad, but in the language of reason. She maintains to the end the calm, objective, and rational style of narration, precisely to the point at which it is the language which dominates her, which makes the signs of her madness most visible. As Derrida writes, in a critique of Foucault's *Madness and Civilization*:

> The misfortune of the mad, the interminable misfortune of their silence, is that their best spokesmen are those that betray them best; which is to say that when one attempts to convey their silence *itself*, one has already passed over to the side of the enemy, the side of order, even if one fights against order from within it, putting its origin into question. There is no Trojan horse unconquerable by Reason (in general). (Derrida 1978, 36)

Derrida's point is part of a critique of Foucault's logic in writing a history of madness, in which his writing is always already the writing of reason. Foucault can only write about madness *rationally*, and so his history of madness is at the same time a history of reason. We can say the same of Gilman's story, that although it is written by a mad narrator she can do nothing other than to betray madness. As soon as she writes of madness, of herself as a patient, with a mental illness, as an object of medical study, she has written of madness in the language and under the terms of reason. The battle between reason and madness was won long ago, and so every representation of madness, every attempt even to figure madness as a defiance of reason, is written from the position of reason, in the language and structure which has resulted from reason's domination over madness. Madness is always already determined by reason, as the other of reason, as the other which makes reason possible, and so every representation of madness takes its place within this language and discourse of domination. Gilman's story is one such representation of madness, threatening the subversion of reason by representing madness as if from the perspective of madness, but in fact replicating the language and structure of reason's domination of madness.

Gilman's 'The Yellow Wall-paper' produces the liberal subject of Western rational discourse. The narrator produces herself in the act of writing, but it is in writing that she is both liberated and constrained. Writing enables her to peel away the layers between herself as author/subject and herself as mad woman/object, and so produces the paradox of a woman free to write, resist, disagree, free even to consider herself free at the very moment, and in the very conditions, in which she is most subject to constraint and control. She is liberated at the point at which she is incarcerated. She is mad when she approaches herself most rationally. In this nexus of liberalism and the carceral, reason and madness, Western society produces the liberal subject. Liberation is only guaranteed by the existence somewhere, in some form, of incarceration. Only by locking up the mad and the bad can the subject experience freedom, reason and morality. Only by being determined and conditioned by a range of discourses and ideologies can the subject really shape and fashion her individuality. Only by resisting power is the liberal subject delivered into the hands of power. For new historicists the signs of resistance, of freedom, of liberalism, are the signs and traces of power, authority and subjection.[2]

A reading of this story from the perspectives of cultural poetics would barely be distinguishable from the new historicist reading above, because, as I argued in the chapter on cultural poetics, the two theories are different only in name. If there is a difference it is, as Louis Montrose argues, that cultural poetics abandons the claim to be historicising literature and takes on more of the form of 'the synchronic text of a cultural system' (Montrose in Veeser 1989, 17). Cultural poetics tends to be more insistent on the idea that culture is a hermetic system of signs, complete in itself, and that any notion of reality or history was an effect of this sign system and entirely determined by representations. A cultural poetic analysis is unlikely to attempt an 'archaeology', or 'genealogy', of madness, because this implies the existence of a discourse continually changing and shifting through the past to reach its form in the present. It will be less interested, then, in the implications that Gilman's story would have for the construction of madness and reason for us in the present, as it is in the location of Gilman's story in the discourse on madness in late nineteenth-century USA, or Western society.

A cultural materialist reading would focus on how the text is the site of struggles which do not necessarily conclude with the co-option of the subversive within the dominant discourse or ideology. Cultural materialists are interested in two sites of struggle, the society (or moment in time) in which the text was first produced and first interacted with other texts and cultures, and the present function of the text in ideological struggle. In terms of the latter interest, it is mostly to 'canonical' texts and authors that cultural materialists will pay attention, simply because Shakespeare, Wordsworth or Tennyson are more likely to have a definite function in current ideological discourses (through the media, education, theatre, government, etc.) than more obscure authors. Gilman is unlikely to have a secure place in current ideological discourse, and so a cultural materialist reading would be more prone to analysing the potential for dissidence and struggle in the relationship between 'The Yellow Wall-paper' and the society in which it was first produced. This may simply take the form of cultural materialists giving more credence, and indeed more scope for success, to the dissident voices in the story. Where new historicism always sees subversion appropriated and contained by powerful discourses, cultural materialism often sees in the struggle between subversion and power a potential for disturbance of the operations of power, a potential for change. If new historicists believe that every culture or discourse finds the means of making safe the subversive voices which emerge from textual representations, cultural materialists work from the more positive belief that even where subversion is contained, traces of it remain which enable the dissident (i.e. cultural materialist) critic to raise the spectre of this subversion again, and thereby contest the location and interpretation of that text in current discourses.

The reading of Gilman's 'The Yellow Wall-paper' practised above applies the ideas and methods of Foucauldian analysis to a literary text, and imagines the place which Gilman's story might have occupied in the discourse on madness in late nineteenth-century USA. The uses of this kind of reading lie principally in seeing how the text functions within a discourse which is dispersed and deployed throughout a given culture or society, and how the text replicates the structures and technologies of producing the subject within a powerful nexus of discourses and ideologies. The primary aim of such analyses, then, is to make visible the ideological function of a literary text, how it is produced and shaped, and what, in turn, it produces and shapes. In the case of the reading above, we examined the function of madness in Gilman's story, and the function of the story in the discourse on madness. Such a reading problematises the disciplinary boundaries erected in modern academic practice, but as Foucault makes clear, discourses always transgress academic boundaries, and license inter-disciplinary exchanges:

> The linch-pin of *Madness and Civilization* was the appearance at the beginning of the nineteenth century of a psychiatric discipline ... this practice [the discursive practice of psychiatry] is not only manifested in a discipline possessing a scientific status and scientific preten-sions; it is also found in operation in legal texts, in literature, in philosophy, in political decisions, and in the statements made and the opinions expressed in daily life. The discursive formation whose existence was mapped by the psychiatric discipline was not co-exten-sive with it, far from it: it went well beyond the boundaries of psychia-try. (Foucault 1972, 179)

Notes

1. Dimock rehearses this kind of reading, and how it might be used in a new historicist analysis of the story. She then criticises new historicist readings from feminist perspectives on gender, rightly pointing out the failure of new historicism (replicated in this chapter) to treat gender as the site at which both difference and resistance might be mobilised, and may indeed fracture or disturb the Foucauldian grid of power, knowledge and subjectivity. See Wai-Chee Dimock, 'Feminism, New Historicism, and the Reader', *American Literature*, 63:4 (December 1991), 601–22.

2. For another version of the argument that Gilman's story produces the subject, see Walter Benn Michaels's *The Gold Standard and the Logic of Naturalism*, London and Los Angeles: University of California Press, 1987. In his introduction Michaels reads Gilman's 'The Yellow Wall-paper' as a story about the interconnection of the subject and the market-place, arguing that Gilman's narrator produces and consumes herself simultaneously in the act of writing, thereby conforming to a utopian ideal of the market.

8 Cultural Materialism and Reading Dissidence in(to) the Poetry of Alfred Tennyson

> It is the business of literary criticism to reveal the human histories of its subjects, a task which will – which must – include an acknowledgement of literary criticism's own historical limits.
>
> Jerome J. McGann, *The Beauty of Inflections*

This chapter is concerned not just with reading dissidence in Tennyson, as the title professes, or with cultural materialists reading dissidence in Tennyson, but more broadly with the status of the text in the process of reading, or what I will call, after Derrida, the process of 'translation'. The concern is therefore how a text is interpreted within a theoretical or critical framework such as cultural materialism. In particular I want to focus on the act of translation or communication between theory and text, and the responsiveness and resistance of each to this process. In this case it is the political readings of cultural materialism which feature in the communication with Tennyson's poetry, which in itself is an interesting juxtaposition of a critical theory engaged with reactionary discourses in contemporary politics and a writer held to be, in Joanna Richardson's terms, the 'pre-eminent Victorian' (Richardson 1962). Cultural materialism's interest in how writers from the past come to function within contemporary discourses as legitimating agents of the values and power strategies of the dominant culture finds an interesting and fit subject in Alfred Tennyson, whose writings become the ground of contest between the dominant culture and 'dissident critics'. The strategy which critics such as Alan Sinfield, Jonathan Dollimore and Catherine Belsey tend to adopt is one of revealing how certain texts can be seen to expose the operations and masking of power of the dominant culture, or conform to its values and structures. Thus, for cultural materialists, literary texts and writers either lend cultural authority to reactionary discourses or challenge such discourses. It is this aspect of the condition of politics in literature that I want to test out in the relationship between text and theory.

The first part of the chapter rehearses a cultural materialist reading of Alfred Tennyson's poetry, stressing the characteristics and conventions of such a reading. This rehearsal borrows heavily from the work of Alan Sinfield and will focus upon three of Tennyson's works, *In Memoriam, Idylls of the King* and 'Ulysses'.[1] Following this, the reading will be dissolved in a consideration of the communicative relationship between the theoretical and the textual, exposing the underlying assumptions of cultural materialist readings with regard to an examination of the textuality of Tennyson's poetry. Further to this the chapter develops some ideas on textuality, locating these ideas theoretically and teleologically. As a closing gesture, I wish to elaborate upon disputes foregrounded with cultural materialism and suggest some implications for textuality and theory from these disputes.

Keeper of the margins

In 1990, Carolyn Porter wrote, in an article subtitled 'After the New Historicism': 'To believe that literature might have social or political weight as a form of cultural agency entails also believing that such agency as it has is by definition already co-opted by "power". What is thus excluded is the possibility that literature might well – at least occasionally – occupy an oppositional cultural site at specific cultural moments' (Porter 1990, 262). This could be read as one of the defining differences between cultural materialism and new historicism, that the latter excludes the possibility of effective dissidence, whereas cultural materialism attempts to define how dissidence is articulated. Richard Wilson discerns the origin of cultural materialism as the belief that not only do representations shape history, as with new historicism, but that representations are also shaped by history; what he calls the 'historicity of representations' (Wilson and Dutton 1992, 1–18).[2] Two points then emerge as characteristics of cultural materialism as a way of reading. First, that literature at particular moments may offer a dissident perspective, and, second, that the potential for either dominance or dissidence in a text will be shaped by history and will change according to the historical context in which the text is read.

Alan Sinfield's book on Tennyson largely exemplifies these points in critical practice, and three main arguments about Tennyson's function within cultural politics emerge. First, Tennyson supposedly serves the needs of imperialist discourse when he incorporates remote and exotic places into the dominant vein of his poetry. Second, as Poet Laureate he plays the crucial domestic role of masking the operations of power in the Victorian state. And third, Tennyson's poetry occasionally threatens a dissident perspective but is eventually incorporated with the dominant order and is contained.

We can see the first of these in Tennyson's early concern with the remote in his prize-winning 'Timbuctoo', where he simultaneously evokes the beauty and the threat of the 'dusky band' of 'sturdy black-amoors'. He goes on to write 'the time is well-nigh come / When I must render up this glorious home / To keen *Discovery*'. The idea of moving out in lament from a home of glory to the margins is repeated in many of his later works, reconstructing the move of imperialism. This is, of course, the move of 'Ulysses'. Sinfield compares Tennyson's 'Ulysses' to the operation of imperialism as described by Edward Said in *Orientalism*: 'Tennyson's use of remote places was in the service of a wider project, calculated to help Europe handle its own ideological problems, and especially those associated with its domination of the rest of the world' (Sinfield 1986, 51–2).

> It little profits that an idle king,
> By this still hearth, among these barren crags,
> Match'd with an aged wife, I mete and dole
> Unequal laws unto a savage race,
> That hoard, and sleep, and feed, and know not me. ...
>
> I am a part of all that I have met;
> Yet all experience is an arch wherethro'
> Gleams that untravell'd world whose margin fades
> For ever and ever when I move.
> How dull it is to make a pause, to make an end,
> To rust unburnish'd, not to shine in use!
>
> Tennyson, 'Ulysses', ll. 1–5, 18–23

Ulysses is the coloniser, who requires more and more marginal spaces in order to define his own enterprise, and to redefine his sense of self. Imperialism cannot stand still, must not 'rust unburnish'd', but instead must move outwards to the remote and the marginal, constantly pushing the boundaries of empire further and further away. Standing still, the unequal laws and foreignness of the coloniser become apparent, but it is the constant project of imperialism to move on and outward, the continued globalisation of the British empire which keeps these unequal laws and savage races in the imperialist perspective. Tennyson, in the cultural materialist discourse, is in the textual vanguard of the historical movement of imperialism. With these projected metaphors of discovery and advance, Tennyson's poetry primes the idea of the remote and the marginal for the imperial project. His poetry prepares the Victorian consciousness, if such a phenomenon can be said to exist, for the first landings on the beach of the marginal space, preceding the fleets, armies and laws of imperial Britain.

In terms of 'domestic' politics too, Tennyson's poetry serves to reinforce the operation of 'power'. Sinfield says of *Idylls of the King*:

> Tennyson's personal involvement in the patterns of deference which sustained a social hierarchy and, to a degree, masked the realities of power, only marks him as a man of his time – along with many others of note. But it may also lead us to expect a certain asymmetry in the relation between his writing and the hegemonic class. At the risk of being simplistic, I would derive part of the appeal of *Idylls of the King* in Victorian culture from its compatibility with the aristocratic display which was admired in that culture. (Sinfield 1986, 163–4)

The *Idylls* follow the legends of King Arthur and the Round Table, bringing to public consciousness a tale of ancient English royalty (and also, of course, feudal behaviour), and when fully collected as a complete edition in 1874 came with an opening dedication to Prince Albert, who died in 1861, and a concluding offering 'To the Queen', which entreated Victoria not to let the Empire slip. Placing the tales of romance, legend and greatness within the framework of Victorian royalty, of course, immediately romanticised and idealised the power of Victoria. As Elaine Jordan says of the *Idylls*: 'The recovery of legend, romance and early texts had always been political, concerned to produce a sense of nationhood' (Jordan 1988, 179). As such, then, the *Idylls of the King* serve to forge through legend a mythical unity and to play out a scene of greatness and power designed to link attractive Arthurian legend to the realities of power in Victorian Britain. Tennyson renders culture to tell a tale of a progressive, legitimate, unbroken link between Arthur and Victoria, masking the realities of disruption, discontinuity and contest. Simultaneously, of course, Tennyson is exporting these images to the remote frontiers of the British Empire, providing, as Sinfield says, a feeling of proximity between the margins and the authority of the centre (Sinfield 1986, 164). As Poet Laureate, then, Tennyson serves the crucial function of national poet with remarkable efficiency, helping to forge national unity with his poetry.

Yet the very poem which brings him to the role of Poet Laureate is the poem to which many, including Sinfield, attribute a dissident perspective, or at least the potential for dissidence. *In Memoriam* was published in 1850, written in fragments as a series of memories, laments and emotional investigations of the loss in 1833 of his friend Arthur Hallam. In relation to its contexts, the poem is uneasy and can be read as affording certain dissident perspectives. 'The developing bourgeois hegemony was aggressive', Sinfield writes, 'but it was also anxious and insecure' (Sinfield 1986, 132). The result of this anxiety and insecurity was an '[i]nsistence on a rigid ideology of male and female characteristics and behaviour' (132). Hegemonies as such are never totalised and complete but always in an historical state of flux and change. It is this movement which results in excesses and 'fault-lines', cracks in the dominant ideology through which dissident perspectives can be formulated and represented. In the case of *In Memoriam*, Tennyson is able to articulate dissident perspectives on gender roles. The idea of a male femininity that the intimate confessions of the poet opens up troubles the gender divisions aspired to in the Victorian dominant order. In particular the intimacy of Tennyson and Arthur Hallam introduces 'threatening' hints of homosexual love, and as Sinfield says, threatens to reverse the move from homosexual to heterosexual love in Western culture (Sinfield 1986, 127). In the context of this specific position in Victorian culture a dissident perspective is articulated, but the dominant order then reasserts itself, transforming itself to maintain its authority and subsume the dissident voice of Tennyson's poetry. *In Memoriam* concludes with the homely image of a wedding celebration, masking the dissidence which has preceded it. To return to Sinfield's view, 'The domestic image domesticates, the ground of disturbance becomes the ground of incorporation. To use my earlier terms, the marginal emotional disturbance is re-assimilated to the ideology of the centre' (Sinfield 1986, 151). Of course, other perspectives in the poem have already reinforced dominant constructions. In particular the poem reinforces national oppositions and identities:

> cix
> A love of freedom rarely felt,
> Of freedom in her regal seat
> Of England; not the schoolboy heat,
> The blind hysterics of the Celt;

> cxxvii
> Proclaiming social truth shall spread,
> And justice, even tho' thrice again
> The red fool-fury of the Seine
> Should pile her barricades with dead.

> Tennyson, *In Memoriam*

Referring back to the Romantic period, and the constructions of oppositional identities resulting from the turbulent social events in France and Ireland during that period, Tennyson brings to consciousness the otherness and primitive passion of the French and Irish which reinforce the centrality and superiority of English culture. In terms of national identity, Tennyson reinforces once more the boundaries and stereotypes which perpetuate the sustaining myths of the dominant order in Victorian Britain, and sustain the whole Darwinian discourse of evolution, with Britain naturally at the top of the scale. From certain angles a dissident perspective can be articulated, but literature moves within the confines of the social structure always towards incorporation and assimilation. The margins are kept at bay, and for this reason Alan Sinfield writes: 'The laureate is official keeper of the margins' (Sinfield 1986, 155).

'Crossing the Bar'

The reading that I have rehearsed does to a certain extent misrepresent the complexity of the cultural materialist arguments, but the important characteristics of cultural materialist readings are here. Dominance and dissidence are opposed positions in a relationship that is obviously unequal and heavily weighted towards sustaining the dominant order. But dissidence is threatening, and occasionally its strategies and messages must be accommodated. The dominant order occasionally must compromise. As a less gloomy version of new historicism, as it is sometimes reported to be,[3] cultural materialism serves well as a discourse which recognises the possibility, even if limited, of effective dissidence. This dissidence is mostly read as part of a counter-strategy against the canonisation, or canonical reading, of the literary text. As a counter-strategy then, cultural materialists claim to present oppositional readings and to consciously render texts to tell dissident and oppositional stories, and there is within this practice, of course, the admission that dissidence and dominance exist alongside each other in one text.

The practice of interpreting a text then becomes, in Sinfield's own words, 'a theatre of war' (Sinfield 1992),[4] where strategies and counter-strategies are played out, with the text acting as some kind of bargaining chip or pawn. It is to the status of the text that I think we should pay attention, for within this theatre of war the text appears only as object, and the practice of interpretation is a practice of subsuming the text into one's interpretative context or strategy. The strategy or counter-strategy of reading determines the interpretation of the text, so that a dominant or canonical reading of Tennyson constructs the interpretation of his poetry in a manner that will suit the dominant discourse, such as Tennyson as national or public poet, voicing the universal and moral conditions of humankind, whereas a dissident or cultural materialist reading constructs the interpretation of his poetry in a manner which exposes its relationship to the dominant culture, be that a conformist or a critical relationship. But this is where I want to raise a problem for cultural materialist reading, in that its underlying assumption is that the readings around the text are allowed to be formed without the textuality of the text coming into play. The process of interaction with the text is assumed to be passive and silent on matters which the strategy of reading constructs. For cultural materialism, reading takes place as the ongoing contest between opposed meanings, but what it ignores, as I hope to demonstrate now, is the ongoing interpretability of the text:

Crossing the Bar

Sunset and evening star,
And one clear call for me!
And may there be no moaning of the bar,
When I put out to sea,

But such a tide as moving seems asleep,
Too full for sound and foam,
When that which drew from out the boundless deep
Turns again home.

Twilight and evening bell,
And after that the dark!
And may there be no sadness of farewell,
When I embark;

For tho' from out our bourne of Time and Place
The flood may bear me far,
I hope to see my Pilot face to face
When I have crost the bar.

In the first two lines the sun going down darkens the sky to the degree
that we can see the Evening Star, Venus, and so the poem opens with
the marking of the passage of day to night. The third line introduces
ambivalence into the interpretation of the poem in the choice of the
word 'bar'. The 'bar' could refer to any number of possibilities: it could
be the sand bar, marking the passage from shore to sea, the bar as
barrier between life and death, it could be bar as the strip of twilight
which divides night from day. Moreover, the phrase 'may there be no
moaning of the bar' introduces ambiguity itself. Is it the bar itself that
should not moan or present difficulty for those passing through it? Is
it that the unspecified addressee of the poem should not moan about
the bar, or about the person passing through the bar? The 'clear call'
that the poet receives is followed by a lack of clarity about the experience which we are being drawn towards. The first line of the second
stanza, 'such a tide as moving seems asleep', conjures up two possibilities at least, of the sea before the poet appearing calm, and also of
the poem itself seeming to be asleep. The poem appears to be a
passive lament, or contemplation of leaving or death, but the movements of the poem are quite dramatic – 'sound and foam', 'boundless
deep', 'the flood', 'the dark'. The text is constructing not only varying
and deceptive degrees of movement, but also is constructing move-

ment through three related metaphors – the maritime metaphors of a voyage on the sea, which is both the metaphor of British imperial strength, and 'otherness' to the land, the temporal metaphors of passing from day to night, from light to darkness, and the existential metaphors of passing from life to death, and these states in themselves are metaphorical. There is also, of course, the more scandalous 'mis'-reading of the 'bar' as a public-house bar. Tennyson the drunken sailor stands in the 'sound and foam' of the bar, hearing the 'clear call' of the 'evening bell'. The calling of time in the public bar resonates delightfully with the 'HURRY UP PLEASE IT'S TIME / Goonight Bill. Goonight Lou' of Eliot's *The Waste Land*, and drawing the last from 'the boundless deep' quenches the thirst of the dry tongues of the damned sailors in Coleridge's *The Rime of the Ancient Mariner*. The last drink-up before setting sail makes a mock epic of the pub as the threshold, of mortality, of social discourse, even of imperialism. The imperial enterprise takes on not the epic proportions of the civilising mission or the humane conquest, but rather of a drunken brawl across the globe. Ulysses leaves the shore with a hangover, and Tennyson laughs at his Lordship. The carnival that is taking place around the 'bar' in this reading has a serious point. Moving from the sublime to the ridiculous shows up one of the shortfalls of cultural materialist readings, in that such readings rely upon similar criterion of plausibility and sensibility as the readings which they are contesting. The textuality and multiplicity of the text produce more than plausibility, more than a logic of dissidence or dominance. Constraint is not in its vocabulary.

The text, to put it briefly, produces the appearance of being passive, facilitating its use as a pawn in strategies of reading, but while allowing itself to be the mediator of contesting strategies, 'Crossing the Bar' actively produces a multiplicity of readings which seduce the reader into distraction. The seduction lies in the relation of all the metaphors, for each of the readings or 'translations' of this poem relies for its effect upon the relationship with other readings. The readings, therefore, are inseparable, and this poem is not about death, a voyage, or about the raucous calling of 'time, please', unless it is about all three, and more.

'Crossing the Bar' promotes itself as the mediation between the dominant and the dissident, as the pawn between the contesting opposites, but in the process has effectively added the noise of its own activity as a text to their readings, disrupting their readings just as it facilitates them.

'A red fire woke in the heart of the town'[5]

The literary text is, then, some kind of incessant babbler, always saying more than it should, and always exposing more than any one reading seeks to expose. The reason for this, I think, is that readings are inseparable, in that they feed off the same text. Readings are the parasites of other readings, existing within and feeding off the host body of the text, which in itself is not a corpse but rather a parasite of culture, constituted by and constituting the endless heterogeneity and parasitism of culture. Any attempts to incorporate or appropriate a text are premised on the idea of a passive, inanimate text, but the problem for these attempts is that the text carries within its body all of its parasitic readings. As the interpreter or critic attempts to communicate her/his own reading to a reader, the readings and cultures parasiting/para-citing the text continue to speak in their many tongues. We might call this ambiguity of meaning, or perhaps the equivocation of the text, and if we return to the texts discussed earlier I want to show how we might listen to the other voices of the text.

The reading produced earlier was one of the language and movement of imperialism being served in Tennyson's 'Ulysses'. The necessity of the imperial culture to push the margins further and further back, and to homogenise its culture, is served by the unstoppable advance of the metaphors 'To strive, to seek, to find and not to yield'. Yet within the body of this empire-building reading is the parasite reading of the exposure of imperial motivations:

> Little remains ...
> ... this grey spirit yearning in desire ...
> When I am gone. ...
> Death closes all ...
> ... my purpose holds
> To sail beyond the sunset ... until I die.
> We are not now that strength which in old days
> Moved earth and heaven, that which we are, we are;
> One equal temper of heroic hearts,
> Made weak by time and fate, but strong in will
> To strive, to seek, to find, and not to yield.

The traditional explanation of the movement and actions of colonisation were grounded in ideas of superiority and paternal nurturing -

the burden of the white man to bring culture, industry and education to the savage. This superiority is supported by the lone voice of Ulysses the coloniser in this poem – the coloniser is still the one who can push back the margins, yet the language also reveals partially obscured motivations within this reading. The poem exposes the feeling of loss and fear in the coloniser and the consequent desire to conquer for the sake of relieving this sense of loss (or even drinking to relieve this sense of loss – the last few heroic lines of 'Ulysses' being the exuberant proclamations of the drunken coloniser). Neither is the language reflective of the effortless superiority supposed to characterise imperialism. In the heart of the poem there are two simultaneous beats then – one of the movement of imperialism, the other of its psychological motivations of loss and desire. This is not a case of reading and alternative reading, as in cultural materialism, but instead an oscillation of meanings, an ambiguity which is not passively dual, but active and equivocal in its coexistence.

So too, in *Idylls of the King* we have the previous reading of the legitimation of royalty and the masking of state power. But throughout the *Idylls* there are interrelated voices calling into question the legitimacy of the King. In the opening 'Coming of Arthur', the lords and barons of the kingdom cry out 'Who is he that should rule us? who hath proven him King Uther's son? for lo! we look at him and find nor face nor bearing, limbs nor voice, are like those of Uther whom we knew. This is the son of Gorloïs, not the King; This is the son of Anton, not the King.' Until in the concluding Idyll 'The Passing of Arthur', it is Arthur himself who says 'on my heart hath fallen confusion, till I know not what I am, Nor whence I am, nor whether I be King; Behold, I seem but King among the dead'. Doubt is an important element of the *Idylls*, and of Tennyson's poetry. T. S. Eliot, of course, expressed his preference for the doubts of Tennyson as against his faiths. But it is not as simply dichotomous as this, for the mists and screens which pervade the poem's images of Arthur feed off the idea of royalty itself. They eat into this, dependent upon legitimacy yet crucially weakening legitimation.

It is important to distinguish between the idea here of the oscillation and coexistence of meanings as they are constructed around a text, and the cultural materialist idea of dominance and dissidence appearing in the same text. The earlier reading of *In Memoriam* was intended to prepare for this very distinction, for the dissidence of hybridised gender identities was read as being in conflict with, and contradiction to, the final dominant wedding images and the reinforcing of national stereotypes. It is this idea of conflict and contradiction in cultural materialist readings that prepares the ground for incorporation of the dissident within the body of the dominant. The power of the dominant culture can only be seen in its containment of the threat of dissidence. In cultural materialism dissidence is a phenomenon occurring at specific junctures of the history of a text, which is then subsumed, hence the necessity of cultural materialist revitalisations of the dissident perspective. One reading comes into prominence or comes into conflict with others at any given time. Cultural materialism is concerned to relate texts 'to the conditions in which they were and may be read' (Dollimore and Sinfield 1990, 99), but what is apparently neglected is the condition of the text itself. A reading of *In Memoriam* as a poem which expresses dissident doubts in order to reinforce faith in the social order may be ignoring the condition of the text:

> At length my trance
> Was cancell'd, stricken thro' with doubt.
>
> Vague words! but ah, how hard to frame
> In matter moulded forms of speech,
> Or even for intellect to reach
> Thro' memory that which I became ...
>
> 'The dawn, the dawn', and died away;
> And East and West without a breath,
> Mixt their dim lights, like life and death,
> To broaden into boundless day.
>
> *In Memoriam*, xcv, ll. 43–8, 61–4

Doubt is not just a reinforcement of faith, as Tennyson says it is in reference to Arthur Hallam later in the poem, but doubt also blurs boundaries and clouds faith. Doubt, expressed almost as a second voice in the poem, serves to question the body of faith from within the body of faith, not as contest or contradiction but as parasite of faith. Doubt feeds off faith, accepting the existence of faith but also weakening the boundaries of thought. The condition of the text is affecting the reading, clouding the essence of a reading with doubts and the blurring of boundaries.

What is in dispute here is the very idea of how the 'condition' of a text affects its reading. My argument is that cultural materialism constructs an alternative 'knowledge' of the text which is potentially as reductive as the reading which it is contesting. True, cultural materialists commendably attempt to understand the text not in its form as fetishised commodity, but as its materiality in the process of production and reception. The text for Sinfield is incorporated in the power structures through which it comes to materiality and to consciousness, or alternatively it is marginalised outside the social structure. Tennyson is then one writer who polices the boundaries of 'normality' and social acceptability. The problem with this becomes apparent in my attempt above to reread Tennyson on the basis of a revised conception of the condition of the text, that the text continues to read beyond the critical construction of a voice for the text. Even a wayward Tennyson emerges. In cultural materialism the text is monumentalised as the tablets of stone that are owned and read by either the dominant culture or the dissident critic. The 'allegiance' of the text is determined by the critic conducting the reading. 'Allegiance' is perhaps one of the most crucial terms in understanding the debates around contemporary theoretical readings of 'the text', especially around ideas of translation and interpretation. Cultural materialism relies upon the idea of transforming the allegiance of a text from dominant to dissident by bringing that text to consciousness within dissident critical conditions, but the text speaks both the language of seduction and of betrayal, betraying not just 'its readers' (as if they were any kind of community), but also betrays itself. *In Memoriam* constructs its own boundaries only in order to blur them, confuses identities only in order to distinguish them, so that textuality precisely involves an eternal babble of both the perpetuation and the extinction of 'meaning'.

Where this chapter attempts to intervene in contemporary theoretical constructions of allegiance is not to herald the text back to its true home of meaning, but instead to add to the 'critical knowledge', in Lyotard's terms,[6] of textuality, of society. Since Leavis, particularly, criticism has been engaged in promoting and contesting canons and canonicity, both in status and interpretation, and thus engaged too in referring to the text as object, as pawn within strategic moves, critical gaming. Thomas Docherty calls upon readers to 'betray the text', which 'proposes a mode of criticism which explicitly demands a revision of the prevalent understanding of literary history' (Docherty 1987, 264). This is in a sense the dissident reading of cultural materialism, the rewriting of canonical lists on the basis of alternative (both alternatively plausible and plausibly alternative) interpretations. Extending this, however, beyond a simple betrayal of the meaning or function of a text within prevalent discourses, to a betrayal of modes of textual understanding might produce more radical results, perhaps even the deconstruction of the function of critical apparatus in their appropriation of the text as object. We might speak anachronistically of the textuality of the Tennysonian text functioning as a telephonic cable facilitating the transmittance of the 'text' to the contemporary 'context'. This is not to speak of communication between past and present, or author to reader, but, as in cultural materialism, of text to text. We are on the same lines, but as Derrida reminds us, 'we must pause to consider translation' (Derrida 1991, 267), by which I mean that the act of translation that we necessarily perform as readers/authors/texts is a space through which information passes, and that this space is capable of adding noise to the textuality of the text. Reading/translating never exists in conditions that exclude this space, and therefore it is crucial to recognise what 'betrayal' of the text may be going on here. It seems that this space is the space of proliferation, as well as of perforation, of the text, and that each reading is an event of transgressing the unknowability of text (because of the inexhaustibility and extinction of meaning), and because of this transgression, a pretence at knowledge, at communication. The telephone conceals the existence of distance, and of the electronic disturbance, and since textuality functions on a much more complex and chaotic level than telephonic exchange ('the tongue no longer occupies one place', Critical Art Ensemble 1994, 64), the possibility of 'noise', 'interference', increases beyond containment. Within the host cable of literature we have the furious oscillation of meanings and forms, the incessant babble of voices, the parasitic noise of the endless configurations and interrelated possibilities. The space of translation, the communication carrier, is itself communicative.

The basis of my dispute with cultural materialism is the belief that the relationship between text and context is not a simple condition of different, contesting meanings negotiated through different periods or moments of history, but instead the relationship is a complex condition of shifting meaning, never isolatable as singular readings, but always in relation to other meanings. This multiplicity and relational concept of meaning is what I would propose as the site of the equivocation of dissidence. The contention in cultural materialism that dissidence can be unproblematically incorporated, that 'marginal disturbances can be re-assimilated into the ideology of the centre' (Sinfield 1986, 151), is flawed in that its underlying assumption is that dissident writing or dissident textual effects are passive and inanimate. Far from this, dissidence feeds endlessly from the body of the dominant, fully implicated simultaneously in its perpetuation as well as transformation and disruption of the dominant, fully interactive with and inseparable from the dominant. In this sense it is possible to read dissidence entwined around every form of dominance, hence inclining always towards the failure of the centre to communicate unproblematically with its margins. Literature promotes itself as the mediation between the dominant and the dissident, seducing readers to its apparent passivity, but in the process adds the noise of its own oscillating meanings to their readings, disrupting their readings just as it hosts them. The equivocation of the dissident, and the ambivalent nature of text and meaning, actively prevent the desired homogeneity of which incorporation and assimilation are supposedly the instruments. If the text is the site of the oscillation and equivocation of meaning, then it is possible that 'literature', in the words of Ross Chambers, 'is available as the piggyback for the silenced' (Chambers 1991, 4). Tennyson, possibly despite himself, enables a constant challenging of the attempted imposition of readings on the text, a constant questioning of appropriations of his poetry.

Notes

1. All references to and quotations from Tennyson's poetry are taken from the Norton Critical Edition, *Tennyson's Poetry*, selected and edited by Robert W. Hill Jnr, New York: Norton, 1971, with the exception of references to 'Timbuctoo', which are taken from Alfred Lord Tennyson, *Selected Poems*, London: Penguin, 1991, 1–8.
2. For one of the most lucid theorisations of the 'historicity of representations', see Thomas Docherty's *After Theory*, London: Routledge, 1990, 97–119.
3. Wilson and Dutton, for example, describe cultural materialism as 'the mainly British wing of New Historicism' (228). Prefacing Wilson's essay, they write: 'If New Historicism followed Foucault in seeing power as monolithic, Cultural Materialism responded that the dominant do not control the whole of culture' (145).

4. See Chapter 1 of Sinfield's *Faultlines: Cultural Materialism and the Politics of Dissident Reading*, Oxford: Oxford University Press, 1992.

5. Tennyson, 'Song – The Promise of May'.

6. See Lyotard's *The Postmodern Condition: A Report on Knowledge*, trans. G. Bennington and B. Massumi, Manchester: Manchester University Press, 1984, 12–14. Lyotard argues that two interrelated kinds of knowledge exist, that of functional knowledge and that of critical knowledge. All too often, I think, literary criticism has been complicit in considering literature a functional form of knowledge, and this I think is further exemplified in cultural materialist writings. My question is, really, is a text not more of a form of critical knowledge?

9 'I Write It Out in a Verse': Power, History and Colonialism in W. B. Yeats's 'Easter 1916'

> Like all the poets of decolonization Yeats struggles to announce the contours of an 'imagined' or ideal community, crystallized not only by its sense of itself but also of its enemy.
>
> Edward Said, 'Yeats and Decolonization'

Neither new historicism nor cultural materialism have yet dealt with decolonisation from the perspective of the colonised. The problem for both critical practices is that decolonisation presents an epistemological dilemma, insofar as it usually entails a successful process of resistance to power. It may ultimately succeed only in replicating structures of power after independence, but initially decolonisation is a process of activating and articulating dissent and subversion. Edward Said sees Yeats as a poet involved in this process of bringing about the downfall of imperial domination in Ireland, and Said implies that poetry can have a crucial role in the business of politics. Yeats is not alone in delineating the 'contours of an "imagined" or ideal community' (Said 1990, 86). His poetry is in circulation with other cultural representations, political documents and speeches, or social and political acts. Said's view of Yeats is just one example of a number of interpretations which have brought a historical perspective to the study of Yeats's poetry, and in this chapter I will demonstrate how we might read Yeats's poetry from the vantage-point of a form of historical reading which does not replicate the faults of new historicist and cultural materialist practices.

The problem for both new historicism and cultural materialism when dealing with the question of resistance, particularly successful resistance, is that within the historicist schema of power there are only two categories in which resistance can be conceptualised: resistance which is an illusory effect of power, which closely mirrors the operations of power; and resistance which is effective outside a specific epistemé and cultural system, which is therefore not represented within it. What is not possible, therefore, within the historicist schema is a concept of resistance as a form of potential within discourse for altering and renegotiating power relations. In Greenblatt's *Marvelous Possessions*, for example, he argues that European colonists were able to gain control over the peoples of the 'New World' within the European system of representation:

> The marvelous is a central feature then in the whole complex system of representation, verbal and visual, philosophical and aesthetic, intellectual and emotional, through which people in the late Middle Ages and the Renaissance apprehended, and thence possessed or discarded, the unfamiliar, the alien, the terrible, the desirable, and the hateful. (Greenblatt 1991, 22)

But Greenblatt, or any other historicist critic, never allows for the possibility that 'the other' also enters this complex system of representation and is able, not by individual effort or will, to manipulate and negotiate a position within that system which is yet pliable and offers the potential for change. It is this possibility which I want to demonstrate in this chapter, taking Yeats's poetry as one form of representation in which both power and its radical others are at work. I wish to demonstrate also that the limits which I am suggesting exist in historicist theories and practices should allow us to see some ways in which to avoid the pitfalls of a too rigid approach to the relationships between literature, history and politics. New historicism and cultural materialism are primarily responsible for some of the most significant and praiseworthy changes in the practice of literary studies – the turn to history and politics, the move away from the reductive use of historical detail as background information in literary analyses, to the more fruitful approach of placing literary texts in circulation with texts of all kinds, and the use of contemporary interdisciplinary sources to reconstruct the cultural and social discourses in which literary texts participate – but they also consist of theoretical and practical blind spots, and rigid conceptions of power, history, textuality and culture.

The best historical criticism is sensitive to historical difference, and

to the many relationships which a literary text may have with an
historical event or trend. These relationships between literature and
history are made even more problematic in the case of Yeats's poetry
which tends to respond to historical events in a very personal
manner. In the poems in which Yeats represents the impact of the
Easter Rising of 1916 even the rebels are remembered for their
personal significance to Yeats. The second stanza of 'Easter 1916'
illustrates this well:

> That woman's days were spent
> In ignorant good-will,
> Her nights in argument
> Until her voice grew shrill.
> What voice more sweet than hers
> When, young and beautiful,
> She rode to harriers?
> This man had kept a school
> And rode our wingèd horse;
> This other his helper and friend
> Was coming into his force;
> He might have won fame in the end,
> So sensitive his nature seemed,
> So daring and sweet his thought.
> This other man I had dreamed
> A drunken, vainglorious lout.
> He had done most bitter wrong
> To some who are near my heart,
> Yet I number him in the song;
> He, too, has resigned his part
> In the casual comedy;
> He too, has been changed in his turn,
> Transformed utterly;
> A terrible beauty is born.

Yeats does not mention any names in this stanza, and yet he has
referred to Constance Markievicz, Padraig Pearse, Thomas
MacDonagh, John MacBride and, of course, Maud Gonne. With the
exception of Gonne, all of those represented took part in the fighting
against the British Army in the centre of Dublin on Easter week of
1916, and for their part Pearse, MacDonagh and MacBride were
executed, while Markievicz was imprisoned. Yeats's poem advertises

its interest in the significance of the event, and its refrain of 'A terrible beauty is born' suggests the political and historical power of this event, but for all that the rebels are represented not for their actions, speeches or achievements, but for circumstances which brought them to the personal attention of Yeats. Markievicz is remembered for her shrill voice and her hunting, Pearse remembered for his school, MacDonagh for his nature and thought, MacBride for hurting Maud Gonne: none are remembered for their part in leading, forming or participating in the historical event supposedly being foregrounded.

The move which Yeats makes in his poetry, as Denis Donoghue has argued, is one in which 'the rhetoric of his poems ... draws experience to a distinctly personal centre and takes possession of it there' (Donoghue 1986, 65). The problem with a poem by Yeats for a new historicist analysis is that the poem must be read at a biographical as well as historical or political level. The poem cannot be divorced from the personal meanings which Yeats invested in it without making many of the references in the poem unclear. If one of the major assumptions behind new historicist work is that powerful discourses both make and manipulate the individual in society, Yeats seems to defy this assumption in the way in which he masters history and politics, and indeed promotes the idea that he has been a cause of some of the historical trends and events around him. For new historicism and cultural materialism, and indeed for Marxism and structuralism, the idea that the individual is the maker of his own destiny, and, further, the maker of history, is a fabulation of bourgeois ideology. For each of these theoretical schools the actions, beliefs and language of an individual are determined by a wide range of social, economic, historical and cultural factors. It is very difficult, however, to treat Yeats's works as if they have been determined and shaped solely by forces outside the poet.

Yeats rarely missed an opportunity to publicise his own writings and person as an influence on great historical and political events and trends. This is usually suggested in the form of a question. When in his *Autobiographies* he recounts the details of a riot which took place in Dublin, he writes: 'I count the links in the chain of responsibility, run them across my fingers, and wonder if any link there is from my workshop' (Yeats 1955, 368). So, too, in the late poem 'The Man and the Echo', he wonders of his play *The Countess Cathleen*: 'Did that play of mine send out / Certain men the English shot?' (Yeats 1989, 469). Yeats's suggestions of his own importance have gathered momentum into a critical commonplace, in which he is seen as the indispensable creator of the Irish literary, cultural, and, perhaps, ultimately, political revival. Declan Kiberd has noted that 'Oliver St. John Gogarty, one of the first senators of an independent Ireland, could stand and suggest, in full seriousness, that without the poetry of W. B. Yeats, he and his colleagues would not be representatives of an independent state' (Kiberd in Foster 1992, 230–1). And this view, that Yeats, with a handful of other poets, playwrights and intellectuals, created the cultural and political base of a decolonised state, has found its way into most accounts of the Irish revival period. Even Adrian Frazier's new historicist book on Yeats's plays accepts the view that the Irish revival is 'an instance of a literary movement leading to a social and industrial movement for self-reliance' (Frazier 1990, 51). In one sense this confirms the new historicist practice of treating literary texts as inseparable from texts of other kinds. But Frazier also argues that it is one individual who is exercising control of the literary text and its effects:

> For a work to make an impression, the impresario has to create the ways in which the work is perceived, not simply the work itself, which may well remain invisible until one is taught how to see it. Indeed, the very materials of the work – the words of the language – always already belong to a polity of discourse about many topics that seem external to the work, and using those words, the writer is performing an act of power over others, defining how they are seen, and how they see themselves, just as in receiving those words from others, the writer is an effect of the way others have constituted a world and him out of words. From the first word that is written, then, the author enters upon a long conversation that continues until the last word is said, a conversation that is continuous with other acts of language and acts of power in the society. The immense volume, scope, and ambition of Yeats's activities in every aspect of this polity of discourse is one main reason his plays and poems have such great meaning for us. (Frazier 1990, 22–3)

From a range of discourses and materials, Yeats fashions a powerful legend of culture as the engine of historical change. Frazier locates Yeats as the source of power, as the master of discourse, as well as the medium through which language and power pass. Frazier pushes the new historicist conception of power towards the Bakhtinian idea of dialogism, whereby literature is not just the passive vehicle of power relations but takes an active part in conversing with and converting those power relations. By doing so, Frazier avoids the tendency of new historicist criticism to see power as the determining, totalising formula behind every facet and nuance of culture and history.

A reading of Yeats's poetry which aims to adopt a historical approach must first avoid this new historicist tendency to inflate the capacity of power to determine cultural meaning. A literary text is not a passive vehicle of ideological meaning. It generates and multiplies meaning, and therefore must be accounted for as an active participant in the process of fashioning and interpreting society, culture and history. Again, Yeats's 1916 poems are good examples of poems which participate in making sense or meaning from social and historical events. The fourth stanza of 'Easter 1916' asks a series of questions about the meaning of the Easter Rising and the execution of the rebels which followed it:

> Too long a sacrifice
> Can make a stone of the heart.
> O when may it suffice?
> That is Heaven's part, our part
> To murmur name upon name,
> As a mother names her child
> When sleep at last has come
> On limbs that had run wild.
> What is it but nightfall?
> No, no, not night but death;
> Was it needless death after all?
> For England may keep faith
> For all that is done and said.
> We know their dream; enough
> To know they dreamed and are dead;
> And what if excess of love
> Bewildered them till they died?
> I write it out in a verse –
> MacDonagh and MacBride
> And Connolly and Pearse
> Now and in time to be,
> Wherever green is worn,
> Are changed, changed utterly:
> A terrible beauty is born.

To see this poem as a pawn in the game of power relations, as a
passive vehicle of ideological forces, is to ignore the extent to which
this poem is itself questioning the meaning of the historical event it
foregrounds. The stanza above seems to raise serious doubts and
questions about the actions of the rebels. In the first lines of the
stanza it suggests that sacrifice can make 'a stone of the heart',
turning the rebels' hearts cold and passionless, and asks 'when may it
suffice?' – when will nationalist insurrections and the rhetoric of
martyrdom end? It then considers the rebels like children whose
'limbs ... had run wild'. The rebels seem to be giddy with the excitement of talk of adventure, and the rebellion seems to be no more than
a childish game. The stanza raises the possibility that the rebellion
was in any case a futile and imprudent gesture, since England had
already promised Home Rule to Ireland, and in 1916 there may have
been no reason why it should not 'keep faith'. A series of images in
this stanza suggest that the rebellion was futile, badly planned and
misconceived strategically, and that the motivations for the rebellion
were an 'excess of love', dreams and wild childhood fantasies. The
rebels, it suggests, were not prudent, honourable leaders, but were
bewildered children. The stanza then moves beyond its questions and
doubts to the recognition that, whatever the nature of the rebels and
the rebellion, all has 'changed, changed utterly'.

But despite the fact that these questions are troubling, and do
suggest reproaches to the actions of the rebels, we might also notice
that almost every single doubt raised can be read in another way. It is
not clear what the line 'Too long a sacrifice' refers to: it could be the
acts and rhetoric of nationalist martyrdom, as suggested above, or
indeed it could be the sacrifice which Ireland has been forced to make
under colonialism. In the context of the third stanza, in which the
poem uses the metaphor of 'the living stream' to allude to the
inevitability of historical forces, and uses the metaphor of the stone in
the living stream to allude to something capable of disturbing those
historical forces, it is possible to interpret the use of the stone
metaphor in the final stanza to refer not to the coldness of rebel
hearts but to their resoluteness, their determination. And the question
'when may it suffice?' might not be despairing in search of an end to
nationalist violence, but may in fact be wondering when it will
succeed, when the violence will be sufficient to result in liberation.
The poem certainly considers the rebels like children – giddy and wild
– but it also considers 'our part' as that of the child's mother. This is

an interesting revision of the colonial image of mother country and its child colony, in which as Fanon says:

> colonialism did not seek to be considered as a gentle, loving mother who protects her child from a hostile environment, but rather as a mother who unceasingly restrains her fundamentally perverse offspring from managing to commit suicide and from giving free rein to its evil instincts. (Fanon 1967, 169–70)

'Our part', as it is suggested in 'Easter 1916', is to replace the colonial mother with the gentle, loving mother. And the children in this case are not the dysfunctional barbaric children of the colonial image which Fanon depicts, but instead are adored children whose only fault is an 'excess of love'. They may not even be guilty of imprudence, since the suggestion that 'England may keep faith / For all that is done and said' may be ironic, particularly in the context of the executions and backlash which followed the rising, and when the poem rhymes 'said' with 'dead'. Indeed, in the lines which precede and succeed these two there are found the words 'death' (twice), 'dead' and 'died', all of which may be offsetting the suggestion that 'England may keep faith'. So, for each of the doubts which this final stanza of 'Easter 1916' may raise, it may equally cancel out those doubts.

A formalist analysis of this poem would delight in the structure which this final stanza employs – thesis and antithesis, point and counterpoint, question leading to doubt, and all moving towards the resolution that 'a terrible beauty is born'. The whole poem might be seen to move towards this formal reconciliation of opposites in this image of a 'terrible beauty' being born out of death. But an historical analysis is not primarily interested in the formal qualities at work in the poem, but in how those formal qualities interact with history. The poem is embedded in history, as part of what forms the historical discourse of Irish decolonisation. But the ways in which the poem sustains and supports a variety of interpretations, and holds a series of 'conversations', as it were, with its historical subject matter, makes it possible to consider the poem as an active participant in shaping history rather than being the passive bearer of historical scars. The poem is ambivalent about the Easter Rising of 1916, but is ambivalent in such a way as to enable several different readings, ranging from its status as a nationalist poem, to a poem which criticises rebellion and holds out hope for England.

The point to be made here is that the poem does not have a fixed identity, and no amount of historicising can fix its identity. It supports colonial and anti-colonial readings, nationalist and anti-nationalist readings, as well as feminist, Marxist, formalist and historical readings. It supports all these readings not because it is an empty receptacle of any and every interpretive agenda, but because 'Easter 1916' is comprised of a series of words and formal qualities which construct and shape these readings in the first place. To historicise a poem, a complex verbal and linguistic structure, is to find that there is more than one way in which the poem fits into, and participates in, history. Or, to put it another way, when we try to do what Greenblatt suggests of the practice of cultural poetics – to 'ask how collective beliefs and experiences were shaped' (Greenblatt 1988, 5) – we will find that there is not one way, and one way only, in which literary texts can be seen to 'shape' collective beliefs and experiences. The relationship between literature and history is not a matter of a simple determination of the effects which a text has on historical change. To historicise a poem is to discover the varieties and histories of the interpretations and meanings of that poem, always in relation to the experiences and events in which the poem is embedded, and is to recognise that the poem converses endlessly with those experiences and events. To believe that we can determine the part which the poem plays in shaping history, however, is to ignore the dialogic nature of the relationship between the poem and history, and to ignore the multiple interpretive possibilities which a poem like 'Easter 1916' offers, even within a defined historical context.

For Bakhtin the concept of dialogism referred to the 'double-voicedness' of language in the novel form.[1] Bakhtin analysed the incorporation of different social discourses (legal, medical, pedagogic) as voices in prose texts, and argued that they combined to make the novel a hybrid construction in which many languages were in dialogue – the language of the author, and the various languages which are incorporated into the author's language. Any novel, in Bakhtin's view, was a dialogue between two voices. Although he was reluctant to extend this view to the poetic genre, I believe that a similar process can be seen at work in Yeats's 'Easter 1916'. Yeats incorporates the voices of others into his poem. This is particularly noticeable in the final stanza, in which Yeats incorporates a series of words and metaphors borrowed from the rhetoric of contemporary Irish nationalism. The word 'sacrifice' had much resonance in nationalist discourse of the time, referring partly to the sacrifice which every nationalist was expected to make for the cause, and partly to the 'blood-sacrifice' of dying for the cause – the martyrdom for which the 1916 rebels became renowned. So too, 'our part' echoes the language of duty, loyalty and acting for a cause which became so much a feature of the nationalist rhetoric of Pearse, Markievicz, Connolly, MacDonagh and the other 1916 leaders. The image of 'us', Ireland, as mother is rife in the rhetoric of the rebels, and forms the first line of the 'Proclamation of the Republic' which Pearse read on the steps of the General Post Office on commencing the Easter rebellion: 'Irishmen and Irishwomen: In the name of God and the dead generations from which she receives her nationhood, Ireland, through us, summons her children to her flag and strikes for our freedom' (*Field Day* 1991, II: 733). The 'Proclamation' concludes by calling on these children of 'Mother Ireland' to 'sacrifice themselves for the common good' (734).

There are other voices incorporated into this stanza too. The poetic metaphor of death as a form of sleep, which we might easily identify as a Shakespearean, or, perhaps even more clearly, a Keatsian image, appears in the form of the question: 'What is it but nightfall?' But the poem refuses this image ('No, no, not night but death'), and refuses to allow the deaths of the rebels to become a metaphor. Yeats also incorporates Maud Gonne's voice by repeating her view that the Easter Rising, and the carnage caused by the Rising, may have been 'needless', given that England had promised Home Rule to Ireland in 1914. And even the refrain of the last line, 'A terrible beauty is born', intimates a recurrent theme of Pearse's speeches, articulated in his graveside speech on the Fenian, O'Donovan Rossa, in 1915, in the words: 'Life springs from death; and from the graves of patriot men and women spring living nations' (*Field Day* 1991, III: 294).

There are two points to be raised immediately about the incorporation of other voices into the poem.[2] The first is that the presence of these other voices suggests that Yeats is never independent of (and indeed is formed in and from) the whole gamut of social discourses and public representations proliferating around him. The second is that the poem is as much a dialogue between voices (dramatised most effectively with the four questions which the final stanza raises but cannot answer), as much a double-voiced text, as is the genre of the novel in Bakhtin's view. Bakhtin argued that the dialogic novel 'presumes a deliberate feeling for the historical and social concreteness of living discourse, as well as its relativity, a feeling for its participation in historical becoming and in social struggle' (Dentith 1995, 224). So too, Yeats's 'Easter 1916' presumes a feeling for its participation in social and historical discourse, and indeed for the shifting social and historical conditions of Ireland after the Easter Rising. The poem is aware of its own participation in historical change. It specifies that 'our part' is 'to murmur name upon name', and then it closes by carrying out 'our part' by murmuring 'name upon name': 'MacDonagh and MacBride / And Connolly and Pearse'. The poem is indicating that it performs *actions* in history, and is part of history itself, rather than simply reflecting history, or being determined by historical forces. It is not a passive pawn in the game of power relations, but instead is a space in which power relations are mediated.

The literary text cannot be determined by historical forces, precisely because the literary text is inseparable from history, and in fact is part of what forms and shapes historical forces. The relationship between literature and history is dialogic. They are interrelated and mutually dependent, but also double-voiced. They shape each other in more than one way, on more than one level. 'Easter 1916' intervenes in social and historical discourses, and one of those discourses is that of colonialism. In the poems Yeats wrote in response to the Easter Rising, he gives the space of those poems over to debate the significance and meaning of the event for national and colonial history. 'Easter 1916' reveals its position in this debate by taking up its own call to 'murmur name upon name', but in the process of arriving at this position it allows for a series of questions, doubts, debates and conversations to take place. This is the dialogic space of the poem, the 'double-voicedness' of the poem.

The dialogism of 'Easter 1916' affirms that the colonial relationship is based both on communication and miscommunication. The coloniser needs to communicate its rule, its laws, its culture, its religion, to the colonised, but as Homi Bhabha has argued persuasively, in order to preserve its superiority it must also ensure miscommunication, so that it remains the origin and master. Colonialism depends upon this contradiction. The colonised must understand the coloniser in order to obey and to conform, but the colonised must always remain in a position of subservience, and therefore must at some point fail to be capable of understanding and mastering the communication of the coloniser. According to Bhabha this ambivalence which is at the heart of the relationship between coloniser and colonised cannot be resolved:

What threatens the authority of colonial command is the ambivalence of its address – father and oppressor or, alternatively, the ruled and reviled – which will not be resolved in a dialectical play of power. For these doubly inscribed figures face two ways without being two-faced. Western imperialist discourse continually puts under erasure the civil state, as the colonial text emerges uncertainly within its narrative of progress. Between the civil address and its colonial signification – each axis displaying a problem of recognition and repetition – shuttles the signifier of authority in search of a strategy of surveillance, subjection, and inscription. Here there can be no dialectic of the master-slave for where discourse is so disseminated can there ever be the passage from trauma to transcendence? From alienation to authority? Both colonizer and colonized are in a process of miscognition where each point of identification is always a partial and double repetition of the *otherness* of the self – democrat and despot, individual *and* servant, native and child. (Bhabha 1994, 97 – Bhabha's italics)

'Easter 1916' demonstrates the ambivalence of colonial communication at work. The poem refers obliquely to the prowess at hunting, an English aristocratic pursuit, for which Markievicz was renowned, and to MacDonagh's potential as a lecturer, and poet, in English literature. And yet these signs of English culture have evidently been misread and misunderstood by the colonised, since Markievicz and MacDonagh have taken up arms against England. The poem refers directly to the possibility that 'England may keep faith', a line which suggests that a relationship of trust, respect, even love, existed between England and Ireland. And yet this sign of England's political will is certainly ambivalent when sixteen men have been executed, and the only certainty which the final stanza seems capable of confirming is death. The poem, then, is dialogic in that it converses with the historical forces of colonisation, and also in that it dramatises subtly a conversation between the coloniser and the colonised.

Bhabha sees this ambivalence in colonial communication as the factor which makes resistance against colonial power possible. Resistance will never be totally effective (just as power, contrary to new historicist assumptions, will never be totally effective) because colonialism is always a powerful force, even when it becomes a powerful legacy after independence. The history of the relationship between independent Ireland and Britain may yield an ample number of examples of the dependency, ambivalence of communication,

stereotypical identifications, trauma and subjection which characterised the same relationship prior to independence. But resistance is
a force, mobilised by the colonised, which counters and makes apparent the power and brutality of the coloniser, and at the same time
utilises the instruments of colonial ideology – chiefly cultural, political
and military instruments – to renegotiate the state of power relations.

A poem can be a part of this process of renegotiating power relations, and is in that respect somewhat similar to a political movement
or an army. What is striking in many ways about the drive for independence in Ireland in the early twentieth century is that poets and
artists became as deeply and widely involved in politics and military
affairs as they were in poetry and art. But we should not forget that
although poetry (and art and literature in general) are inseparable
from political, from military, indeed from social and historical
discourses, they are also in dialogue with these discourses, and that
the dialogue is always double-voiced, and can be interpreted in very
different ways. New historicism and cultural materialism charged
themselves with the task of challenging the extent to which formalism
had denied any significance to the relationships between poetry and
the outside world. But they have lurched towards an equally damag-
ing dogma, and have come to insist that poetry is determined by, and
a product of, the outside world. They are partly right, in that poetry is
inseparable from social and historical forces, but poetry also plays an
active part in mediating those forces, and in the process it may be
read as shaping, interrupting and renegotiating those forces. Yeats's
poetry did not alter the course of Irish history, but neither was it
entirely without its own modicum of power to manipulate, and negotiate, and shape the course of that history.

Notes

1. See M. M. Bakhtin, 'Heteroglossia in the Novel', in *Bakhtinian Thought:
   An Introductory Reader*, ed. Simon Dentith, London and New York:
   Routledge, 1995.
2. Conversation, dialogue, seems to be an important theme in the poems
   in which Yeats responds to the 1916 Rising. The two poems which
   follow 'Easter 1916' in the collection *Michael Robartes and the Dancer*
   which Yeats published in 1921, 'Sixteen Dead Men' and 'The Rose Tree',
   highlight the significance of dialogue. 'Sixteen Dead Men' suggests that

the time for talking has ended as a result of the executions of the sixteen leaders of the Rising. Lynn Innes, in the chapter on Yeats's response to the Easter Rising in her excellent book, *Woman and Nation in Irish Literature and Society*, reads 'The Rose Tree' 'as a drama in which Yeats's own voice has been entirely silenced as poet and politician ... it is a poem which both acknowledges the power of that populist tradition and refuses comment on it' (Innes 1993, 88).

Part III

Afterwords

Afterwords

the literary institution has 'fictioned' a criticism which uncritically protests its own truth; we must instead 'fiction' a literature which renders up our true history in the interests of a politics of change.

Catherine Belsey, 'Literature, History, Politics'

Both new historicism and cultural materialism read literary texts for the history which they might reveal in the expectation that the history produced by such readings will alter our conceptions of political and historical change, and of the political and historical possibilities of change. In this sense, both are directed towards what may emerge in the aftermath of their readings. We need, then, to examine this aftermath, the time of after new historicism and after cultural materialism, to know more fully what it is that new historicist and cultural materialist practitioners are producing.

This part of the book is titled 'Afterwords', and contains two chapters which consider the future of new historicism and cultural materialism. The title refers to the position of these two chapters, coming after the main discussion, demonstration and criticism of the critical practices of new historicism and cultural materialism. It also refers to the status of the two chapters as considerations which come, historically and theoretically, in the wake or aftermath of these critical practices, which are only possible after new historicism and cultural materialism have emerged and mutated. But this part of the book, unlike most conventional 'Afterwords', is not an attempt to make general and definitive conclusions of the two critical practices, not an attempt, therefore, at determining finally what both practices mean and signify. The two chapters which follow are speculations on the work which remains to be done in new historicism and cultural materialism. They are, therefore, invitations to these critical practices to continue, to foster new work, to open up new possibilities for reading and scrutinising texts, and to continue to challenge and provoke our conceptions of the relationship between literature and history.

10 After History: Textuality and Historicity in the New Historicism

> I began with the desire to speak with the dead.
>
> Stephen Greenblatt, *Shakespearean Negotiations*

> The great project of historicist criticism is liberation, and only through its work in the world – its interpretation of culture and its critique of power's presence – will it become not a discipline but a gift, one of power's presents.
>
> Jeffrey N. Cox and Larry J. Reynolds, *New Historical Literary Studies*

When Stephen Greenblatt announced the arrival of the new historicism in 1982, he defined it as a practice which was 'set apart from both the dominant historical scholarship of the past and the formalist criticism that partially displaced this scholarship in the decades after World War Two' (Greenblatt 1982, 5). New historicism represented (itself as) a significant shift away from the kind of literary studies wherein the literary text was conceived to be an ahistorical linguistic structure, or the literary text was measured against a crude historical background. Along with some Marxist and feminist critics, and cultural materialism in Britain, the new historicism came to be known as the turn to history in literary studies. In his presidential address to the Modern Language Association in 1986, Hillis Miller claimed that the turn to history was dominating literary studies:

> As everybody knows, literary study in the past few years has undergone a sudden, almost universal turn away from theory in the sense of an orientation toward language as such and has made a corresponding turn toward history, culture, society, politics, institutions, class and gender conditions, the social context, the material base in the sense of institutionalization, conditions of production, technol-

ogy, distribution, and consumption of 'cultural products', among other products. This trend is so obvious everywhere as hardly to need description. How many symposia, conferences, scholarly convention sessions, courses, books and new journals recently have had the word *history, politics, society* or *culture* in their titles? (Miller 1991, 313)

This trend is still obvious everywhere, of course. Although many of the first practitioners of the new kinds of historical criticism which emerged in the early 1980s have since moved into other areas of study (for example, Goldberg and Orgel moving into gender and sexuality studies), or have given a new label to their work (cultural poetics), the relationship between literature and history still dominates the attention of literary critics and scholars. Indeed, the tendency to think of literature as history has led to other concerns: literature as geography, as architecture, as political community. The new historicism has succeeded in bringing this relationship between literature and history into the mainstream of literary studies. Perhaps the most important achievement which we can attribute to the turn to history is the recognition that the text is an event. For new historicists, and for others too, literary texts occupy specific historical and cultural sites, at which, and through which, historical forces clash, and political and ideological contradictions are played out. The concept of the text as event allows us to recognise the temporal specificity of the text, the definite and contingent function of a text in a particular discourse under particular historical conditions. It recognises also that the text is part of the process of historical change, and indeed may constitute historical change. This has shifted critics away from approaching the text as a simple reflection or rejection of historical trends, and instead has led critics to explore what Montrose called 'the historicity of texts and the textuality of history' (Montrose in Veeser 1989, 20).

It is this claim, that new historicism is examining 'the historicity of texts and the textuality of history', which I want to interrogate in this chapter. Since the mid-1980s new historicism has been criticised increasingly for its failure to read literary texts, and its reductive conception of history. This chapter will trace the new historicist critical practice and conception of history back to Foucault, and will speculate on what a revision of the relationship between new historicism and Foucault might produce. The aim of this chapter is, then, to ask about the future of new historicist practice, to speculate about what comes after the new historicism, after the turn to history. The title of this chapter, 'After History', refers not just to what we might clumsily call 'post-new historicism', however, but also refers to the end of history, or the post-history of which new historicism appears to be a part. New historicism was apparently also part of the recognition that history, in terms of the narrative of enlightenment progress, had not only come to an end, but had lost its unity, had dissolved into a multiplicity of histories. 'This dissolution', writes Gianni Vattimo in *The End of Modernity*,

> marks an end to historiography as the image, albeit a constantly varied one, of a unitary process of events, a process which itself loses all recognizable consistency when deprived of the unity of the discourse that formerly defined it. (Vattimo 1991, 9)

Post-history depends on a dismantling of enlightenment chronology, and on a radical reinterpretation of temporal and historical order. It represents a diverse and bizarre consensus of Western liberalism, after the collapse of communism, with postmodern and post-Marxist thinkers, who claim at the end of modernity that progress is impossible, that the new is only part of a self-perpetuating conservative system. So, in this chapter, I will also investigate the extent to which new historicism is part of this apparent consensus that we are now in a state of 'after-' or 'post-history'.

Louis Montrose certainly believed that new historicism was part of post-history, part of the recognition that historians could no longer look upon the past as if they were not looking at the image of the present, as if they were dealing with an objective reality outside their own representations of it. Montrose explains that to recognise the historicity of texts is to specify the cultural and historical differences at work in both the literary text and the critical text, and that to recognise the textuality of history is to assume that nothing exists outside language, outside representations:

> By *the historicity of texts*, I mean to suggest the cultural specificity, the social embedment, of all modes of writing – not only the texts that critics study but also the texts in which we study them. By *the textuality of history*, I mean to suggest, firstly, that we can have no access to a full and authentic past, a lived and material existence, unmediated by the surviving textual traces of the society in question – traces whose survival we cannot assume to be contingent but must rather presume

to be at least partially consequent upon complex and subtle social processes of preservation and effacement; and secondly, that those textual traces are themselves subject to subsequent textual mediations when they are construed as 'documents' upon which historians ground their own texts, called 'histories'. (Montrose in Veeser 1989, 20)

But if new historicism emerged in opposition to types of literary criticism and of historical investigation which failed to theorise cultural and historical differences in their own work, and failed to recognise the temporal and generic specificity of texts and events, new historicism was also subject to the same criticisms by the mid-1980s. From that time onwards, the criticisms of new historicism have proliferated and become stronger. In particular, these criticisms have focused on the new historicist tendency to reduce all representations of history to the same basic model of power relations, and the tendency to subject texts to a superficial and generalised reading, locating the ostensible positions of texts in the grid of discursive formations without interrogating the interpretability of those texts.

To take the first criticism, Carolyn Porter has articulated this particularly well in her article from 1988, 'Are we being historical yet?':

new historicism projects a vision of history as an endless skein of cloth smocked in a complex, overall pattern by the needle and thread of Power. You need only pull the thread at one place to find it connected to another. (Porter 1988, 765)

Porter argues that new historicism has succeeded in displacing the grand narrative of progress which dominated the old historicism, and indeed which shaped the development of empirical history, only to replace it with another grand narrative, that of power. Moreover, she suggests that the effect of this model of power relations in new historicism is to consider all historical events the subject of an elusive, but generalised and universal condition of power. To Porter it seems ironic that a practice which claims to be historicising texts and events ends up making them the product of an ahistorical, universal, and apparently omnipotent force. Frank Lentricchia attributes the centrality of this ill-defined and seemingly rampant and universal 'power' in new historicist analyses to the influence of Foucault, whose 'depressing message' of a power 'saturating all social relations to the point that all conflicts and "jostlings" among social groups become a mere show of political dissension' is repeated uncritically by the new historicists (Lentricchia in Veeser 1989, 235).

It is certainly the case that, whether examining pastoral poems in the Elizabethan period, confessions of an Italian heretic in the sixteenth century, the realist novel in Victorian England, or the encounters between colonisers and natives in the new world, new historicists seem to find the same model, whereby power produces its own subversion in order to contain and control subversion more effectively. Power is everywhere, in every facet of Western society and culture, but nowhere is it clear what power is, how it is made, where it fails or ends, what is outside of power, or even how power emerges. Clearly, this conception of power is borrowed from Foucault's *History of Sexuality, Volume 1.* Lentricchia's claim that it is accepted uncritically by the new historicists is shared by Lee Patterson, who sees the new historicist interest in circularity demonstrated in their critical practice when he writes: 'There is no space outside power because power is the only term in the analyst's arsenal' (Patterson in Ryan 1996, 96). Power is everywhere, because it is sought for everywhere, and at the same time it erases the specificity of the historical moment. Effectively, new historicism silences dissent and subversion, and eradicates difference, by looking only for power.

The second major criticism of new historicism is that it tends to subject texts to the most superficial and generalised readings as a result of an interest in the function rather than the interpretability of texts. If Stephen Greenblatt can make texts of various genres, from confessional to travel narrative, from drama to political pamphlet, perform the very same function in a general discourse, and if he can take texts from Italy, England, Germany, colonised America and make them repeat the same formulation, it is easy to see why new historicism has been criticised for a lack of sensitivity to the complexity of literary texts. When this criticism has been expressed by formalist critics we might choose to regard it as the result of an opposition to historical criticism. But when Hillis Miller rebuked new historicism as 'an exhilarating experience of liberation from the obligation to read' (Miller 1991, 313), as a flight of fancy away from an ethical obligation to the other, even to the otherness of the past, we may expect his opposition to be based on more than a desire to return to an ahistorical practical criticism. And when Kiernan Ryan argues that new historicism 'is undoubtedly the poorer for its reluctance to meet the complex demands of a text's diction and formal requirements' (Ryan

1996, xviii), he does so from the desire to see a radical historical criticism which engages with the detail of the text in order to show even more clearly the historical and political implications and locations of the text.

Here, too, we can trace the new historicist focus on the function of a text rather than its interpretability to Foucault. In *The Archaeology of Knowledge*, Foucault advocates a kind of analysis which depends on avoiding interpretation:

> The analysis of statements, then, is a historical analysis, but one that avoids all interpretation: it does not question things said as to what they are hiding, what they were 'really' saying, in spite of themselves, the unspoken element that they contain, the proliferation of thoughts, images, or fantasies that inhabit them; but on the contrary it questions them as to their mode of existence, what it means to them to have come into existence, to have left traces, and perhaps to remain there, awaiting the moment when they might be of use once more; what it means to them to have appeared when and where they did – they and no others. From this point of view, there is no such thing as a latent statement: for what one is concerned with is the fact of language. (Foucault 1972, 109)

Foucault is describing here the analysis of discursive formations, and the focus of this analysis is the position of texts and statements within discursive formations. Texts are, in Foucault's conception, pawns in the game of discursive transformations, and are therefore subject to an interrogation of what position they occupy, but not of what they mean. Foucault's archaeological analysis seeks to uncover the participation of texts and statements in discourse, not to scrutinise the varieties of meaning which may be produced from texts and statements. Reading the text is not, it seems, a necessary part of this process, and is certainly not as necessary as a knowledge of how texts connect with other texts, how the textuality of history forms a kind of discursive fabric. If new historicism fails to read literary texts, and seems to be completely insensitive to the differences between texts, between genres, and indeed between textual and historical events, it is a product of following the Foucauldian model of discursive analysis.

Of course, I am also doing an injustice to new historicism in ignoring differences between its various practitioners. On the relationship between their own practice and Foucault, new historicists have differed widely, from Stephen Greenblatt, who has been influenced by Foucault's ideas on power and discourse in the Renaissance, to D. A. Miller, who has applied Foucault's ideas on the carceral, on discipline and on policing to the Victorian novel. But Foucault's presence, as argued in the section above, is pervasive in new historicist thinking, and indeed seems to be responsible for many of the faults for which new historicists have been attacked. Brook Thomas argues that new historicist uses and abuses of the concepts of power and discourse can be traced to Foucault, and Thomas counsels against following the Foucauldian model when he writes that 'to become a disciple to his [Foucault's] thought is, to my mind, to pay too high a cost' (Thomas 1991a, 47). But although the new historicist uses of power and discourse are undoubtedly borrowed from Foucault, where they differ from Foucault is in their conception of history, and it is this, I want to argue, which absolves Foucault of responsibility for the critical short-comings of new historicism.

Foucault's conception of history underwrites his ideas of power and discourse. History is not only the discipline within which Foucault claims to be working, but it is also the practice which he attempts to subvert and to reorient. All of his works claim in some ways to be involved in tracing historical patterns, delineating the structures of the past, or theorising new historical methods. Even in the course of apparently 'doing' history, Foucault is also critiquing historical methods, and in the process restoring singularity to the event, thinking of the event in its uniqueness. He calls this 'effective history':

> 'Effective history' ... deals with events in terms of their most unique characteristics, their most acute manifestations. An event, conse- quently, is not a decision, a treaty, a reign, or a battle, but the reversal of a relationship of forces, the usurpation of power, the appropriation of a vocabulary turned against those who had once used it, a feeble domination that poisons itself as it grows lax, the entry of a masked 'other'. The forces operating in history are not controlled by destiny or regulative mechanisms, but respond to haphazard conflicts ... they always appear through the singular randomness of events. (Foucault 1977, 154)

We could counter Foucault's claim to be studying the 'singular randomness of events' with Simon During's argument that Foucault believed 'that texts can be analysed as if they are produced within knowable strategies' (During 1991, 181). If Foucault thinks of the text as a singular and random event, it certainly seems at odds with his practice of reading texts and events as vehicles of a complex, widely dispersed and highly systematic discursive formation. But in writing the history of discursive formations Foucault is laying stress not on the grand design which might be (falsely, in his view) discerned in their operations, but in the randomness and uniqueness of the emergence and mutation of those discursive formations. In short, Foucault is inviting us to think of history not as the continuous elaboration of a design guaranteed and decreed by an authorial presence – God, the King, the government – but of history as the random appearance and formation of singular discourses which have definite historical effects, of history as the random production and containment of power. He invites us to conceive of 'power without the king' (Foucault 1981, 91), of power without design, and therefore a history of random effects and accidental formations.

The result of this focus on the randomness and singularity of the event is that Foucault's historical insights tend to straddle the actual and the possible. I am thinking here not of the accusations of historical inaccuracy made against Foucault, and discussed by Lois McNay in her book on Foucault (McNay 1994, 24–6), but of those moments in Foucault's work when a specific historical event is recognised as the containment of possibilities. In each case the event is characterised by the transformation of the discourse, the release of possibilities to effect a decisive but unmeditated change in the field of discursive formations. Madness becomes the object of psychological study. Delinquency becomes the subject of penal incarceration. Africa becomes Europe's dark 'other'. In each case a new technology of power is born, quite by accident, and effects a transformation in the system of Western thought. But in each case too Foucault is interested in the other possibilities which may have occurred at specific historical moments, the alternative scenarios, the histories which didn't actually happen but which were nevertheless possible. This is part of Foucault's project of inventing a counter-history, or counter-memory, to Western historical discourse.

What this reveals about Foucault's conception of history is that history is not confined to descriptions of what actually happened, but to the analysis of how events come into existence, what controls and circulates those events, and how events generate discursive formations. Moreover, for Foucault, history does not follow the chronology of 'totalitarian periodization' (Foucault 1972, 148), as he calls it, and instead each discursive formation has its own temporal articulations, its own historical structure. There is in Foucault's history more than one time, more than one temporal order. We need to bear this in mind when examining the relationship between the new historicists and Foucault. It is Foucault's theoretical formulations of time and historical method which distinguishes his practice from the new historicists, and correspondingly, it is the new historicist tendency, as Robert Young has described it (Young 1990, 89), 'to shelve the whole problem' of historical method which produces in their work the problems with 'the historicity of the text and the textuality of history' for which they have been widely criticised.

Ostensibly, Foucault and the new historicists share common conceptions of historical analysis. All of Foucault's concerns – with disruption and discontinuity, with épistemé, with the historicity of discursive formations, with archaeological and genealogical analysis, and with ascribing a definite function to texts or events – are present in a variety of similar forms in the work of new historicists. What is missing from new historicist analysis are two complex and productive tensions in Foucault's conception of his historical analysis, and the absence of these tensions in new historicism, I will argue, denotes the failure of new historicism to engage seriously with 'the historicity of texts and the textuality of history'.

The first tension in Foucault's work concerns the historical and textual condition of the object of study. Foucault argues at various points throughout his work that effectively discursive formations constitute and bring into existence their objects of study. In *The Archaeology of Knowledge*, for example, he claims that each discourse 'constituted its object and worked it to the point of transforming it all together. So that the problem arises of knowing whether the unity of a discourse is based not so much on the permanence and uniqueness of an object as on the space in which various objects emerge and are continuously transformed' (Foucault 1972, 32). So, madness as an object of study is only possible when a discourse on madness has emerged. So too with criminality, homosexuality, witchcraft, or sickness. But note here that for Foucault it is still a 'problem' as to whether the object is permanent or unique, or whether it is coterminous with, and constituted by, the discursive formation. And the problem is important because it indicates a tension running right through Foucault's work. Rudi Visker outlines this tension in Foucault's work:

> On the one hand, he [Foucault] wishes to deny the transhistorical reality of phenomena like homosexuality or madness; on the other, however, he wants also to leave them sufficient objective reality that they remain, none the less, in need of explanation. (Homo)sexuality does not precede its discourse and yet it is also not a discursive illu· sion. In the first case one would fall back into a realism which, after *Histoire de la folie*, Foucault sought to combat with all the resources at his disposal; in the second case, one would be promulgating a kind of discursive idealism which, instead of according too little weight to discourse, would go to the opposite extreme. (Visker 1995, 81)

It is clearly a contradiction in Foucault's work that he insists on both the objective reality of the object, and the construction of that object by an emerging discursive formation, but the price of resolving this contradiction, as Visker suggests, is either to collapse back into empirical history or realism, or to surrender everything to the idealism of an autonomous, omnipotent discourse. Foucault rides this tension, therefore, between objectivity and discursivity, not because he cannot resolve them into a coherent system but because the price of doing so is too high. By holding them in tension, objectivity is constantly countered by the discursivity of the object, and vice versa. Jon Simons finds a similar tension in Foucault's conceptions of power and freedom, arguing that, on the one hand, Foucault seems drawn to a totalising model of power in which we are entrapped totally, while, on the other hand, he also seems drawn to the notion of pure freedom, of escaping all the constraints of power (Simons 1995, 3). In both cases, Foucault is caught between advocating a totalised, closed system and believing in a space 'outside' that system, and, while this occasionally borders on idealism, or perhaps naivety, Foucault sustains this tension as a productive and critical strategy. He rides the tension rather than resolving it, and thereby theorises a space in which critical histories can be generated.

   Robert Young argues that we can trace the emergence of this productive, critical tension in Foucault's work to the aftermath of Derrida's essay on *Madness and Civilization*, in which Derrida had criticised Foucault for maintaining the illusion of a space 'outside' discourse (Young 1990, 72). What is notable too about Derrida's

'Cogito and the History of Madness' is that in it he describes the
attempt to sustain this illusion in the face of a totalitarian concept of
discourse as 'the most audacious and seductive aspect of his venture',
and 'with all seriousness, the *maddest* aspect of his project' (Derrida
1978, 34). After Derrida's essay, Foucault never attempted to resolve
the contradiction between objectivity and discursivity into a free
space of critical insight, as he had done at the end of *Madness and
Civilization* by positing that art and writing were outside, and critical
of, the discourse on madness. As Young argues, in Foucault's later
work, the relationship between writing and history 'would remain
profoundly equivocal' (Young 1990, 72).

Equivocation is seriously absent from the work of new historicists,
however. In the work of Greenblatt, Montrose, Miller, Gallagher,
Tennenhouse and others, what was a productive tension in Foucault's
writing between objectivity and discursivity is resolved completely
into discursive idealism. All objects, all writings, all histories, are
constituted by the discursive formation, and are subject to the totalising and closed system of power. For Greenblatt, for example, there is
in *Renaissance Self-Fashioning* a single process by which identities
were formed and constituted in Renaissance Europe, as there is in
Marvelous Possessions a single European representational practice by
which the New World was constructed and shaped. Nothing exists
outside these discourses of power, and neither self-fashioning nor the
New World exist prior to the European discourse through which they
are represented, contained and controlled. For Greenblatt, then, there
is no tension between objectivity and discursivity, and what justifies
his historical analysis is entirely the distance between his analysis and
the Renaissance modes of power which he is describing, a point
which I'll come back to later. The objects which they describe are
formed entirely within a closed system of power.

Where Foucault differs from the new historicists, therefore, is in
sustaining the tension between the objective existence of the object of
study outside discourse or power and the impossibility of there being
a space 'outside' discourse or power. By sustaining this contradiction,
Foucault evades a model of total closure, and avoids falling into either
realism or idealism. The result of this tension in Foucault's work is
that he remains critical of discursive formations, while entirely implicated in the production of discursive formations. The failure to maintain this tension renders the new historicists entirely complicit in the
production of power, and in the silencing of dissent, and complicit in

the objectification of texts into the passive pawns of power. There is in new historicism no distance between their descriptions of how power operates, and their part in prescribing how power operates.

The second tension in Foucault's work concerns the relationship between discursive time and chronological time. This may be as simple as distinction between how the Victorians lived and how we represent the lives of Victorians, between the act and the representation, or more properly, between the representation and its repetition. Or it may involve a more complex distinction between events and discourses, in which an event in chronological time interacts with its discursive formations in different ways, according to the logical scheme and temporal order of each discourse:

> Thus the French Revolution – since up to now all archaeological analyses have been centred on it – does not play the role of an event exterior to discourse, whose divisive effect one is under some kind of obligation to discover in all discourses; it functions as a complex, articulated, describable group of transformations that left a number of positivities intact, fixed for a number of others rules that are still with us, and also established positivities that have recently disap-peared or are still disappearing before our eyes. (Foucault 1972, 177)

Foucault's discursive analysis cannot reduce the French Revolution to the level of a break with the past, the beginning of new discourses or periods, because the relationship between the event and the discourses surrounding it, and inhabiting it, are more complex. Some have brought the French Revolution as an event into existence, others have only the barest of relationships to it. In any case, because discur-sive formations are networks of relations and technologies, partially defined by 'the way in which they are institutionalized, received, used, re-used, combined together' (Foucault 1972, 115), the time of discourse is, literally, and elusively, unknowable and indefinite. New historicists have occasionally shown the consequences of this conception of indefinite temporal orders by tracing the appearance of Spenserian motifs in the Victorian construction of sexuality, or images of ancient Roman civilisation in revolutionary France, by tracing the presence of an event out of chronological sequence. But new histori-cists do not follow Foucault's concept of temporal disjunction to the full, a point to which I will return in a moment.

For Foucault, then, statements and texts function in discursive formations which are not at all coterminous even with their ostensible chronological positions. Discursive time is not chronological time. Despite this, Foucault suggests that the analysis of discursive formations requires chronological distance when he argues that 'it is not possible for us to describe our own archive', by which he means the system or law of all that is possible to say and do, 'since it is from within these rules that we speak' (Foucault 1972, 130). If it is not possible to describe our own archive, then it suggests that discursive analysis requires the distance of chronological time in order to make sense of the archive of possible statements and representations. But if those statements and representations operate according to the logic of an indefinite time, impossible to predict and know finally, then surely the distance of chronological time matters little to the possibility of analysis. Here is the second contradiction or tension in Foucault's work: the necessity of the difference between discursive time and chronological time, but the impossibility of analysis without chronological time.

Again, I want to argue that this contradiction in Foucault's work is not so much a logical flaw as a theoretical, and strategic, necessity. What this tension indicates is that there are two temporal orders in Foucault's writing, the time of the occurrence and transformation of discursive fields, and the time of Foucault's analysis of them. Foucault's conception of history is, then, diachronic, concerned with both the time of the past and the time of his own writing, and with how the past appears as an effect in the present. In the preface to *The Order of Things*, Foucault explains that his fascination with this diachronicity arose from a passage in Borges on the absurd division of categories of animals in a certain Chinese encyclopaedia:

> In the wonderment of this taxonomy, the thing we apprehend in one great leap, the thing that, by means of the fable, is demonstrated as the exotic charm of another system of thought, is the limitation of our own, the stark impossibility of thinking *that*. (Foucault 1974, xv)

History is 'the thing we apprehend in one great leap'. In history too, told as fable, 'is demonstrated the exotic charm of another system of thought'. In this explanation is contained Foucault's diachronic tension, between history as the exotic other which exposes the limitations of our system of thought, and history as the thing which we apprehend. History is not only the object of study, but, in Foucault's terms, is only possible, is defined solely, as the thing which we apprehend. Our apprehension of history 'in one great leap' is what characterises it as history, and, as he shows in *The Order of Things*, history is brought into existence, as a discipline, as a time, in response to the rise of a discourse of the present, the discourse of modernity. Foucault's conception of historical analysis requires and uses the tension between a time impossibly other for us to conceive, the time of discourse, and a time utterly incapable of being anything other than what we conceive, chronological time. What this enables Foucault to do is analyse the past from the present without pretending that he has discovered the absolute real conditions of the past, and without conceding that we are trapped entirely in the self-image of the present.

New historicism, on the other hand, fails to theorise the use of time in its own practice, and sticks rigidly to a chronological model of time. There is no equivocation in new historicist work on the status of the past. It is the other of the present, without being in dialogue with it. For Stephen Greenblatt, despite explaining the motivation for his work as 'the desire to speak with the dead' (Greenblatt 1988, 1), to recreate a conversation with the past, consistently returns the past to a distant otherness, and fails to theorise the degree to which the images of the past he produces are in fact structured and constituted by the desires and limitations of the present. So, in 'Invisible Bullets', for example, Greenblatt finds in the Renaissance 'a heightened consciousness' of the idea of religion as trickery (Greenblatt 1981, 44), and explains to us what is going on 'in the minds of Renaissance authorities' (45). In short, Greenblatt never abandons the idea that the historian can describe the past as if from an objective position outside history, even though he occasionally makes mention of what the Renaissance might mean in the present. So too, new historicists cling to the chronological time more appropriate to the conventions of literary history than the Foucauldian analysis of discourse, grafting Foucault's idea of epistemic shifts on to the literary periods of Renaissance, Romantic or Victorian.

New historicism collapses the diachronic tension of Foucault's work back into the synchronic uniformity of a period fully knowable and describable, and it is the adherence of new historicists to chronological time which is primarily responsible for this. The result might have been a new historicism which positions literary texts in an orthodox historical framework, was it not for the fact that new historicism subjects its historical analyses to a totalised model of power relations which, as Vincent Pecora (among others) has argued, produces conclusions which are always already assumed in their methodologies (Pecora in Veeser 1989, 268).

Perhaps we have arrived, then, at the point of imagining what comes after the new historicism, what follows in its wake, or what reinvents its concerns. In some ways what I have been tracing in the sections above is the failure of new historicism to address what Derrida referred to, in his criticisms of the new historicism, as 'the problematic of the border and of framing' (Derrida in Carroll 1990, 92). In the new historicism, the borders or frames – of the text, of history, of discourse – were determined according to the logic of a totalising system of power as the untrammelled vehicles of that power, a power without limits. It is naive to assume that a revision of the faults of new historicism could successfully rescue the notion of a place outside, and completely free of, the operations of hegemonic power, but what it might do, as I hope I have demonstrated partially in rereading Foucault's conception of history, is address the absence of equivocation, of diachronicity, and, indeed, of dialogics from new historicist thinking. In part, the work which could address this absence is already being done. It seems to me, for example, that cultural materialism has maintained a diachronic approach to history in some of its work, and that other historical critics, Jerome McGann seems an obvious example, have avoided the pitfalls of totalising models of history and power. But perhaps what is more important, as indeed Hillis Miller argued in 1986, is the exploration of the relationship between historical criticism and deconstructive criticism on the grounds that both are attempts 'to confront what language itself has always already erased or forgotten, namely, the performative or positional power of language as inscription over what we catechrestically call the material' (Miller 1991, 327).

Included in this exploration of the relationship between historical and deconstructive criticism ought to be the analysis of Foucault's conception of history and historical investigation. In Foucault's writings, historical investigation is always subject to the force of historicity itself, always being cross-examined. So, we find Foucault revising his conceptions of history as he writes, reflecting on his methodologies in the course of deploying them, and, in case it appears that his own subjectivity is the stabilising centre of history, historicising his own subject position. In quotation marks, towards the end of *The Archaeology of Knowledge*, Foucault is already erasing his own voice, and allowing another voice to ask:

> Must we admit that the time of discourse is not the time of consciousness extrapolated to the dimensions of history, or the time of history present in the form of consciousness? Must I suppose that in my discourse I can have no survival? And that in speaking I am not banishing my death, but actually establishing it; or rather that I am abolishing all interiority in that exterior that is so indifferent to my life, and so *neutral*, that it makes no distinction between my life and my death? (Foucault 1972, 210)

Like the last line of *The Order of Things*, with its image of man as 'a face drawn in sand at the edge of the sea' (Foucault 1974, 387), this voice at the end of *The Archaeology of Knowledge* makes the author's subjectivity the product of historical forces, implying the imminent disappearance of the self in writing. Everything in Foucault is historical, and historicised, and everything in Foucault is therefore both the product and producer of the historical object. But paradoxically, this is what makes Foucault's work post-historical, in the sense that it recognises the disappearance of a grand narrative of historical change, and its replacement with the proliferation of histories and the temporal disunity of history.

In this sense, new historicism is not fully a part of what we might call post-history, or the dissolution of history, since it replaces one grand narrative of historical progress with another grand narrative of power. And, if it gestures towards the proliferation of histories – women's history, native American history, the history of madness, or of criminality – which might be explored, it tends instead to narrate the history of successive dominations. And, because new historicism clings to a chronological model of time, and projects the play of power relations into the past, it tends not to place itself within the historical, but appears instead to be outside of history. New historicism puts itself in the position, then, of being after or outside history, but not post-historical; immune to historicity and textuality, and therefore ahistorical. For new historicists, to adapt what Greenblatt wrote of subversion at the end of 'Invisible Bullets', which in turn is his adaptation of what Kafka said to Max Brod of hope, there is history, no end of history, only not for us.

11 The Importance of Not Concluding

Piece out our imperfections with your thoughts:
Into a thousand parts divide one man,
And make imaginary puissance.

Shakespeare, Prologue to *Henry V*

Literature regularly invites us to believe in it as a narrative or representation of the past. It needs our belief, or at the very least, the suspension of our disbelief, in order to tell its stories of history, community, the individual, and everything else. When R. G. Collingwood wrote of the similarities between literature and history in his book, *The Idea of History*, the only difference he could find between them was that history was intended to be true (Collingwood 1961, 246). As literary criticism and theories have for several decades now eroded the stability of authorial intention as a guide to the meaning or interpretation of texts, and the notion of truth has always been unstable for philosophers, the differences between literature and history now seem to many literary critics and some historians to be less clear than ever. A major part of the effort to erode further the distinctions between literary and historical writings has been undertaken by new historicism and cultural materialism, and the degree of their success is perhaps easily measured by the prominence of historical issues and contexts now raised in the course of studying and writing about literature.

I do not pretend here that new historicists and cultural materialists were the only critics responsible for the turn to history in literary studies, but what they brought to the party, so to speak, certainly provided, and continues to provide, provocative and challenging ways of reading literature in history, and history in literature. Their ways of reading are not, of course, without their hazards and weaknesses, and what I have attempted to do in this volume is to question the merits, uses and pitfalls of new historicism and cultural materialism, as well as telling stories about how they emerged and mutated across the last two decades. That process of mutation is still ongoing, which is one of the reasons why this final chapter cannot be a conclusion. Literary theories and critical practices are always in transition, because they are always in history, always subject to change and constantly being revised and reused. Every new historicist reading, every reading of a new historicist reading, reinvents the concerns and methods of new historicism. The challenge which literary theories offer the reader is not the necessity of learning how to apply the theory to the text, but is instead the necessity of learning how to reinvent the theory and the text. The challenge of theory is the challenge to invent conversations between texts and theories, between one text and other texts, between texts and the histories and discourses of which they are part. If this sounds like the creation of imaginary friends, it is because there is something of childish play in reading, something of the childish fascination with invention and gaming in the act of conversing with texts.

And yet, at the same time, these acts of playing with texts could not be more serious. All texts are about representations, and representations are about how we see ourselves, are seen by others, and project ourselves to others. One of the claims of new historicism and cultural materialism is that it is how we are represented that shapes our social, political and cultural situation. How it is that native Americans were colonised and subjugated? Because Europeans consistently represented the native Americans as savage, wild people in need of Western civilisation and culture, but in order to avail of the gifts of European civilisation, their savagery had to be tamed, punished and controlled. Hence, European representations of the native Americans justified European colonisation of America. Nothing could be more serious than the deployment of violence to reach political ends, and in each case it is a system of representations which leads to the deployment of violence and indeed constructs political ends.

If texts are the source of our play, then perhaps they are dangerous toys. But it is precisely because literary texts are serious representations, and form with other texts systems of representation, that we need to play with them. As Ross Chambers argues in *Story and Situation*, 'storytelling not only derives significance from situation but also has the power to change human situations' (Chambers 1984, 7). Storytelling – whether this is a novel, a work of history, or a scientific description – has the power to rearrange and reinvent our conceptions of living. It may be that in the course of telling stories we will produce the values and norms of our society, and thereby perpetuate the existing system of representations. It may be that we do not wish to see change in the world, or to see anything other than ourselves reflected in those texts. But we may also encounter something quite unexpected and unpredictable in those texts, something which reorganises our knowledge around different objects and dissident ideas.

New historicism in particular, but also cultural materialism, can often be seen reducing a text to a passive function of power relations. The critics engaged in this practice seem to accept the apparent function of the text for what and where it is. My criticism of this kind of practice is that it does not play with the text enough, and consequently it does not discover the potential of a text to work against the grain of power relations. A literary text does not do this at the command of its author, or even necessarily at the command of its reader, but can behave, on close examination, in quite startling ways towards the ideas and powers which it apparently contains. But if new historicism elides this potential by reading the texts as the function of power relations, its methods and strategies of reading literature in history and history in literature are nevertheless useful. By allowing texts of all kinds equal status as representations of the past, both new historicism and cultural materialism construct productive exchanges between texts. This has been perhaps the most positive feature of their work, and has produced some astounding analyses of cultural systems of the past.

The future of new historicism and cultural materialism lies not in the reproduction and literal application of their methodologies and strategies to texts, but in the capacity of texts to speak back, to counter historical trends as well as confirming them. And only in playing with readings, playing with what texts might say, is it possible to discover and enable that capacity of texts to speak back. It is tempting to predict the future of new historicist and cultural materialist criticism, to describe what Derrida called the 'horizons of potential presence' (Derrida 1976, 67). It is tempting to surmise on what future new historicist practices and future cultural materialist practices might do, or analyse, or react against, but one of the lessons which these theories have already taught us is that to describe the future is to bring it into existence. To predict the future is to begin to prescribe it, and although this book is an intervention in, and an attempt to redirect, the critical practices of new historicism and cultural materialism, it is the task of readers and scholars alone, working on the interface between literature and history, to reinvent and prescribe the practice which they will then be practising *as if for the first time.*

Annotated Bibliography

Belsey, Catherine. *The Subject of Tragedy: Identity and Difference in Renaissance Drama.* London: Methuen/ Routledge, 1985.

First published in 1985, Belsey's book traces the history of modern subjectivity by examining the construction of the human subject in fiction of the sixteenth and seventeenth centuries. Belsey contends that modern understandings of human subjectivity derive from the Renaissance period, and demonstrates the emergence of the individual subject in her readings of Renaissance texts. The book is divided into two parts, the first dealing with 'Man', the second with 'Woman'. Belsey argues that this was the period in which 'Man' became the 'common-gender noun', failing to include women, and defining 'Woman' as having meaning only in relation to 'Man'.

Dollimore, Jonathan. *Radical Tragedy: Religion, Ideology and Power in the Drama of Shakespeare and his Contemporaries.* Hemel Hempstead: Harvester Wheatsheaf, 1984.

One of the first examples of cultural materialist critical practice, Dollimore's *Radical Tragedy* examines the ways in which Renaissance drama represented crises in contemporary ideas of order, religion and subjectivity. Dollimore discusses a wide range of important changes in Renaissance society, including changes to concepts of law, theology, identity, providence, cosmos, class, virtue and sexuality. He also situates these discussions of Renaissance society in relation to twentieth-century debates about literature, subjectivity and society. In the second edition of *Radical Tragedy*, published in 1989, Dollimore added a long introduction which sets out the function and methodology of materialist criticism, as well as reflecting on the reasons why he wrote the book, and on its reception.

Dollimore, Jonathan, and Alan Sinfield, eds. *Political Shakespeare: New Essays in Cultural Materialism*. Manchester: Manchester University Press, 1985.

The appearance of this volume marked the emergence of cultural materialism as a major new critical approach in British literary studies. Sinfield and Dollimore had already established their reputations as materialist (or Marxist) critics, influenced by the writings of Raymond Williams and Louis Althusser. The essays contained in the volume are divided into two parts. The first part, entitled 'Recovering history', includes essays by Jonathan Dollimore, Stephen Greenblatt, Paul Brown, Kathleen McLuskie and Leonard Tennenhouse. All of the essays in part one examine Shakespeare in the contexts of Renaissance culture and society. The second part, 'Reproductions, interventions', includes essays by Alan Sinfield, Graham Holderness and Margot Heinemann. All of the essays in part two examine the twentieth-century contexts of Shakespeare's plays, and how Shakespeare has been deployed in education, cinema and theatre. The volume is introduced by Dollimore and Sinfield with a polemical call to practice a literary and historical criticism with political commitment, and concluded with an 'Afterword' by Raymond Williams. The second edition was published in 1994 and included new essays by Sinfield and Dollimore.

Foucault, Michel. *The Archaeology of Knowledge*. (1969) Trans. A. M. Sheridan Smith. London: Tavistock/Routledge, 1972.

All of Foucault's work has had a significant impact on the theoretical assumptions and critical practices of new historicism, and, to a lesser extent, of cultural materialism. With the exception of the concept of power (which Foucault defines in *History of Sexuality, Volume 1*), *The Archaeology of Knowledge* is perhaps the most important articulation of those assumptions and practices. In that work, published in France in 1969, Foucault defined the principles of archaeological analysis, defined the meaning and structure of discursive formations and defined the function of texts, statements and events within discursive formations.

Foucault, Michel. 'What Is An Author?' *Language, Counter-Memory, Practice: Selected Essays and Interviews by Michel Foucault*. Ed. and intro. Donald F. Bouchard. Ithaca, NY: Cornell University Press, 1977. 113–38.

A formative essay for Foucault's influence on literary studies, it begins by analysing the concept of the author in Western discourse. Foucault proposes to replace the importance of the author in literary analysis with the concept of *écriture*. *Écriture*, for Foucault, represents the attempts in recent literary analysis of the conditions of the text. He concludes by suggesting the following questions as more appropriate to the analysis of texts and discourses in Western society: 'What are the modes of existence of this discourse? Where does it come from; how is it circulated; who controls it? What placements are determined for possible subjects? Who can fulfill these diverse functions of the subject?' (138).

Greenblatt, Stephen. *Renaissance Self-Fashioning: From More to Shakespeare*. Chicago and London: University of Chicago Press, 1980.

Although this was not Greenblatt's first book, it was the first in which he employed the concepts of power, discourse and subjectivity to analyse literary texts, a practice which became known subsequently as new historicism. Greenblatt argues in this book that in the Renaissance period there was a transformation in the social and cultural structures which changed the character of subjectivity. He analyses the ways in which writers and individuals like Thomas More, William Tyndale, Thomas Wyatt, Edmund Spenser and Christopher Marlowe fashioned their self-identities through a network of social, psychological, political and intellectual discourses.

Greenblatt, Stephen. 'Invisible Bullets: Renaissance Authority and its Subversion', *Glyph* 8 (1981): 40–61.

This is one of the most influential new historicist essays, by which I mean that it has been widely discussed and widely anthologised. Greenblatt begins with an anecdote about an Italian heretic, Menocchio, whose radical subversiveness led to his being burned at the stake on the authority of the Inquisition. Greenblatt uses this anecdote to explain his argument that subversiveness is necessary in order for power to become visible and fearsome, and to extend his argument to suggest that seemingly orthodox texts generate subversive insights which are an integral part of a society's policing apparatus. He then proceeds to examine this argument in relation to Thomas Harriot, the author of a report on England's first colony in America, and to Shakespeare's *I Henry IV.* He finds in each case that power produces the appearance of subversion in order to contain and police subversion more effectively.

Greenblatt, Stephen. *Shakespearean Negotiations: The Circulation of Social Energy in Renaissance England.* Oxford: Oxford University Press, 1988.

Many of the chapters in *Shakespearean Negotiations* were published earlier as essays or chapters, including 'Invisible Bullets', which forms Chapter 2 of this book. Greenblatt expresses his preference in *Shakespearean Negotiations* for the term 'cultural poetics' as a description of his own critical practice, instead of the controversial 'new historicism', and he begins to sketch in the first chapter what the concerns of a cultural poetics might be. Another important aspect of this book is its preference for the term 'social energy' over the Foucauldian term 'power'. Greenblatt dismisses 'power' as 'that term implied a structural unity and stability of command belied by much of what I actually knew about the exercise of authority and force in the period' (2), but when he defines 'social energy' it differs in no vital respect from his use of the term 'power'.

Greenblatt, Stephen. *Marvelous Possessions: The Wonder of the New World.* Oxford: Oxford University Press, 1991.

Whereas Greenblatt had occasionally considered the encounter between Europe and the 'new world' in his earlier works, *Marvelous Possessions* is his sustained consideration of the travel writings which constituted the European discourse of discovery. He analyses the writings of Mandeville, Columbus, Díaz and Montaigne, and links them together as a discourse which marked the transformation in the concept of 'wonder' from a sign of dispossession to an agent of appropriation. As such, Greenblatt is investigating an instrument in what he calls 'European representational practice', an instrument which enabled the Europeans to colonise the Americas.

Howard, Jean. 'The New Historicism in Renaissance Studies', *English Literary Renaissance* 16 (1986): 13–43.

This is a good consideration of the rise of new historicism in the study of Renaissance literary texts. Howard seeks to explain why critics of Renaissance texts found constructive models for interpretation and historical analysis in the concepts of power and discourse of Foucault's work. She also analyses the critical practice of new historicists, comparing in detail the work of Greenblatt and Montrose.

Miller, D. A. *The Novel and the Police*. Berkeley, Los Angeles and London: University of California Press, 1988.

Miller differs from the new historicists in Renaissance studies, like Greenblatt and Montrose, in that he applies Foucault's concepts directly and explicitly to literary texts, rather than owing some of his implicit assumptions to Foucault. Miller takes Foucault's work on discipline, punishment, policing and incarceration and explores what kind of readings emerge from the application of those concepts to Victorian novels. Miller focuses on Charles Dickens, Anthony Trollope and Wilkie Collins in his study.

Montrose, Louis. 'Professing the Renaissance: The Poetics and Politics of Culture'. *The New Historicism*. Ed. H. Aram Veeser. London: Routledge, 1989. 15–36.

In this essay (based on an earlier essay published in *English Literary Renaissance*, entitled 'Renaissance Literary Studies and the Subject of History'), Montrose considers the emergence and reception of the new historicism. He also attempts to describe the impact that new historicism has had on Renaissance studies, and to define what new historicism means as a critical practice. This includes his much quoted formulation that new historicism is concerned with 'the historicity of texts and the textuality of history' (20).

Montrose, Louis. '"Eliza, Queene of Shepheardes", and the Pastoral of Power'. *The New Historicism Reader*. Ed. H. Aram Veeser. London: Routledge, 1994. 88–115.

Montrose's essay is reprinted by Veeser as a 'classic' new historicist essay, although it was first published in 1980 in *English Literary Renaissance*. In the essay, Montrose analyses the form of pastoral poetry in the Elizabethan period, arguing that pastoral poetry was a vehicle of state ideology. For example, Montrose claims that pastoral poems were part of the ideological maneouvre to appropriate the Catholic symbolism of the Virgin Mary for use in constructing the image of a virgin queen, capable of uniting church and state and securing the loyalty of the people. Montrose's analysis is part of the new historicist recognition that claims to power, and strategies for appropriating power, are played out in literary texts as much as in more explicit political arenas.

Sinfield, Alan. *Faultlines: Cultural Materialism and the Politics of Dissident Reading.* Oxford: Oxford University Press, 1992.

This is Sinfield's largest and most ambitious book to date. It brings together and refocuses some earlier work on Shakespeare and the early modern period in general, and addresses the debates arising from cultural materialist and new historicist work. It contains ten chapters and a brief photo-essay, all of which address questions of cultural authority and dissident readings ('dissidence' is Sinfield's preference over the new historicist term 'subversion'). Like almost all cultural materialist work, Sinfield's book is primarily interested in challenging the function of literature in the present day, even when it is engaged in reading and interpreting the historical contexts of early modern texts.

Sinfield, Alan. *Cultural Politics – Queer Reading.* London: Routledge, 1994.

In the foreword to this short book, Sinfield states clearly that the key axiom of cultural materialism is simply this: 'culture is political'. In the four chapters which comprise the book Sinfield demonstrates this axiom, that every time culture is invoked, displayed or promoted there are political interests at stake. Throughout the same four chapters, Sinfield also inquires into the contribution of sexual politics to the meaning of culture. He argues that gay and lesbian subcultures provide the most stimulating contexts for political readings of culture at the present time, and demonstrates this position by countering 'mainstream' conservative readings with subcultural readings of literary texts.

Veeser, H. Aram, ed. *The New Historicism*. London: Routledge, 1989.

In this, the first of his collections of essays on the new historicism, Veeser gathers together essays on the emergence, reception and criticism of new historicism, which include contributions from prominent practitioners like Louis Montrose, Joel Fineman, Catherine Gallagher and Stephen Greenblatt to critics like Brook Thomas, Frank Lentricchia, Vincent Pecora and Hayden White. Veeser's introduction attempts to define the characteristics of the new historicism, and in general this anthology is useful for reading debates on what the new historicism represents in literary studies, including its shortcomings and weaknesses.

Veeser, H. Aram, ed. *The New Historicism Reader*. London: Routledge, 1994.

Whereas the first of Veeser's collections published essays about the new historicism, the second anthology published examples of the critical practice of new historicism. It included classic new historicist essays by Stephen Orgel, Stephen Greenblatt, Louis Montrose, Joel Fineman, Walter Benn Michaels, Catherine Gallagher and many others. Some of the essays included, such as the essays by Brook Thomas and Eve Kosofsky Sedgwick, do not follow the classic new historicist formula, which Veeser usefully describes as the process of 'converting details into knowledge' by five measured operations: 'anecdote, outrage, resistance, containment, and the critic's autobiography – all in a tight twenty-five pages' (5).

Williams, Raymond. *Marxism and Literature*. Oxford: Oxford University Press, 1977.

For cultural materialists, Williams's *Marxism and Literature* was an important revision of Marxist ideas on literature, and paved the way for materialist interpretations and analyses of literary texts. Williams's book is divided into three parts. In the first part, Williams traces the evolution and meanings of the concepts 'culture', 'language', 'literature' and 'ideology'. In the second part, he considers the development of Marxist thinking on literature and culture, from early formulations of base and superstructure to emerging work on the sociology of culture, which Williams sees as the promise of a growing field of study. In the final section, Williams turns his attention to discussing

Marxist interventions in literary theory, and what Marxism may have to contribute to ideas of genre, convention, authors and creative practice.

Williams, Raymond. *Keywords: A Vocabulary of Culture and Society.* London: Fontana, 1983.

Much of new historicist and cultural materialist work is similar to the discipline of history of ideas, in that both attempt to trace the emergence and formulation of specific concepts and ideas. The differences tend to lie in the methodological approaches used. In a number of his works, Williams traced the meanings of certain concepts, focusing particularly on the period from the eighteenth century to the present day. *Keywords* is the work in which he brought together short essays on the evolution of words and concepts which have acquired specific and complex meanings in the twentieth century. Neither new historicists nor cultural materialists have done anything similar, but the method of revealing the historical process by which a word or concept acquires powerful significance is evident in much of new historicist and cultural materialist thought.

Bibliography

Althusser, Louis. *Lenin and Philosophy and Other Essays.* Trans. B. Brewster. London: New Left Books, 1971.

—. *Essays on Ideology.* London: Verso, 1984.

Armstrong, Nancy. *Desire and Domestic Fiction: A Political History of the Novel.* Oxford: Oxford University Press, 1987.

—, and Leonard Tennenhouse. *The Imaginary Puritan: Literature, Intellectual Labor, and the Origins of Personal Life.* Berkeley, Los Angeles and London: University of California Press, 1992.

—, eds. *The Violence of Representation: Literature and the History of Violence.* London: Routledge, 1989.

Attridge, Derek, Geoffrey Bennington and Robert Young, eds. *Poststructuralism and the Question of History.* Cambridge: Cambridge University Press, 1987.

Bak, John S. 'Escaping the Jaundiced Eye: Foucauldian Panopticism in Charlotte Perkins Gilman's "The Yellow Wall-paper"'. *Studies in Short Fiction* 31:1 (Winter 1994): 39–46.

Barker, Francis. *The Tremulous Private Body: Essays on Subjection.* London: Methuen, 1984.

—. *The Culture of Violence: Essays on Tragedy and History.* Manchester: Manchester University Press, 1993.

—, Peter Hulme and Margaret Iversen, eds. *Postmodernism and the Re-reading of Modernity.* Manchester: Manchester University Press, 1992.

Belsey, Catherine. *Critical Practice.* London: Methuen/Routledge, 1980.

—. *The Subject of Tragedy: Identity and Difference in Renaissance Drama.* London: Methuen/Routledge, 1985.

—. 'Literature, History, Politics'. *New Historicism and Renaissance Drama.* Ed. Richard Wilson and Richard Dutton. Harlow: Longman, 1992. 33–44.

Bender, John. *Imagining the Penitentiary: Fiction and the Architecture of Mind in Eighteenth-Century England.* Chicago and London: University of Chicago Press, 1987.

Benjamin, Walter. *Illuminations.* (1958) Ed. Hannah Arendt, trans. Harry Zohn. London: Fontana, 1992.

Bhabha, Homi. 'Sly Civility'. *The Location of Culture.* London: Routledge, 1994. 93–101.

Bottomore, Tom, *et al.*, eds. *A Dictionary of Marxist Thought.* 2nd edn. Oxford: Blackwell, 1991.

Boyarin, Daniel. '"Language Inscribed by History on the Bodies of Living Beings": Midrash and Martyrdom'. *Representations* 25 (Winter 1989): 139–51.

Brannigan, John. '"And may there be no moaning of the bar": Cultural Materialism and Reading Dissidence in Tennyson'. *Imprimatur* 1:1 (Winter 1995): 3–10.

—. 'Power and its Representations: A New Historicist Reading of Richard Jefferies' "Snowed Up"'. *Literary Theories: A Case Study in Critical Performance.* Ed. Julian Wolfreys and William Baker. London: Macmillan, 1996. 157–76.

Brantlinger, Patrick. '*Heart of Darkness*: Anti-Imperialism, Racism, or Impressionism?' *Criticism* 28:4 (Fall 1985): 363–85.

Brown, Marshall, ed. *The Uses of Literary History.* Durham, NC: Duke University Press, 1995.

Bruster, Douglas. 'New Light on the Old Historicism: Shakespeare and the Forms of Historicist Criticism'. *Literature and History* 5:1 (Spring 1996): 1–18.

Carroll, David, ed. *The States of 'Theory': History, Art and Critical Discourse.* Stanford, CA: Stanford University Press, 1990.

Chambers, Ross. *Story and Situation: Narrative Seduction and the Power of Fiction.* Manchester: Manchester University Press, 1984.

—. *Room for Maneuver: Reading (the) Oppositional (in) Narrative.* Chicago and London: University of Chicago Press, 1991.

Collingwood, R. G. *The Idea of History.* (1946) Oxford: Oxford University Press, 1961.

Conrad, Joseph. *Heart of Darkness.* (1902) London: Penguin, 1983.

Cox, Jeffrey N. and Larry J. Reynolds, eds. *New Historical Literary Studies: Essays on Reproducing Texts, Representing History.* Princeton, NJ: Princeton University Press, 1993.

Critical Art Ensemble. *The Electronic Disturbance.* New York: Autonomedia, 1994.

Cullingford, Elizabeth Butler. *Gender and History in Yeats's Love Poetry.* New York: Syracuse University Press, 1996.

De Man, Paul. *Blindness and Insight: Essays in the Rhetoric of Contemporary Criticism.* 2nd edn. London: Methuen, 1983.

Dentith, Simon, ed. *Bakhtinian Thought: An Introductory Reader.* London and New York: Routledge, 1995.

Derrida, Jacques. *Of Grammatology.* (1967) Trans. Gayatri Chakravorty Spivak. Baltimore, MD and London: Johns Hopkins University Press, 1976.

—. *Writing and Difference.* (1967) Trans. Alan Bass. London: Routledge, 1978.

—. 'Some Statements and Truisms about NeoLogisms, Newisms, Postisms, Parasitisms, and Other Small Seismisms'. Trans. Anne Tomiche. *The States of 'Theory': History, Art and Critical Discourse.* Ed. David Carroll. Stanford, CA: Stanford University Press, 1990. 63–94.

—. 'Living On: Border Lines'. *A Derrida Reader: Between the Blinds.* Ed. Peggy Kamuf. Hemel Hempstead: Harvester Wheatsheaf, 1991. 254–68.

Dimock, Wai-Chee. 'Feminism, New Historicism and the Reader'. *American Literature* 63:4 (December 1991): 601–22.

Docherty, Thomas. *On Modern Authority: The Theory and Condition of Writing, 1500 to the Present Day.* Brighton: Harvester Press, 1987.

—. *After Theory: Postmodernism/Postmarxism.* London: Routledge, 1990.

—. *Alterities: Criticism, History, Representation.* Oxford: Oxford University Press, 1996.

Dock, Julie Bates. '"But One Expects That": Charlotte Perkins Gilman's "The Yellow Wall-paper" and the Shifting Light of Scholarship'. *Proceedings of the Modern Language Association* 111:1 (January 1996): 52–65.

Dollimore, Jonathan. *Radical Tragedy: Religion, Ideology and Power in the Drama of Shakespeare and his Contemporaries.* Hemel Hempstead: Harvester Wheatsheaf, 1984.

—. *Radical Tragedy: Religion, Ideology and Power in the Drama of Shakespeare and his Contemporaries.* 2nd edn. Hemel Hempstead: Harvester Wheatsheaf, 1989.

—. 'Shakespeare, Cultural Materialism, Feminism and Marxist Humanism'. *New Literary History: A Journal of Theory and Interpretation* 21:3 (Spring 1990): 471–93.

—. *Sexual Dissidence: Augustine to Wilde, Freud to Foucault.* Oxford: Oxford University Press, 1991.

—, and Alan Sinfield. 'Culture and Textuality: Debating Cultural Materialism'. *Textual Practice* 4:1 (1990): 91–100.

—, eds. *Political Shakespeare: New Essays in Cultural Materialism.* Manchester: Manchester University Press, 1985.

—, eds. *Political Shakespeare: Essays in Cultural Materialism.* 2nd edn. Manchester: Manchester University Press, 1994.

Donoghue, Denis. *We Irish: Essays on Irish Literature and Society.* Berkeley, Los Angeles and London: University of California Press, 1986.

Drakakis, John, ed. *Alternative Shakespeares.* London: Methuen, 1985.

During, Simon. 'New Historicism'. *Text and Performance Quarterly* 11:3 (July 1991): 171–89.

Equiano, Olaudah. *The Interesting Narrative.* (1789) London: Penguin, 1995.

Everest, Kelvin, ed. *Revolution in Writing: British Literary Responses to the French Revolution.* Milton Keynes: Open University Press, 1991.

Fanon, Frantz. *The Wretched of the Earth.* (1961) Trans. Constance Farrington. London: Penguin, 1967.

Field Day Anthology of Irish Writing. 3 vols. Ed. Seamus Deane. Londonderry: Field Day Publications, 1991.

Fineman, Joel. 'Shakespeare's *Will*: The Temporality of Rape'. *Representations* 20 (Fall 1987): 25–76.

—. 'The History of the Anecdote: Fiction and Fiction'. *The New Historicism.* Ed. H. Aram Veeser. London: Routledge, 1989. 49–76.

Foucault, Michel. *Madness and Civilization: A History of Insanity in the Age of Reason.* (1961) Trans. Richard Howard. London: Tavistock/Routledge, 1971.

—. *The Birth of the Clinic: An Archaeology of Medical Perception.* (1963) Trans. A. M. Sheridan Smith. London: Tavistock/Routledge, 1976.

—. *The Order of Things: An Archaeology of the Human Sciences.* (1966) London: Tavistock/Routledge, 1974.

—. *The Archaeology of Knowledge.* (1969) Trans. A. M. Sheridan Smith. London: Tavistock/Routledge, 1972.

—. *Discipline and Punish: The Birth of the Prison.* (1975) Trans. A. M. Sheridan Smith. London: Penguin, 1979.

—. 'What Is an Author?', 'Nietzsche, Genealogy, History', 'Theatrum Philosophicum'. *Language, Counter-Memory, Practice: Selected*

Essays and Interviews by Michel Foucault. Ed. and intro. Donald F. Bouchard. Ithaca, NY: Cornell University Press, 1977. 113–38, 139–64, 165–96.

—. *Power/Knowledge: Selected Interviews and Other Writings 1972–1977*. Ed. Colin Gordon, trans. Colin Gordon *et al*. London: Harvester Wheatsheaf, 1980.

—. *The History of Sexuality, Volume 1: An Introduction*. (1976) Trans. Robert Hurley. London: Penguin, 1981.

Frazier, Adrian. *Behind the Scenes: Yeats, Horniman and the Struggle for the Abbey Theatre*. Berkeley, Los Angeles and London: University of California Press, 1990.

Friel, Brian, *Translations*. London: Faber and Faber, 1980.

Gadamer, Hans-Georg. *Truth and Method*. London: Sheed and Ward, 1979.

Gallagher, Catherine. *The Industrial Reformation of English Fiction: Social Discourse and Narrative Form 1832–1867*. Chicago and London: University of Chicago Press, 1985.

—. 'Embracing the Absolute: The Politics of the Female Subject in Seventeenth-Century England'. *Genders* 1 (Spring 1988): 24–39.

—. 'Marxism and the New Historicism'. *The New Historicism*. Ed. H. Aram Veeser. New York and London: Routledge, 1989. 37–48.

—. *Nobody's Story: The Vanishing Acts of Women Writers in the Marketplace, 1670–1820*. Berkeley, CA: University of California Press, 1994.

Geertz, Clifford. *The Interpretation of Cultures*. London: Fontana, 1993.

Gilman, Charlotte Perkins. *The Yellow Wall-paper and Other Stories*. Oxford: Oxford University Press, 1995.

Glenn, Ian. 'Conrad's *Heart of Darkness*: A Sociological Reading'. *Literature and History* 13 (1987): 238–56.

Goldberg, Jonathan. *James I and the Politics of Literature: Jonson, Shakespeare, Donne and their Contemporaries*. Baltimore, MD and London: Johns Hopkins University Press, 1983.

—. *Sodometries: Renaissance Texts, Modern Sexualities*. Stanford, CA: Stanford University Press, 1992.

—. '*Measure for Measure* as Social Text'. *New Historicism and Cultural Materialism: A Reader*. Ed. Kiernan Ryan. London: Arnold, 1996. 117–25.

—, ed. *Queering the Renaissance*. Durham, NC and London: Duke University Press, 1994.

Gramsci, Antonio. *Selections from the Prison Notebooks.* Trans. Quentin Hoare and Geoffrey Nowell Smith. London: Lawrence and Wishart, 1971.

Greenblatt, Stephen. *Renaissance Self-Fashioning: From More to Shakespeare.* Chicago and London: University of Chicago Press, 1980.

—. 'Invisible Bullets: Renaissance Authority and its Subversion'. *Glyph* 8 (1981): 40–61.

—. 'Introduction: The Forms of Power'. *Genre* 7 (1982): 3–6.

—. 'Murdering Peasants: Status, Genre, and the Representation of Rebellion'. *Representations* I:1 (February 1983): 1–30.

—. *Shakespearean Negotiations: The Circulation of Social Energy in Renaissance England.* Oxford: Oxford University Press, 1988.

—. 'Towards a Poetics of Culture'. *The New Historicism.* Ed. H. Aram Veeser. London: Routledge, 1989. 1–14.

—. *Learning to Curse: Essays in Early Modern Culture.* New York and London: Routledge, 1990.

—. *Marvelous Possessions: The Wonder of the New World.* Oxford: Oxford University Press, 1991.

Hamilton, Paul. *Historicism.* London: Routledge, 1996.

Harpham, Geoffrey Galt. 'Foucault and the New Historicism'. *American Literary History* 3 (Summer 1991): 360–75.

Hartley, L. P. *The Go-Between.* Harmondsworth: Penguin, 1958.

Hawkes, Terence. *Meaning by Shakespeare.* London: Routledge, 1992.

—, ed. *Alternative Shakespeares Volume 2.* London: Routledge, 1996.

Hawkins, Hunt. 'Joseph Conrad, Roger Casement and the Congo Reform Movement'. *Journal of Modern Literature* 9 (1981/82): 65–80.

—. 'Conrad's *Heart of Darkness*: Politics and History'. *Conradiana* 24:3 (1992): 207–17.

Hawthorn, Jeremy. *Cunning Passages: New Historicism, Cultural Materialism and Marxism in the Contemporary Literary Debate.* London: Arnold, 1996.

Herbert, T. Walter, Jr. 'The Erotics of Purity: *The Marble Faun* and the Victorian Construction of Sexuality'. *Representations* 36 (Fall 1991): 114–32.

Hoggart, Richard. *The Uses of Literacy.* (1957) London: Penguin, 1971.

Holderness, Graham. *Shakespeare Recycled: The Making of Historical Drama.* Hemel Hempstead: Harvester Wheatsheaf, 1992.

—, ed. *The Shakespeare Myth*. Manchester: Manchester University Press, 1988.

Howard, Jean. 'The New Historicism in Renaissance Studies'. *English Literary Renaissance* 16 (1986): 13–43.

—. 'Feminism and the Question of History: Resituating the Debate'. *Women's Studies: An Interdisciplinary Journal* 19: (1991): 149–57.

Howell, Martha C. 'A Feminist Historian Looks at the New Historicism: What's So Historical about It?' *Women's Studies: An Interdisciplinary Journal* 19:2 (1991): 139–47.

Hulme, Peter. *Colonial Encounters: Europe and the Native Caribbean 1492–1797*. London: Methuen, 1986.

Humphries, Reynold. 'The Discourse of Colonialism: Its Meaning and Relevance for Conrad's Fiction'. *Conradiana* 21:2 (1989): 107–33.

Innes, C. L. *Woman and Nation in Irish Literature and Society*. Hemel Hempstead: Harvester Wheatsheaf, 1993.

Jefferies, Richard. *After London, or Wild England*. (1885) Oxford: Oxford University Press, 1980.

Jordan, Elaine. *Alfred Tennyson*. Cambridge: Cambridge University Press, 1988.

—, ed. *Joseph Conrad*. London: Macmillan, 1996.

Joseph, Gerhard. *Tennyson and the Text*. Cambridge: Cambridge University Press, 1992.

Kiberd, Declan. 'Irish Literature and Irish History'. *The Oxford History of Ireland*. Ed. R. F. Foster. Oxford: Oxford University Press, 1992. 230–81.

—. *Inventing Ireland: The Literature of the Modern Nation*. London: Jonathan Cape, 1995.

Kingsley, Mary. *Travels in West Africa*. (1897) London: Everyman/ J. M. Dent, 1993.

Klancher, Jon. 'Romantic Criticism and the Meanings of the French Revolution'. *Studies in Romanticism* 28 (Fall 1989): 463–91.

Knapp, Jeffrey. *An Empire Nowhere: England, America, and Literature from* Utopia *to* The Tempest. Berkeley, Los Angeles and London: University of California Press, 1992.

Leavis. F. R. *The Great Tradition*. (1948) Harmondsworth: Penguin, 1962.

—. *The Common Pursuit*. (1952) London: Hogarth Press, 1984.

—. *D. H. Lawrence: Novelist*. (1955) Harmondsworth: Penguin, 1964.

Lee, John. 'The Man Who Mistook His Hat: Stephen Greenblatt and the Anecdote'. *Essays in Criticism: A Quarterly Journal of Literary Criticism* 45:4 (October 1995): 285–300.

Lentricchia, Frank. *After the New Criticism*. London: The Athlone Press, 1980.

—. 'Foucault's Legacy – A New Historicism?' *The New Historicism*. Ed. H. Aram Veeser. London: Routledge, 1989. 231–42.

Levinson, Marjorie. *Wordsworth's Great Period Poems*. Cambridge: Cambridge University Press, 1986.

—, Marilyn Butler, Jerome McGann and Paul Hamilton. *Rethinking Historicism: Critical Readings in Romantic History*. Oxford: Blackwell, 1989.

Lewis, Tom. 'The New Historicism and Marxism'. *Journal of the Midwest Modern Language Association* 24:1 (Spring 1991): 14–23.

Liu, Alan. 'The Power of Formalism: The New Historicism'. *English Literary History* 56:4 (Winter 1989): 721–71.

Lukács, Georg. *History and Class Consciousness: Studies in Marxist Dialectics*. (1968) Trans. Rodney Livingstone. London: Merlin Press, 1974.

Lyotard, Jean-François. *The Postmodern Condition: A Report on Knowledge*. (1979) Trans. Geoff Bennington and Brian Massumi. Manchester: Manchester University Press, 1984.

Marx, Karl, and Friedrich Engels. *Selected Works in One Volume*. London: Lawrence and Wishart, 1991.

McAlindon, Tom. 'Testing the New Historicism: "Invisible Bullets" Reconsidered'. *Studies in Philology* 92:4 (Fall 1995): 411–38

McGann, Jerome J. *The Romantic Ideology: A Critical Investigation*. Chicago and London: University of Chicago Press, 1983.

—. *The Beauty of Inflections: Literary Investigations in Historical Method and Theory*. Oxford: Oxford University Press, 1985a.

—. *Towards a Literature of Knowledge*. Oxford: Oxford University Press, 1989.

—. *The Textual Condition*. Princeton, NJ: Princeton University Press, 1991.

—, ed. *Historical Studies and Literary Criticism*. Madison, WI: University of Wisconsin Press, 1985b.

McNay, Lois. *Foucault: A Critical Introduction*. Cambridge: Polity Press, 1994.

Megill, Allan. 'The Reception of Foucault by Historians'. *Journal of the History of Ideas* 48:1 (January/March 1987): 117–41.

Michaels, Walter Benn. *The Gold Standard and the Logic of Naturalism: American Literature at the Turn of the Century.* Berkeley, Los Angeles and London: University of California Press, 1987.

Miller, D. A. 'Discipline in Different Voices: Bureaucracy, Police, Family and *Bleak House'. Representations* 1:1 (February 1983): 59–90.

—. *The Novel and the Police.* Berkeley, Los Angeles and London: University of California Press, 1988.

Miller, J. Hillis. 'Presidential Address 1986: The Triumph of Theory, the Resistance to Reading, and the Question of the Material Base'. *Theory Now and Then.* Hemel Hempstead: Harvester Wheatsheaf, 1991. 309–27.

Milner, Andrew. *Cultural Materialism.* Victoria: Melbourne University Press, 1993.

Montrose, Louis. '"Shaping Fantasies": Figurations of Gender and Power in Elizabethan Culture'. *Representations* 1:2 (Spring 1983): 61–94.

—. 'Renaissance Literary Studies and the Subject of History'. *English Literary Renaissance* 16 (1986): 5–12.

—. 'Professing the Renaissance: The Poetics and Politics of Culture'. *The New Historicism.* Ed. H. Aram Veeser. London: Routledge, 1989. 15–36.

—. '"Eliza, Queene of Shepheardes", and the Pastoral of Power'. *The New Historicism Reader.* Ed. H. Aram Veeser. London: Routledge, 1994. 88–115.

Morgan, W. John, ed. *Raymond Williams: Politics, Education, Letters.* New York: St Martin's Press, 1993.

Mullaney, Stephen. 'After the New Historicism'. Ed. Terence Hawkes. *Alternative Shakespeares Volume 2.* London: Routledge, 1996. 17–37.

Murfin, Ross C., ed. *Heart of Darkness.* 2nd edn. New York: St Martin's Press, 1996.

Newton, Judith. 'History as Usual? Feminism and the "New Historicism"'. *Cultural Critique* 9 (Spring 1988): 87–121.

Nietzsche, Friedrich. *The Birth of Tragedy and The Genealogy of Morals.* Trans. Francis Golffing. New York: Doubleday, 1956.

—. *Thus Spake Zarathustra.* Trans. R. J. Hollingdale. Harmondsworth: Penguin, 1961.

Nussbaum, Felicity A. *The Autobiographical Subject: Gender and Ideology in Eighteenth-Century England*. Baltimore, MD: Johns Hopkins University Press, 1989.

—. *Torrid Zones: Maternity, Sexuality, and Empire in Eighteenth-Century English Narratives*. Baltimore, MD and London: Johns Hopkins University Press, 1995.

O'Hara, Daniel T. *Radical Parody: American Culture and Critical Agency after Foucault*. New York: Columbia University Press, 1992.

Orgel, Stephen. *The Illusion of Power: Political Theater in the English Renaissance*. Berkeley, CA: University of California Press, 1975.

—. *Impersonations: The Performance of Gender in Shakespeare's England*. Cambridge: Cambridge University Press, 1996.

Patterson, Lee, ed. *Literary Practice and Social Change in Britain, 1380–1530*. Berkeley, Los Angeles and London: University of California Press, 1990.

—. 'Historical Criticism and the Claims of Humanism'. *New Historicism and Cultural Materialism: A Reader*. Ed. Kiernan Ryan. London: Arnold, 1996. 92–102.

Paxson, James J. 'The Green(blatt)ing of America: Reflections on the Institutional Genealogy of Greenblatt's New Historicism'. *Minnesota Review* 41/42 (Fall 1993/Spring 1994): 221–35.

Pechter, Edward. 'The New Historicism and Its Discontents: Politicizing Renaissance Drama'. *Proceedings of the Modern Language Association* 102:3 (May 1987): 292–303.

Pecora, Vincent P. 'The Limits of Local Knowledge'. *The New Historicism*. Ed. H. Aram Veeser. London: Routledge, 1989. 243–76.

Plato. *The Republic*. Trans. Desmond Lee. London: Penguin, 1987.

Porter, Carolyn. 'Are We Being Historical Yet?' *South Atlantic Quarterly* 87:4 (Fall 1988): 743–86.

—. 'History and Literature: "After the New Historicism"'. *New Literary History* 21 (1990): 253–72.

Prendergast, Christopher, ed. *Cultural Materialism: On Raymond Williams*. Minneapolis, MN: University of Minnesota Press, 1995.

Richardson, Joanna. *The Pre-Eminent Victorian*. London: n.p., 1962.

Rosenberg, Brian. 'Historicizing the New Historicism: Understanding the Past in Criticism and Fiction'. *Modern Language Quarterly: A Journal of Literary History* 50:4 (December 1989): 375–92.

Ryan, Kiernan, ed. *New Historicism and Cultural Materialism: A Reader*. London: Arnold, 1996.

Said, Edward. *Orientalism*. London: Routledge and Kegan Paul, 1978.
—. 'Yeats and Decolonization'. *Nationalism, Colonialism and Literature*. Intro. Seamus Deane. Minneapolis, MN: University of Minnesota Press, 1990.
—. *Culture and Imperialism*. London: Vintage, 1994.
Simons, Jon. *Foucault and the Political*. London and New York: Routledge, 1995.
Sinfield, Alan. *The Language of Tennyson's 'In Memoriam'*. Oxford: Blackwell, 1971.
—. *Literature in Protestant England 1560–1660*. London: Croom Helm, 1982.
—. 'Four Ways with a Reactionary Text'. *Journal of Literature Teaching Politics* 2 (1983b): 81–95.
—. *Alfred Tennyson*. Oxford: Blackwell, 1986.
—. *Literature, Politics and Culture in Postwar Britain*. Oxford: Blackwell, 1989.
—. *Faultlines: Cultural Materialism and the Politics of Dissident Reading*. Oxford: Oxford University Press, 1992.
—. *The Wilde Century: Effeminacy, Oscar Wilde and the Queer Moment*. London: Cassell, 1994a.
—. *Cultural Politics – Queer Reading*. London: Routledge, 1994b.
—, ed. *Society and Literature 1945–1970*. London: Methuen, 1983a.
—, and Jonathan Dollimore, eds. *Political Shakespeare: New Essays in Cultural Materialism*. Manchester: Manchester University Press, 1985.
—, *Political Shakespeare: Essays in Cultural Materialism*. 2nd edn. Manchester: Manchester University Press, 1994.
Singh, Jyotsna G. 'Afterword: Shakespeare and the Politics of History'. *Literature and History* 5:1 (Spring 1996): 78–85.
Stallybrass, Peter, and Allon White. *The Politics and Poetics of Transgression*. London: Methuen, 1986.
Stanley, Henry M. *Through the Dark Continent*. 2 vols. (1878) New York: Dover Publications, 1988.
Straub, Kristina. *Sexual Suspects: Eighteenth-Century Players and Sexual Ideology*. Princeton, NJ: Princeton University Press, 1992.
Strier, Richard. *Resistant Structures: Particularity, Radicalism, and Renaissance Texts*. Berkeley and Los Angeles: University of California Press, 1995.
Tennenhouse, Leonard. *Power on Display: The Politics of Shakespeare's Genres*. London: Methuen, 1986.

Tennyson, Alfred. *Tennyson's Poetry*. Ed. Robert W. Hill, Jr. New York: Norton, 1971.

—. *Selected Poems*. London: Penguin, 1991.

Thomas, Brook. *The New Historicism and Other Old-Fashioned Topics*. Princeton, NJ: Princeton University Press, 1991a.

—. 'Walter Benn Michaels and the New Historicism: Where's the Difference?'. *Boundary 2: An International Journal of Literature and Culture* 18:1 (Spring 1991b): 18–59.

—. 'Preserving and Keeping Order by Killing Time in *Heart of Darkness*'. *Heart of Darkness*. 2nd edn. Ed. Ross C. Murfin. New York: St Martin's Press, 1996.

Thompson, E. P. *The Making of the English Working Class*. Harmondsworth: Penguin, 1968.

Tillyard, E. M. W. *The Elizabethan World Picture*. (1943) London: Penguin, 1963.

Vattimo, Gianni. *The End of Modernity*. (1985) Trans. Jon R. Snyder. Cambridge: Polity Press, 1991.

Veeser, H. Aram. 'Re-Membering a Deformed Past: (New) New Historicism'. *Journal of the Midwest Modern Language Association* 24:1 (Spring 1991): 3–13.

—, ed. *The New Historicism*. London: Routledge, 1989.

—, ed. *The New Historicism Reader*. London: Routledge, 1994.

Visker, Rudi. *Michel Foucault: Genealogy as Critique*. (1990) Trans. Chris Turner. London: Verso, 1995.

Watson, William. 'England and Her Colonies'. (1890) *The White Man's Burden: An Anthology of British Poetry of the Empire*. Ed. Chris Brooks and Peter Faulkner. Exeter: University of Exeter Press, 1996. 275.

Wells, H. G. *The Time Machine*. London: Pan Books, 1953.

White, Hayden. 'New Historicism: A Comment'. *The New Historicism*. Ed. H. Aram Veeser. London: Routledge, 1989. 293–302.

Williams, Jeffrey, ed. *PC Wars: Politics and Theory in the Academy*. New York: Routledge, 1995.

Williams, Raymond. *Culture and Society 1780–1950*. (1958) Harmondsworth: Penguin, 1961.

—. *The Long Revolution*. (1961) Harmondsworth: Pelican, 1965.

—. *Communications*. (1962) Harmondsworth: Pelican, 1968.

—. *The Country and the City*. (1973) London: Hogarth Press, 1993.

—. *Marxism and Literature*. Oxford: Oxford University Press, 1977.

—. *Problems in Materialism and Culture*. London: Verso, 1980.

—. *Keywords: A Vocabulary of Culture and Society.* London: Fontana, 1983.

Wilson, Richard, and Richard Dutton, eds. *New Historicism and Renaissance Drama.* Harlow: Longman, 1992.

Wilson, Scott. *Cultural Materialism: Theory and Practice.* Oxford: Blackwell, 1995.

Wolfreys, Julian. *Being English: Narratives, Idioms and Performances of National Identity from Coleridge to Trollope.* New York: State University of New York Press, 1994.

Yeats, William Butler. *Autobiographies.* Dublin: Gill and Macmillan, 1955.

—. *Yeats's Poems.* Ed. A. Norman Jeffares. Dublin: Gill and Macmillan, 1989.

Young, Robert. *White Mythologies: Writing History and the West.* London and New York: Routledge, 1990.

Index

243

CPSIA information can be obtained at www.ICGtesting.com
Printed in the USA
LVOW07s1743111115

462081LV00009B/886/P